MR. DOOLEY & MR. DUNNE

The Literary Life
of a
Chicago Catholic

by

Edward J. Bander

Sketches by Hal Zamboni

THE MICHIE COMPANY
LAW PUBLISHERS

CHARLOTTESVILLE,
VIRGINIA

To my sister Nettie,
who plays Sancho Panza
to my Don Quixote

FOREWORD

I think I know why Mr. Dooley's comments are viable after these many years: their essence is truth. Also, their truth relates to the most fundamental of our human and institutional weaknesses. These things do not change in a year, or a century.

I have paid special attention to Mr. Dooley's musings on lawyers, judges, the courts and the law. I have heard legal gatherings receive Dooley with delight. They all but verbalize it: "That's true! That's us!" Mr. Dunne was neither a lawyer nor a judge. If he strikes so close to this one core, should we fear that he misses his mark as he attacks any other entrenchments? We rest assured that he has read the inner secrets of every discipline, every subject, just as certainly as he has with the law and the courts as, for example, he states the three issues phrased by the jury: Did the defendant kill his wife? Did she look as though she ought to be killed? Isn't it time we went to supper?

Mr. Dooley is called a cynic, and a skeptic. He is both. There is a temptation to call him a misanthrope, because no group, no person, no institution, is safe from his lash. Surely he is no more than a quasi-misanthrope, because he hates only the worst that is in us. Mr. Hennessy, on the other hand, has been called simply a boob. Of course he is not; no boob can consistently find the great issues, and ask the crucial questions. I need not defend Hennessy, though; he spells his name without the noble, ultimate "e." He is obviously of the other branch of the family.

Incidentally, I have told Ed Bander, and I meant it, that this book is a tour de force. It brought me so much that is new about my old, old friends, Mr. Dunne and Mr. Dooley. For his depth of research, and the wisdom of his comments, Ed

v

Bander has my gratitude, and he will have the thanks of many others.

EDWARD F. HENNESSEY
Chief Justice
Supreme Judicial Court
   for the Commonwealth
   of Massachusetts

PREFACE

This book is not an epitaph for the corpus of Finley Peter Dunne. His Mr. Dooley essays are a live and viable literature that still have a role to play in American life and letters. When *Look* devoted its June 11, 1968 issue to the problems of cities, it quoted from Mr. Dooley's devastating attack on the hordes of people who leave the convenience of the city for the so-called pleasures of country living. "We ought to live where all the good things iv life comes fr'm," says Hogan. "No," says I. "Th' place to live in is where all the good things iv life goes to. Ivrything that's worth havin' goes to th' city, th' counthry takes what's left." [1] When the Greenwich Village *Villager* of New York City wanted to give advice to incoming Mayor Lindsay, it devoted in two issues two full columns to Mr. Dooley's political musings for his edification.[2] When columnist Peter Lisagor offered advice to Democratic presidential candidate Senator George McGovern, he headed his column with a Dooleyism, "Politics ain't beanbag," and he concluded with "McGovern . . . should be acquainted with Mr. Dooley, the fictitious Irish bartender created by Peter Finley Dunne. . . ." [3]

When Martin Mayer wrote his journalistic study of *The Lawyers,* Mr. Dooley was called on four times as a character witness, including this sample to illustrate a chapter on the "Personality of the Judge": "If I had me job to pick out," said Mr. Dooley, "I'd be a judge. I've looked over all th' others an' that's th' on'y wan that suits. I have th' judicyal temperamint. I hate wurruk." [4] When John F. Kennedy was belittled for being too young to run for President, the *Boston Globe* reprinted Mr. Dooley's essay on "Young Presidents" (the remarks originally concerned Theodore Roosevelt) which concluded, "Well," said Mr. Dooley, "a man is old enough to vote whin he can vote, he's old enough to wurruk whin he can wurruk. An' he's old enough to be Prisidint whin he becomes Prisidint. If he ain't, 'twill age him." [5]

When the Democratic National Convention met in 1976, it featured Edward Asner as Mr. Dooley in the television presentation.[6] On election day 1980, the *New York Times* oped page featured Mr. Dooley who, from the grave, predicted that the Democrats would once again be chasing "rapublicans into th' tall grass." [6.1] In fact, a journalist unfamiliar with Mr. Dooley's ". . . th' supreme coort follows th' eliction returns," will be minus an ideal opening line for one of his political commentaries.[7]

When Mort Sahl was riding high as the postwar comic-satirist, *Time* magazine ran a cover feature on the comic situation in America and had this to say:

> Finley Peter Dunne, whose Mr. Dooley is the all-time choice of many political connoisseurs, swaddled his man in an Irish dialect that magically permitted him to speak his mind. He once called John D. Rockefeller 'a kind iv society f'r th' prevention iv croolty to money,' and had a skill in reworking slogans that has turned up again in Sahl. 'Hands acrost th' sea and into somewan's

pocket," said Mr. Dooley. Sahl rallied for Ike with the line: 'He kept us out of Mars.' [8]

Again when *Time* crowned Russell Baker humorist of the 1970's, it traced his genealogy back to Dunne.[9]

When *Life* made gentle fun of computer language, it editorially recalled Mr. Dooley's comments on marriage: "A marrid man gets th' money, Hinnissy, but a bachelor man gets th' sleep." [10] In reviewing a book about muckrakers of the 1920's, Herbert Mitgang recalled a famous line of Mr. Dooley's "that summed up the spirit of the times . . . 'It looks to me,' said Mr. Hennessy, 'as though th' counthry was goin' to th' divvle.' And Dooley replied, 'Put down that magazine, Hinnissy!' " [11] Denis Brogan, the British scholar, who has a chapter on Mr. Dooley in his book, *American Themes*,[12] wrote to his readers in the London *Spectator:* "The most acute commentator on the American scene, the legitimate successor to Mr. Dooley, Mr. Art Buchwald. . . ." [13] When the *New Republic* editorially had its say about the Central Intelligence Agency, it recalled Mr. Dooley's "A lie with a purpose is one of the worst kind and th' most profitable." [14] Bergen Evans, the Thomas Huxley of the English language and the Edwin Newman of another generation, in his article "Now everyone is Hip about Slang," quotes Mr. Dooley's comments on how Americans have enlivened the English language: "When Americans are through with the English language," Mr. Dooley boasted, "it will look as if it had been run over by a musical comedy." [15] And finally, to point up the broad appeal of America's greatest humorist, both the sophisticated *Times Literary Supplement* [16] and Ann Landers[17] of advice-to-the-lovelorn fame, found Mr. Dooley's marriage advice apropos to their purpose: "Up here whin a marrid couple get to th' p'int where tis impossible f'r thim to go on livin' together they go on livin' together." Both neglected Mr. Dooley's closing lines on the topic: "Ill-mated couples?" says Father Kelly. "Ill-mated couples? What ar-re ye talkin' about? Ar-re there anny other kinds?"

Aphorism for aphorism, no American humorist — Josh Billings, Artemus Ward, Mark Twain, Groucho Marx, Mort Sahl, Art Buchwald — can stand comparison to Mr. Dunne. His deadly wit could hold an arrogant businessman to scorn; he could ridicule a pompous politician with a line; in a short pithy essay he could sum up what a foundation-funded sociologist would take tomes not to say; and he could write a line of pure, delicious humor. No amount of critical praise can replace the original and this volume is an attempt to bring as much of it together as possible.

This book is divided into two sections. The first part attempts to put Mr. Dooley and Mr. Dunne in perspective. It is also a collection of Dunne's greatest lines. The appendix is a chronological arrangement of all Dunne's Mr. Dooley essays. Dunne's comments about vice presidents stand alone. But who was the vice president? What historical event, political battle, or intellectual announcement prompted a Dunne comment? I believe that the short extracts will make a good part of Mr. Dooley's humor, lost up to now in newspapers and magazines, available to a public always hungry for literary delights.

Acknowledgements: Fran Bander for her assistance and forbearance in this project; and David and Lida Bander for doing many, many distasteful tasks. When I recently returned to Boston as law librarian at Suffolk University, I fortuitously discovered that my dean was a Dooley fan. I have been fortuitously discovering Dooley fans all over America — Mr. Dooley's America — and this book is an acknowledgement of them.

Edward J. Bander

1. For the complete essays, *see The City as a Summer Resort*, MR. DOOLEY'S OPINIONS 50 (N.Y., 1901).

2. *See* the issues of December 23, 1965, at 16 and January 20, 1966, at 4.

3. New York Post (July 1, 1972). Mr. Dooley often equated politics with sport, and it is interesting that the beanbag analogy was used by

Richard F. Schier in "Take Me Out to the Pol Game," New York Times, A17 (July 17, 1979).

4. MARTIN MAYER, THE LAWYERS, 488 (N.Y. 1967).

5. Boston Globe, 18 (Jan. 25, 1960).

6. *See* New York Post, 4 (June 14, 1976).

6.1. New York Times (Nov. 4, 1980).

7. Some current examples: Tom Wicker, *No Sunshine in Court,* New York Times, A21 (July 6, 1979); Paul Freund, *"Bakke, The Choices That Remain,"* New York Times, E17 (July 9, 1978); Martin F. Nolan, *The Role of Politics in the High Court Decisions,* Boston Globe, 27 (June 29, 1978); *A Matter of Intent,* Wall Street Journal, 14 (March 2, 1977); Michael Harrington, *Hiding the Other America,* NEW REPUBLIC, 15 (Feb. 26, 1977); *Busing,* FORTUNE, 115 (Oct. 1975). It is interesting to note that Mr. Dooley belongs to no political group when it comes to quoting him.

8. TIME, 42 (Aug. 15, 1960).

9. TIME, 51 (June 4, 1979).

10. LIFE, 41 (March 3, 1961).

11. New York Times, 35 (Nov. 30, 1961).

12. DENIS W. BROGAN, AMERICAN THEMES, 47-50 (N.Y. 1947). The late Mr. Brogan's affection for Mr. Dooley is alluded to in *Denis Brogan, Americanist,* ENCOUNTER, 40 (July 1974).

13. London Spectator, 11 (Jan. 6, 1968).

14. NEW REPUBLIC, 5 (March 4, 1967). If one reads this Mr. Dooley essay on lying (*Mr. Dooley's Opinions,* 87) in the context of the brouhaha occasioned by Professor Raiffa's course on "lying" at the Harvard Business School, one would experience the pleasant sensation of déjà vu. *See* Charles L. Whipple, *What Lies Behind 'Lies' at Harvard,* Boston Globe, (Feb. 16, 1979). Harvard, Dr. Eliot, and intellectuals, in general, were an easy target for Mr. Dooley.

15. New York Times (Magazine), 22, 99 (March 22, 1964).

16. Times (Literary Supplement), 780 (Aug. 31, 1967).

17. Syracuse Herald Journal 6 (March 21, 1964).

CONTENTS

CHRONOLOGY

1867   Peter Dunne born in Chicago of Irish parents on July 11. Peter's twin died in infancy.

1884   First newspaper job is on the Chicago *Evening Telegram.*

1888   Preferred Finley, his mother's family name, to his given name. His signature becomes F.P. Dunne and finally F.P.D. in this introduction to the collection, *Mr. Dooley At His Best.* Changed to the *Chicago Times* where he became city editor.

1889   Member of the Whitechapel Club which did much for Dunne's later development.

1892   Achieved local fame for his editorial work on the *Chicago Evening Post.*

1893   First Mr. Dooley piece written in the *Chicago Post.*

1897   Became managing editor of the *Chicago Journal.*

1898   Mr. Dooley pieces on Spanish-American War brought Dunne fame. *Mr. Dooley in Peace and War* published with items on the Spanish-American War, politics and topical items.

1900   Dunne left Chicago for New York City. Published *Mr. Dooley's Philosophy.* This volume contains Mr. Dooley's review of a book by Theodore Roosevelt which resulted in a friendship that did not end Mr. Dooley's satirizing the future President. Other topics included the Negro problem, politics and the education of the young.

1901   *Mr. Dooley's Opinions.* This volume included Mr. Dooley's famed comment on the Supreme Court following the election returns. Also more politics, New York City, vice and the Booker T. Washington incident.

1902   Editor of the *New York Morning Telegraph.*
       Published *Observations of Mr. Dooley.* More politics,
       the habits of the rich, art and a constant theme, that
       no one wants to know about the scandals of the poor
       as illustrated in "One Advantage of Poverty."
       Married Margaret Abbot on December 9.

1905   Published *Dissertations by Mr. Dooley;* topics
       included politics, labor, Socialism, vacations and the
       famous "The Carnegie Libraries" essay.

1906   Joined the American Magazine (until 1913), along
       with William Allen White, Ida M. Tarbell, Lincoln
       Steffens and others.

1910   Published *Mr. Dooley Says.* Essays on women,
       imperialism, literature and "The Big Fine," a fine
       spoof on John D. Rockefeller.

1913   Mr. Dunne wrote for *Collier's Weekly;* subsequently
       edited the publication.

1919   Published *Mr. Dooley on Making a Will and other
       Necessary Evils.* Essays on sports, old age, as well as
       the essay that made up the title.

1926   Dunne now wrote Mr. Dooley items for the Bell
       Syndicate, but time had taken its toll. Essays on the
       income tax and a book review of a work by Colonel
       House showed signs of the old Mr. Dooley.

1927   Dunne was left a half million dollars by Payne
       Whitney which assured his financial needs for the
       rest of his life.

1936   Dunne died on April 24.

Chapter 1

INTRODUCING MR. DUNNE

When asked by Mr. Hennessy whether he would rather be rich or famous, Mr. Dooley answered: "I'd like to be famous, an' have money enough to buy off all threatenin' bi-ographers." [1] Mr. Dooley's biographic apprehension was not warranted as far as his creator, Finley Peter Dunne, was concerned. Elmer Ellis has written an authorized biography, *Mr. Dooley's America,* which gives no indication that Ellis searched "th' bureau dhrawers, old pigeon-holes, th' records iv th' polis coort, an' th' recollections iv th' hired girl." [2] Mr. Dunne's son, Philip, published *Mr. Dooley Remembers,* a combination of the elder Dunne's memoirs and the younger's own commentary that is a model of an older person's exercise of privacy and of a son's affection for his father.

Although Dunne, through the use of his alter ego Mr. Dooley, abused, castigated, ridiculed and satirized the great and near-great of his time, the record shows few reciprocal criticisms of Finley Peter Dunne and an almost universal adulation of him by the leading lights of the period. Although Dunne led an interesting life, in fact an enviable life, it was not what he did but what he wrote that was in the public's eye. It is not unusual for a famous author to have led an unspectacular life, free of petty disputes and publicized domestic quarrels. In fact, doing so is to his credit. No known scandals with the ladies marked Mr. Dunne's career, although he may have had to offer a few explanations to his bride, Margaret Abbott, to explain his frequent comments on bachelorhood, such as, "A married man gets th' money, Hinnissy, but th' bachelor gets th' sleep." A few months before his marriage, Dunne had even written an essay, "Mr. Dooley on the Home Life of Geniuses," [3] which Mrs. Dunne might have found prophetic:

Now, what kind iv a man ought a woman to marry: She oughtn't to marry a young man because she'll grow old quicker thin he will; she oughtn't to marry an old man because he'll be much older befure he's younger; she oughtn't to marry a poor man because he may become rich an' lose her; she oughtn't to marry a rich man because if he becomes poor, she can't lose him; she oughtn't to marry a man that knows more thin she does, because he'll niver fail to show it, an' she oughtn't to marry a man that knows less because he may niver catch up. But above all things she mustn't marry a janius [genius]. A flurewalker, perhaps, a janius niver.

I. Incidents in an Author's Life.

Despite Mr. Dooley's advice, Margaret and Finley married in 1902; and they had four children: Finley Peter (1903), Philip (1908), and the twins, Leonard and Margaret (1910). Dunne's star was ascending, and the children enjoyed the best of schooling, acquaintanceships as high and mighty as President Theodore Roosevelt, and a life style only associated with the very rich. There were private clubs, trips abroad, and a demand for service that could only be learned from association with the very wealthy. When Dunne moved East, he took up residence in Southampton, an exclusive community, and became a member of Southampton Club and the Union Club in New York City. He had arrived. The mighty made friends with Dunne, he was a charter member of Mark Twain's Human Race Luncheon Club,[4] was in demand for his wit and camaraderie, and had an inordinately strong pull to the bottle.

If Dunne ever committed an indiscretion, it was his character testimony for the indicted Harry Daugherty in the infamous Teapot Dome investigation of the 1920's. Daugherty had led Dunne into the Harding camp, and

Dunne admitted to playing a role in the nomination of Warren Harding for President and to being seduced by the siren calls of being a power behind the throne. Dunne did no more for Daugherty than Dean Acheson did for Alger Hiss, and one can only fault Dunne for not accepting the advice of Mr. Dooley that "politics ain't beanbag."

Dunne did not swim the Hellespont, crusade for women's suffrage ("What does a woman want iv rights whin she has privileges?" is a statement that would get him in a lot of trouble today), or strike a Norman Mailer pose. Dunne in fact led a life of ease, even complacency, that could well brand him as a Consciousness II person. However, even if wealth, fame, family and friends can be claimed to have limited his productive years from 1898 to 1914, there is still good reason to say that even a vow of penury and abstinence could not have added to those five hundred or so jewels he bequeathed to American literature.

II. Whitechapel Club.

If a story needs telling about Dunne, it is the mad capers of the Chicago "Whitechapel Club," a name coined by Dunne after a famous English murder of the period. The bar of the club was shaped like a coffin; its decor included a sword that had decapitated an unfaithful wife and a tankard made of the skull of a streetwalker. Jack the Ripper was its patron saint. A "Bohemian, Rabelesian, and macabre" club, to quote Ellis, its members included George Ade, Edwin Markham and Chicago journalists of the period; and among its honored guests one could find Sarah Bernhardt, Rudyard Kipling and the ubiquitous Chauncey Depew. Merciless ribbing and open intimidation were hallmarks of the club, and a thick skin and a quick wit were as necessary to attendance as a karate chop to prevent a mugging in a back alley. The membership was limited to twelve, and the test of eligibility was the ability to consume forty glasses of beer without losing command of one's faculties.[5]

Typical of the antics of the club was a drinking bout with the Clover Club of Philadelphia, won hands up by the Whitechapels in that the Chicago club was "raided" by the police at its own instigation; and the Philadelphians found themselves sobering up in the paddy wagons. Dunne, his fellow wits and the Chicago police, all conspirators in the affair, considered this prank the coup of the season. More gruesome, however, was the story of the one remaining member of a suicide club, who, amid the hangman relics of the Whitechapel Club, was advised to fulfill his pledge, end it all and will his body to the club. This was done and the body was cremated in fine style: "The five hour ceremony, with countless toasts to the departed was described in several columns in the *Herald* and read by subscribers on their return from church." [6] Macabre as this story is, a biographer of George Ade provides another version:

> The principal activities of the club were talking, smoking, drinking, and scorning commercialism. It was not unusual for the police to come and testify to the success of the club's activities. And everybody in Chicago remembered Club Member Collins.
>
> Collins was a penniless intellectual who loved the poor and hated everybody who wasn't starving. His theory was that America needed martyrs to awaken the national conscience to the horrors of capitalist exploitation. Collins proposed that the members organize a mass suicide to pound home the lesson. He argued eloquently that dramatically planned suicides for a high purpose would be both effective and satisfying. While expatiating on his gory plan, one of the Whitechapel members suggested that he kick off the festivities. Collins greeted the suggestion with

4

enthusiasm and agreed to be the first if the others wouldn't think it pushy.

With a vote of confidence Collins returned to his shabby hotel room on Clark Street and downed a tankard of poison. He died slowly and passed the time writing an impassioned account of his immediate sensations and the more universal pains of mankind. He bade farewell to all and asked that the Whitechapel members collect his remains and cremate them "on account of" he was broke.

The membership approved Collins' last request and took what was left of him to Miller's Station, Indiana, on the shore of Lake Michigan. There they built a funeral pyre, drenched it with coal oil, capped it with Collins, made a few speeches before touching it off, and then went in swimming until the ashes cooled enough for them to gather up the martyr's charred remnants. Collins' skull and a few odds and ends were put in a flour sack and brought back to the club rooms. Everyone conceded that Collins was a great guy with "lousy" ideas.[7]

Above all, the club was a spawning ground for intellectual ferment. Fred C. Kelly's description is evidence that its iconoclastic, tradition mocking, antiestablishment motif provided the kind of perspective that made possible the wise old Irish bartender who was not fazed by wealth, fame, novel ideas or the status quo:

One source of entertainment for George Ade in 1892 came from his membership in the Whitechapel Club, whose rooms faced the alley at the rear of the office of the *Daily News*. George has called it "a little group of thirsty intellectuals who were opposed to everything." The more conservative favored a redistribution of property, while the radicals believed in the free use of dynamite. The club had a couple of managing editors and a few judges and a sprinkling of millionaires who were verbally scalded every time they ventured an opinion. In the list including painters, poets and architects was the most famous magician of his time, Alexander Hermann. About half of the members were newspaper toilers who were having plenty of fun in life even when complaining most vigorously about what was wrong with the world.

Sometimes the club gave a party. Rudyard Kipling was once the guest of honor. Talk at the tables near a coffin-shaped bar was a principal club activity and the most brilliant of the talkers was "Pete" Dunne, reporter on the *Herald,* not yet the famous "Mr. Dooley." He was the club's Dr. Johnson. When he talked the others listened. They were unsparing in their shots even at a distinguished guest if he uttered any banality. With equal candor they assailed any member whose newspaper story, poem or book failed to win their approval. The novelist and newspaperman, Opie Read, couldn't "take it" and left the club.[8]

An unsigned item in the Boston Globe, September 17, 1899, as much as any other, supplies the critical information necessary to understand the creator of Mr. Dooley:

FACTS ABOUT PETER DUNNE*

"Dooley" Suggested by an
Actual Character.

Thousands Have Laughed at His Quaint
and Original Sketches.

Amusing Instances of Mr. Dunne's Quick
Wit on Many Public Occasions.

"So you are Peter Dunne," said Richard Harding Davis when he was introduced to the brilliant young Chicago newspaper man on the American Line dock in New York last summer. "I am surprised; I expected to find the author of the Dooley papers wore red galway sluggers."

"And I expected to find you in a shirt waist and sailor hat," retorted Mr. Dunne.

A clever bit of repartee, wasn't it? But perhaps you have heard it before. A lot of newspapermen were present when it was said, and they thought it so good that they published it far and wide. Still, it is good enough to tell again.

But, at that, I don't think it half so funny as the remark Peter Dunne made to an Illinois state senator at one of the famous old Whitechapel Club dinners. The senator was a newly made statesman. Nobody knew exactly how he had broken into politics, but he had done it some way, and in the same mysterious manner he got himself elected to the state senate.

---

* Facts About Peter Dunne, Boston Globe (September 17, 1899).

7

He was a lawyer, noted chiefly for his poses, his willingness to orate anywhere, at any place, and upon any subject, his transparent straining for theatrical effect, and a mass of long, heavy jet black hair, which he combed back from his forehead and with studied carelessness allowed to fall over his coat collar.

The statesman was late for the Whitechapel dinner. When he arrived he "made an entrance," as the actor says, which was spectacular. A speech was in progress when he strode across the floor and tossed his overcoat to ... [the] steward. Then he stepped forward and paused as if waiting for a welcome cheer.

He was in full evening costume, a thing which the Whitechapelers were not partial to anyway, and the whiteness of his shirt and waistcoat made his great mass of hair look all the blacker.

President Dunne arose from his seat at the head of the coffin-shaped table and pounded for order with a thigh bone which had been given the club by a medical member. The statesman smiled at the compliment and struck another attitude.

"Will the senator kindly remove his furs?" asked Mr. Dunne. The crowd yelled and the senator sank into a vacant chair, and, except to put something in it, didn't open his mouth all evening.

That's the kind of fellow Pete Dunne is. The man who attempted to cross the sabers of retort with him soon found that he was dueling with a fencing master. With him it is as much the way he says a thing as the thing itself. I heard him spike the guns of the late Moses P. Handy, the head of the famous Clover Club of Philadelphia, and noted as a wit and after-dinner speaker.

It also was at a Whitechapel dinner. The late Gov. Russell of Massachusetts was there, and so were Buffalo Bill and Dr. Edward Bedloe, who is back in this country to answer

8

charges brought against him of aiding the Filipinos while he was U.S. consul at Canton, China. Maj. Handy had fired a good shot at Peter and when Pete later referred to him as Maj. Handy, the president of the "jute trust," it finished the comments upon his flowing, carroty side whiskers, but he had never heard them called "jute" before.

Pete always was funny. He was the pioneer of baseball slang. Many words which we could not get along without in discussing baseball were coined by Pete Dunne. It was as a baseball reporter on the Chicago Tribune, back in the early eighties, that Mr. Dunne first showed the stuff in him. Don't think him an old man because he was writing for a newspaper 20 years ago. He began young. He was about 17 years old, fresh from school, when he got his first reportorial position. The city editor of the Tribune decided Pete was too good to write about ball games, and transferred him from the sporting department to do general reporting.

It wasn't long before Pete was known as the Tribune's best man — the star reporter. He remained with the Tribune until the old Times, which was then at the height of its great influence, sent for him. He was in the city editor's chair when he left the Times to go to the Herald.

This was in '87 or '88. I am not sure which. At that time a favorite meeting place for the Chicago newspapermen was old Jim McGarry's saloon, in Dearborn St., near the corner of Madison; it was but a stone's throw from the Tribune office and directly across the street from the Inter Ocean office. You could always find a crowd of reporters there. When the city editor of a paper was in need of some men who didn't happen to be in he called the office boy and said:

"Run over to McGarry's and tell Smith to come here." McGarry himself was the attraction of the place. He was — and is yet, for he's alive, though the old Dearborn St. place is closed — one of the quaintest characters you could meet in a search over the globe. Big, broad and brawny, sandy-haired, his red face showing his redder arteries streaking like a railroad map, and a "far-down brogue," that was Jim McGarry.

Jim had ideas of propriety and honor that were as rigid as they were unique. He never broke his word with a man and he demanded that every one else be as honest with him. . . .

Such things as that amused Pete Dunne, and he started in to write stories about McGarry. Jim didn't see them till a dozen or so character sketches had appeared in the Herald. When a friend pointed it out to him, and when Jim saw his name and some of his sayings in print, he was wild.

He sent word to Pete that he would kill him, and he threatened to lop off Pete's privilege of credit. The old fellow carried on at such a rate that Pete promised to quit, and the riot was quelled.

When Pete ceased contributing his Irish stories the editor demanded to know why it was thus. Pete explained but the editor, who knew good stuff when he saw it, refused to let Pete discontinue them.

Pete was in a fix. He had promised McGarry to stop, but his boss said no. Then he hit on the compromise which has made him famous on two continents and a fortune besides. Dooley! He dropped old Jim McGarry and began to write about Mr. Dooley. For some time Mr. Dooley was only McGarry.

Old Jim spotted the subterfuge one day when he read his own words as those of Mr. Dooley: "I don't trust a man who makes no noise with his heels whin he walks." Then there was more trouble. Mr. McGarry almost cried that Pete should have deceived him, though ever so little.

The two friends patched up another truce and Pete never wrote another McGarry story. But he continued on Mr. Dooley and made Mr. Dooley say what Pete thought old Jim McGarry ought to say, and there you have the story of the clever little sketches which have made thousands of people laugh.

III. Newspaper Career.

Chicago, then and now, was a city in need of redeeming, which explains in good measure Finley Peter Dunne's lack of reforming instinct. Dunne saw Chicago as it was; and his wit, humor and satire were directed at showing Chicagoans what they really were and not what they thought themselves to be. By no coincidence, greed, avarice, innocence and idiocy are common to people and societies outside of Chicago, and Dunne's essays were everywhere a sensation at the turn of the century. While the Spanish-American War provided the spur to Dunne's fame, his depicting of celebrities as local Chicagoans brought out the weaknesses of businessmen, generals and politicians and laid them bare to the public. Admiral Dewey was Cousin Dooley (Mr. Dooley, by the way, rather liked the Admiral), international conflicts were battles between Schwarzheimer in the German ward and Dorsey from Archey Road, and a review of Rostand's *Cyrano de Bergerac* became a description of a wild Irish brawl. Dunne described conduct, he never explained it; and what Shakespeare did with the kings of England and Chaucer with the Canterbury pilgrims, he did with the people of Chicago, making a credo of Mr. Dooley's "There's no news in bein' good."

Dunne's career as a newspaperman began while he was still in his teens and he rose rapidly in his profession. As a cub reporter, he covered fires, election campaigns and sports. He is credited with coining the term "southpaw" and with being one of the first to dramatize sporting events, thus creating, if not a new literature, a new industry. In

11

fact, Dunne's Mr. Dooley essays on sports rank him with Ring Lardner, Westbrook Pegler, Grantland Rice, Red Smith, and that small bank of journalists who make the Sunday papers worth reading.

Dunne, who progressed quickly from reporter to editorial assignments, became an editor at a time when aspiring journalists of that time were still attending college. Dunne was not college educated, though he was far better read than most collegians; and one finds in the Mr. Dooley essays a condescending attitude toward higher education and college professors, even an anti-intellectualism. Mr. Dooley has remarked that one can lead a student to a university, but one cannot make him think; moreover, the only reason he would send a boy to college was because at that age he would not have him around the house (Dunne's children had the best of educational opportunities — the two eldest went to Harvard, an institution frequently satirized by Mr. Dooley). As for college professors, he thought that if they wrote for the press, their columns should always appear on the same page so that readers would not have to hunt for the day's humor columns. As an editorial writer, Dunne could be sharp and effective, as Elmer Ellis has observed. The success of his Mr. Dooley material made it possible for Dunne to expand into non-dialect essays as well as into publishing.

As Dunne himself points out, the word "great" never attached to his name as a publisher. At the peak of his reputation, he contributed solid, if not durable, essays to the *American* and other magazines. Louis Filler's *The World of Mr. Dooley* reprinted six of these essays; and, with the possible exception of the one on capital punishment, they make one long to see Mr. Dooley, rather than Dunne himself, address these issues. When one reads Dunne's essays in the King's English, his literary debt to Michel de Montaigne, Charles Dickens, Ralph Waldo Emerson and other

12

stalwarts of the general Victorian period becomes evident. While admirable models, they are heavy-handed, moralistic, aside-throwing essays that do not sit well with an impatient American public. As Mr. Dooley once boasted, "When Americans are through with the English language it will look as if it had been run over by a musical comedy." Only as Mr. Dooley did Finley Peter Dunne fulfill that prophecy.

IV. Decline and Fall.

World War I was the dividing line in Mr. Dunne's career. Although he revived the Dooley series on occasion, it never met with the success of the series during the Spanish-American War through Theodore Roosevelt's term of office. One war brought Finley Peter Dunne to fame in 1898 and another ended his career in 1914. Dunne continued to be a well-known literary figure, but only for his past performances. Receipts and royalties from his columns and books were no longer able to maintain him and his family in the grand style. However, Dunne was left a half-million dollars by his friend Payne Whitney because Dunne was a dear friend and because he had honorably refused a legacy of a magazine so that it would go to the hard-pressed, ungrateful widow of the donor. Dunne himself attributes his declining reputation to his economic condition:

One bright morning in late May or early June I awoke with a consciousness that I had much important work to do. Accordingly, I took a long time over breakfast, studied the morning papers with the greatest care and having exhausted all other devices for postponing labor, like playing with the dog and winding the clock, settled down to work, when suddenly it occurred to me that I had still a small balance left in

13

the bank. It was not only small, it was puny, but large enough to shut the door on Inspiration. Every great artist knows that without inspiration he can't create; so letters and art are left to the working classes.... Anyhow, with the thought of my bank balance all Inspiration fled and there was nothing left for a sensible man to do but practice his mashie shots.[9]

Upton Sinclair, at whom Dunne had taken pot shots via Mr. Dooley and in his editorial columns, was convinced that Dunne's literary output was diminished by his drinking.[10] Franklin P. Adams saw Dunne as an artist frustrated by his striving for perfection,[11] and this interpretation may account for Dunne's rapidly declining output. To Lincoln Steffens, "He could not make himself write. I never knew a writer who made such a labor of writing; he seemed to hate it; he certainly ran away from it whenever he could.... There was nobody so boring as Dunne himself when he was thinking out a Dooley article. He would talk about it from this view and the other and still another angle for days, at dinner, at lunch; and you could hardly stand it or stop him." [12]

On the other hand, no one can read about Dunne's life among the upper classes without suspecting that he had lost his critic's eye. A club member of clubs that discriminated against Jews (Blacks were not yet an issue; and, although Dunne thought the restriction a disgrace, he never gave up his memberships), lord of a houseful of servants and a chauffeur, and a power broker, however slight, in the making of a less-than-distinguished president, Dunne had suddenly become not the author of Mr. Dooley, but a subject for Mr. Dooley. He was caught in the tide of the 1920's that made the good life too good to miss. There was enough for everyone — or so it seemed until the crash exploded dreams and made the wealthy aware of poverty in America in the form of their own condition. To criticize Dunne would be to curse the sunset, for it is a rare personality who can pay his dues to two generations.

There are some, including Dunne himself, who believed that the times had grown too evil for humorists and satirists. World War I, the rise of Fascism, Hitler, anti-Semitism, and the approaching World War II had made humor seemingly impossible. But Will Rogers managed to ridicule Congress; Charlie Chaplin's *The Great Dictator* is a classic about the Axis partners; Mort Sahl made a living from President Eisenhower's administration; and, while an atom bomb and an ecological disaster threaten civilization, Russell Baker and Art Buchwald manage to make readers choke with pure, clean, harmless laughter. None compare with Finley Peter Dunne's Mr. Dooley, and one may never see his like again; but it is as idiotic to say that a humorist of genius is not possible in the post-World War eras as it would be to say that one was possible in the *opera bouffé* period of the Spanish-American War that was characterized by imperialism and fortune hungry barons. The genius of Finley Peter Dunne needs no excuse in time, place or period. His humor may yet stand as the only monument to a not very humane period of American history.

The simple fact is that for a generation Dunne had ground out, sometimes on a week-by-week basis, column after column on a variety of topics — a World's Fair, a prize fight, a political convention, a book review, current news topics — which, while predicated on specific events, spoke in terms of humanity. It is not that events had overtaken him; it is more likely that there was little that he could say that he had not said before.

V. Imitations.

Dunne's success with Mr. Dooley bred many imitations. Dunne's essays were pirated and imitations made their way

15

into print. The syndication of Mr. Dooley to newspapers throughout the country and to England had its impetus in the newspapers that innocently copied the material, a common practice of the day. The *Boston Globe* was one of the first to make arrangements to pay for the essays. In a letter from Willard de Lue of the *Globe,* "This led General Taylor to make a definite arrangement with Dooley [*sic*] to have each story wired to us in advance, but there was so much confusion over transmitting the dialect by telegraph that General Taylor urged Dooley to make some regular syndication of his stories — which led to his becoming a national figure." [13]

Dunne's son Philip bemoans the many Mr. Dooley imitations. He has a point when he criticizes those who write in Irish dialect and maintain they are writing as the old master would have had he known what they know. But it is questionable whether most of the imitators even considered how Mr. Dunne would have felt. It is the device of Mr. Dooley that they are imitating. The Mr. Dooley essay portraying a poor, ill-educated immigrant bartender taking on the high and mighty is too good a "shtick," to borrow from the entertainment industry, to bury with its originator. Mr. Dooley got away with well-aimed shafts at the Carnegies, Roosevelts, Yarkes, Baers, McKinleys, the literary crowd and a vast assemblage of puncture-vulnerable people. Mr. Dooley did not have to prove his point or footnote it, he had only to make it, which is all one can ever ask of a bartender. Some Mr. Dooley imitations are, in fact, so good that they have been mistaken for the real thing.[14] As Mr. Dooley once wrote, "Larceny is the sincerest form of flattery."

One of the harsh realities of Dunne's life was that he became overshadowed by his own creation. Like Charles Brown (Artemus Ward), Arthur Conan Doyle (Sherlock Holmes), and Arthur Train (Mr. Tutt), he is recognized only in terms of his fictional alter ego. No one, not even Philip Dunne, would dare write about Finley Peter Dunne without putting "Mr. Dooley" in the title. Paradoxically, Mr. Dunne omitted his own name from the title pages of his books. Understandably, Finley Peter Dunne resented playing second fiddle to Mr. Dooley. In a letter to Richard Watson Gilder, editor of *The Century*, he suggested a new series as "I fear that Dooley's 'pipe is out.' He keeps on puffing at the ashes after the manner of Archey Road but it is a dry smoke. I think I ought to get away from him, not too far, at least put him in the third person." [15] That letter was written on December 17, 1898, before some of the best Mr. Dooley

17

pieces had been written. Dunne never began the series he had in mind, and one is grateful, in this instance, for his procrastination.

1. FINLEY PETER DUNNE, MR. DOOLEY SAYS, 24 (N.Y., 1910). This quotation has been used in ELMER ELLIS, MR. DOOLEY'S AMERICA, vii (N.Y., 1941); and PHILIP DUNNE, MR. DOOLEY REMEMBERS, 3 (Boston, 1963).
2. MR. DOOLEY AT HIS BEST, 198 (Elmer Ellis, ed., N.Y., 1938).
3. FINLEY PETER DUNNE, OBSERVATIONS, 159 (N.Y., 1902).
4. *Organized to damn the species.* M. Meltzer, MARK TWAIN HIMSELF, 246 (N.Y., 1960). *See also* II MARK TWAIN-HOWELLS LETTERS, 828, 842 (Henry H. Smith and William M. Gibson, eds., N.Y., 1960).
5. New York Herald Tribune, April 25, 1936. A clipping in the New York Herald Tribune morgue located at New York University.
6. JOHN J. MCPHAUL, DEADLINES AND MONKEYSHINES, 152 (Englewood Cliffs, N.J., 1962).
7. LEE COYLE, GEORGE ADE, 28-29 (N.Y., 1964).
8. FRED C. KELLY, GEORGE ADE, 100, 101 (Indianapolis, 1947).
9. PHILIP DUNNE, MR. DOOLEY REMEMBERS, 164 (Boston, 1963).
10. UPTON SINCLAIR, AUTOBIOGRAPHY, 252 (N.Y., 1962).
11. MR. DOOLEY AT HIS BEST, xiii (Introduction to Elmer Ellis, ed., N.Y., 1938).
12. LINCOLN STEFFENS, AUTOBIOGRAPHY, 536 (N.Y., 1931).
13. Letter to the author from Willard de Lue (Feb. 16, 1959).
14. Some examples of imitations, as well as items attributed to Mr. Dooley, will be shown in Chapter 5.
15. Letters in New York Public Library, Manuscript Division.

Chapter 2

INTRODUCING MR. DOOLEY

I. Antecedents.

Dialect writing has a long and honored tradition in American literature, and Finley Peter Dunne may well be its most noted exponent. Dialect had an attraction for that vast pioneer stock that went West, leaving behind it the literate English publications or the stately and Brahmin *Atlantic*. While James Russell Lowell's *Biglow Papers* might satisfy the Bostonian, it was Petroleum V. Nasby, Artemus Ward, Josh Billings, and Mark Twain who utilized the local press and Chautauqua platform to amuse and educate the masses. Unafraid of the lowly pun[1] and exaggerated language, these spokesmen for a new breed of American enjoyed the earthy episodes and the language that fitted their tongue. As Constance Rourke explains:

> Mimicry and travesty belonged to them all; they caught the scattered life of the time not realistically but with preposterous inflation. They offered talk in a familiar tone, the next thing to conversation; and they were heard and read with an absorbed delight, as if their wide public transferred the burden of uncertain selves to these assured and unabashed provincials. These oracles were indeed profoundly social in their effect as they attacked abuses and foibles and idiosyncrasies of the time; most of them kept that salty and satirical view of the affairs of the nation which had belonged to the earlier figures. Sumner thought that the political value of the Nasby papers could hardly be overestimated. Lincoln pored over all that Nasby wrote and kept the pamphlets near him. "For the genius to write these things I would gladly give my office," he said; and he read Artemus Ward's *High-Handed Outrage at Utica* as sheer comedy — as comic relief —

19

before the members of his cabinet in 1862, when he was about to lay before them the final draft of the Emancipation Proclamation.[2]

The dialect humor of the new immigrants was not a progression of that plied by Artemus Ward, but a natural means of communication with a people learning the American language. A thumbing through of the newspapers of the cities with large numbers of immigrants uncovers many feeble attempts at dialect humor by the Irish, Germans, Jews and Scandinavians. Only a scholar would be interested in these attempts because whatever interest they may have had for local citizens, they were not so durable as the paper on which they were printed.

Although Finley Peter Dunne was probably aware of dialect humor, at least the Pat-and-Mike type, he showed no early interest in it. There is no evidence that he knew the creator of Artemus Ward, although books about Ward were published during Dunne's lifetime. Dunne stumbled upon dialect writing; and, while it was a natural medium for his genius, he wished that he could outlive it, just as Oliver Wendell Holmes, Jr., strove to obtain a reputation independent of his father's.

II. Mr. Dooley is Born.

Dunne's first attempts at dialect were fillers for the *Chicago Sunday Post,* although at this stage he was not so much writing dialect as repeating the wise words of a local bartender who ran a bar that Dunne and his fellow journalists frequented. Dunne changed the name of the bartender from McGarry to a fictional Col. McNeery, and he progressed from quoting McGarry to writing his own material. He chose to use dialect because, "It occurred to me that while it might be dangerous to call an alderman a thief in English no one could sue if a comic Irishman denounced the statesman as a thief." [3]

The notoriety Dunne achieved from his Col. McNeery blasts at politicians and businessmen had an unexpected side effect. When McGarry thought he was being ridiculed and reported the episode to Dunne's editor, Dunne agreed to eliminate any association with McGarry. He wisely kept the same format, simply changing the name of his bartender to Martin Dooley, and his locale to Archer Avenue ("Archey Road"), another section of Chicago.[4]

The Mr. Dooley pieces began on October 7, 1893, some nine months after Dunne's first experiment with Col. McNeery. The topics of discussion were very similar. Immediately before the Mr. Dooley essays, McNeery railed at newspaper reports that President Cleveland had cancer, discussed Irish home rule, ridiculed a world religious congress, and wondered where all the brave people were during a train robbery. As Mr. Dooley, he questioned the celebration of events such as the Chicago Fire, gave points to "Grover," and was not sorry to see the Chicago Fair close. There was more description in the early essays, which later gave way to almost exclusive dialogue.

Although Dunne did not elaborately describe his bartender, he comes to life with the dialogue with which Dunne clothed him. He is Irish, of course, with a sparkle in his eye and, when he talks all listen or he silences them. He almost always has the last word. He is old but ageless, an inveterate reader of the newspapers ("I see be th' pa-apers" was the obvious forerunner to Will Rogers' "All I know is what I read in the papers"), and one who, though aware of his Irishness, has had contact with the Black, the Jew, the German, the Anglo-Saxon and is none the worse for it. Cartoonists of the period, including James Montgomery Flagg and E.W. Kemble, were commissioned to "draw" Mr. Dooley for newspapers, magazines and books, but none could capture the intangible quality of the man who could say, "All men are ME. Th' little tape line that I use f'r mesilf

21

is long enough an' acc'rate enough to measure anny man in th' wurruld . . . ." [5]

Dunne describes the setting for the Mr. Dooley essays as follows:

Archey Road stretches back for many miles from the heart of an ugly city to the cabbage gardens that gave the maker of the seal his opportunity to call the city "urbs in horto." Somewhere between the two — that is to say, forninst th' gas-house and beyant Healey's slough and not far from the polis station — lives Martin Dooley, doctor of philosophy.

There was a time when Archey Road was purely Irish. But the Huns, turned back from the Adriatic and the stockyards and overrunning Archey Road, have nearly exhausted the original population — not driven them out as they drove out less vigorous races, with thick clubs and short spears, but edged them out with the more biting weapons of modern civilization — overworked and undereaten them into more languid surroundings remote from the tanks of the gashouse and the blast furnaces of the rolling-mill.

But Mr. Dooley remains, and enough remain with him to save the Archey Road. In this community you can hear all the various accents of Ireland. . . . Here also you can see the wakes and christenings, the marriages and funerals, and the other fêtes of the old counthry somewhat modified and darkened by American usage. . . .

. . . He reads the newspapers with solemn care, heartily hates them, and accepts all they print for the sake of drowning Hennessy's rising protests against his logic. From the cool heights of life in the Archey Road, uninterrupted by the jarring noises of crickets and cows, he observes the passing show, and meditates thereon. His impressions are transferred to the desensitized plate of Mr. Hennessy's mind, where they can do no harm. Mr. Hennessy says he was a "grown man whin th' pikes was out in forty-eight, an' I was hedgehigh, an' I'm near fifty-five." Mr. Dooley says Mr. Hennessy is eighty. He closes discussion on his own age with the remark, "I'm old enough to know better."

He has served his country with distinction. His conduct of the important office of captain of his precinct (1873-75) was highly commended, and there was some talk of nominating him for alderman. "Politics," he says, "ain't bean bag. 'Tis a man's game; an' women, childher, an' pro-hybitionists'd do well to keep out iv it." Again he remarks, "As Shakespeare says, 'Ol' men f'r th' council, young men f'r th' ward.' " [6]

III. *Cast of Characters.*

But the setting for Mr. Dooley is incomplete without his revolving cast who, but for Hennessy, make infrequent appearances. In an affectionate essay on Mr. Dooley, John V. Kelleher describes these characters:

> Dooley is a unique invention: the only mythical philosopher I can think of with a philosophy. He is also Dunne's only major character. With the exception of Hennessy, who somehow manages a vivid existence on little more than silent bewilderment, the other people in the essays are as shadowy as the fall guys in Plato's dialogues; they exist only through Dooley's quotations or descriptions of them. Hogan, the gullible intellectual; Father Kelly, the humane and humorous priest; Dock O'Leary, the agnostic; Schwartzmeister, the foreign element and Dooley's German rival; the various cops, plumbers, misers, lovers, housewives, aldermen, reformers, and bums, who are mentioned transiently — all exist to feed Dooley information it would be out of character for him to find in his

23

newspaper, or to enable him to point and illustrate a moral.[7]

There were other characters. Mr. McKenna began the series with Mr. Dooley but was replaced by Mr. Hennessy. Dochney, the rich old skinflint, comes hilariously to life in "On Making A Will." And the Jews and Blacks are either nameless or treated as summarily as one would expect in a bar in any unassimilated neighborhood. It is also interesting to note that Father Kelly was possibly based on a real priest by the same name.[8]

IV. Dissecting the Mr. Dooley Essay.

The mechanics of Mr. Dooley's essay are so simple that one can understand ready imitation by others. Mr. Dooley comments on a matter of interest, usually in the manner of: " 'I see in this pa-aper,' said Mr. Dooley. . ." or " 'It's goin' to be gr-reat times f'r us Germans whin Prince Hinnery comes over,' said Mr. Dooley." Mr. Hennessy responds with some inane remark, although he does occasionally get the better of an argument; and Mr. Dooley is off and running. Dunne's selection of topics covered a wide array of human activities, and on occasion he reverted to an old topic. He would discuss the Spanish-American War, all aspects of politics, the Irish, foreign affairs, women, poverty and wealth, the Dreyfus case, alcohol, the law, sports and such out of the way topics as dieting, health fads, playing cards, Theodore Roosevelt on a hunting expedition, after dinner speakers and so on. The bar on Archey Road was a window to the world.

The Dooley essay was short, clever, topical, humorous and complete. On occasion Dunne became sentimental, even brought a tear to the eye, but this type of essay disappeared early from his repertoire. In the Franklin P. Adams and Lewis Gannett dispute about the nature of the essays, Adams writes:

And when the Dunnes and the Lardners die the

papers print editorials saying that there was no malice in their writing and no bitterness in their humor. Few popular writers ever wrote more maliciously and bitterly than Lardner and Dunne. They resented injustice, they loathed sham, and they hated the selfish stupidity that went with them.

Anger, and a warm sympathy for the underprivileged underlay almost all the "Dooley" sketches.[9]

Gannett, on the other hand, did not find malice in the essays.[10] He cites Dunne's essays on Theodore Roosevelt and the Supreme Court to indicate that, while they hit home, they did not bring on the wrath of those "institutions." It is a fact that Dunne and Roosevelt became good friends (some suggest that this friendship was a defensive measure taken by the then governor and soon-to-be President), and also that Mr. Dooley was a favorite of Justices Holmes, Hughes, and Frankfurter — three men who would not have thought kindly of one bent on destroying the Supreme Court.

In a sense, both Adams and Gannett were right. When George F. Baer refused to settle the coal strike, Dunne wrote with hatred and rancor about this exercise of privilege at a time when workers and their families went hungry; and Mr. Dooley's frequent references to William Jennings Bryan can be cruel and even offensive (Mr. Dooley was not averse to referring to one's physical characteristics, such as obesity). There is no record of either Baer's or Bryan's striking back (an indication of the power Mr. Dunne may have wielded). One has to realize these two men were exceptional targets because Mr. Dooley was not one to make outcasts of human beings, being quite convinced that there was not that much difference among them. The miracle of Mr. Dooley is that he was above the battle, and it may have been that his leavening produced more understanding on both sides.

The crowning glory of the Dooley essay is its exquisite ending. Many of the Dooley quotes that have become part of the English language were once summations to a Dooley essay. The essays must have been eagerly scanned by Mr. Dooley's America to get to these surprising and unique endings. Not only did they conclude an essay, but they afterwards took wing and made their way alone.

V. The Tale-end that Wags the Dog.

If readers were aware that a cherished Dooley quote is but the tale-end of a Mr. Dooley essay, it might revive their interest in seeking the original. Unfortunately, most Dooley quotes, many of them by scholars, are not associated with the original essay. If this fate befell the scholarly perpetrator, he would be the first to cry foul and consider bringing suit. The reason for this oversight may be that many people consider a "Dooleyism" part of the American language. Others, one suspects, are very possessive about their Dooley quotes; and they give the reader an option of quoting them as the "finder" of the Dooley quote or of finding the quote themselves. This procedure is all the more ironic in that Dunne's first efforts were pirated by an English publisher, and his *Mr. Dooley in the Hearts of His Countrymen* was dedicated to those "who, uninvited, presented Mr. Dooley to a part of the British public."

Few of the Dooley essays are protected by copyright. In 1963, three collections of the essays were published with much duplication and according to the taste of each editor. The ideal solution is a definitive edition of Mr. Dooley, fully indexed, and containing a glossary and concordance, so that scholars and popular writers, journalists and politicians, readers and quotation compilers can find the original source. The collection would include not only the books but the newspaper and magazine essays that have never been published in book form.

The foregoing discussion has been prefatory to an inclusion in this chapter of a compilation of Mr. Dooley's more famous closing lines; they are arranged by volume and fully cited, but a number have been selected to illustrate the range of his wisdom and talent.

Mr. Dooley in Peace and in War (1898)

ON THE POWER OF LOVE (Corbett-Fitzimmons fight):

" 'Well,' [Father] Doyle says, 'I guess ye're right,' he says. 'Afther all,' he says, 'an' undher all, we're mere brutes; an' it on'y takes two lads more brutal than th' rest f'r to expose th' sthreak in th' best if us. Foorce rules th' wurruld, an' th' churches is empty whin th' blood begins to flow,' he says. 'It's too bad, too bad,' he says. 'Tell me, was Corbett much hurted?' he says." (169)

ON WAR PREPARATIONS:

"We're a gr-reat people," said Mr. Hennessy, earnestly.

"We ar-re," said Mr. Dooley. "We ar-re that. An' th' best iv it is, we know we ar-re." (9)

ON BOOKS:

" 'Well,' says I, 'whin I was growin' up, half th' congregation heard mass with their prayer books tur-rned upside down, an' they were as pious as anny. Th' Apostles' Creed niver was as con-vincin' to me afther I larned to r-read it as it was whin I cudden't read it, but believed it.' " (110)

Mr. Dooley in the Hearts of his Countrymen (1899)

HANGING AN ALDERMAN:

"Now, Hinnissy, that there man niver knowed he was bribed — th' first time. Th' second time he knew. He ast f'r it. An' I wudden't hang Dochney. I wudden't if I was sthrong enough. But some day I'm goin' to let me temper r-run away with me, an' get a comity together, an' go out an' hang ivry dam widdy [widow] an' orphan between th' rollin' mills an' th' foundlin's' home. If it wasn't f'r thim raypechious crathers [creatures], they'd be no boodle annywhere...." (29).

LEXOW:

"Niver steal a dure-mat," said Mr. Dooley. "If ye do, ye'll be invistigated, hanged, an' maybe rayformed. Steal a bank, me boy, steal a bank." (40)

Mr. Dooley's Philosophy (1900)

A Book Review:

"I think Tiddy Rosenfelt [Theodore Roosevelt] is all r-right an' if he wants to blow his hor-rn lave him do it," said Mr. Hennessy.

"Thrue f'r ye," said Mr. Dooley, "an' if his valliant deeds didn't get into this book 'twud be a long time befure they appeared in Shafter's histhry iv th' war. No man that bears a gredge again' himsilf 'll iver be governor iv a state. An' if

29

Tiddy done it all he ought to say so an' relieve th' suspinse. But if I was him I'd call th' book 'Alone in Cubia.' " (18)

THE TRANSVAAL:

"What wud ye have done?" Mr. Hennessy asked.

"I'd give thim th' votes," said Mr. Dooley. "But," he added significantly, "I'd do th' countin'." (41)

THE WAR EXPERT:

"Well annyhow," said Mr. Dooley thoughtfully, "Th' expert is sarvin' a useful purpose. Th' pa-apers says th' rapid fire gun'll make war in th' future impossible. I don't think that, but I know th' expert will." (61)

THE BOER MISSION:

"... Th' enthusyasm iv this counthry, Hinnissy, always makes me think iv a bonfire on an ice-floe. It burns bright so long as ye feed it, an' it looks good, but it don't take hold, somehow, on th' ice." (75)

ALCOHOL AS FOOD:

"D'ye think ye-ersilf it sustains life?" asked Mr. Hennessy.

"It has sustained mine f'r many years," said Mr. Dooley. (153)

31

HIGH FINANCE:

"Cassidy," I says, "ye've been up again what th' pa-apers call hawt [high] finance," I says. "What th' divvle's that?" says he. "Well," says I, 'It ain't burglary, an' it ain't obtainin' money be false pretinses, an' it ain't manslaughter," I says. "It's what ye might call a judicious seliction fr'm th' best features iv thim ar-rts," I says. . . . (160)

Mr. Dooley's Opinions (1901)

CHRISTIAN SCIENCE:

"I think," said Mr. Dooley, "that if th' Christyan Scientists had some science an' th' doctors more Christyanity, it wudden't make anny diff'rence which ye called in — if ye had a good nurse." (9)

32

THE SUPREME COURT'S DECISIONS:

"That is," said Mr. Dooley, "no matther whether th' constitution follows th' flag or not, th' supreme coort follows th' iliction returns." (26)

AN EDITOR'S DUTIES:

"I shud think th' wurruk wud kill thim," said Mr. Hennessy, sadly.

"It does," said Mr. Dooley. "Manny gr-reat iditors is dead." (59)

SOME POLITICAL OBSERVATIONS:

"... A rayformer thries to get into office on a flyin' machine. He succeeds now an' thin, but th' odds are a hundherd to wan on th' la-ad that tunnels through." (177)

YOUTH AND AGE:

"Well," said Mr. Dooley, "a man is old enough to vote whin he can vote, he's old enough to wurruk whin he can wurruk. An' he's old enough to be prisidint whin he becomes prisidint. If he ain't, 't will age him." (186)

COLLEGES AND DEGREES:

"D'ye think th' colledges has much to do with th' progress iv th' wurruld?" asked Mr. Hennessy.

"D'ye think," said Mr. Dooley, " 't is th' mill that makes th' wather run?" (204)

Observations by Mr. Dooley (1902)

THE LAW'S DELAYS:

"I don't see," said Mr. Hennessy, "why they have anny juries. Why don't they thry ivry man before th' supreme coort an' have done with it?"

"I have a betther way than that," said Mr. Dooley. "Ye see they're wurrukin' on time now. I wondher if they wudden't sthep livelier if they were paid be th' piece." (19)

IMMIGRATION:

"Well," said Mr. Hennessy, "divvle th' bit I care, on'y I'm here first, an' I ought to have th' right to keep th' bus fr'm bein' overcrowded."

"Well," said Mr. Dooley, "as a pilgrim father on me gran' nephew's side, I don' know but ye're right. An' they'se wan sure way to keep thim out."

"What's that?" asked Mr. Hennessy.

"Teach thim all about our instichoochions befure they come," said Mr. Dooley. (54)

EUROPEAN INTERVENTION:

". . . F'r, Hinnissy, I tell ye, th' hand that rocks th' scales in th' grocery store, is th' hand that rules th' wurruld." (111)

WORK AND SPORT:

"No, sir, what's a rich man's raycreation is a poor man's wurruk. . . ."

"Why do they do it?" asked Mr. Hennessy.

"I dinnaw," said Mr. Dooley, "onless it is that the wan great object iv ivry man's life is to get tired enough to sleep. Ivrything seems to be some kind iv wurruk. Wurruk is wurruk if ye're paid to do it an' it's pleasure if ye pay to be allowed to do it." (179)

THE NEWS OF A WEEK:

"Th' newspapers have got to print what happens," said Mr. Hennessy.

"No," said Mr. Dooley, "they've got to print what's diff'rent. Whiniver they begin to put headlines on happiness, contint, varchoo [virtue], an' charity, I'll know things is goin' as wrong with this counthry as I think they ar-re ivry naytional campaign." (188)

THE END OF THE WAR:

"An' so th' war is over?" asked Mr. Hennessy.

"On'y part iv it," said Mr. Dooley. "Th' part that ye see in th' pitcher pa-apers is over, but th' tax collector will continyoo his part iv th' war with relentless fury. Cav'lry charges are not th' on'y charges in a rale [real] war." (195)

NEWPORT:

"Oh, well," said Mr. Hennessy, "we are as th' Lord made us."

"No," said Mr. Dooley, "lave us be fair. Lave us take some iv th' blame oursilves." (202)

MACHINERY:

"What d'ye think iv th' man down in Pinnsylvanya [George F. Baer] who says th' Lord an' him is partners in a coal mine?" asked Mr. Hennessy, who wanted to change the subject.

"Has he divided th' profits?" said Mr. Dooley. (219)

Dissertations by Mr. Dooley (1906)

ROYAL DOINGS:

"I don't see annything beautiful about it," said Mr. Hennessy. "It's just a crazy-headed ol' lunytic iv a woman runnin' away fr'm her childher."

"Hinnissy," said Mr. Dooley sternly, "ye f'rget Sophy's station. Whin an ol' crazy-headed lunytic iv a woman skips out 'tis a crime; whin an ol' crazy-headed lunytic iv a duchess does it, it's a scandal; but whin an ol' crazy-headed lunytic iv a princess does it, it's a romance." (15)

SHORT MARRIAGE CONTRACTS:

"... In me heart I think if people marry it ought to be f'r life. Th' laws ar-re altogether too lenient with thim." (47)

THE LABOR TROUBLES:

"They ought to get together [labor and management]," said Mr. Hennessy.

"How cud they get anny closer together thin their prisint clinch?" asked Mr. Dooley. "They're so close together now that those that ar-re between thim ar-re crushed to death." (64)

40

THE AUTOMOBILE:

"I think they ought to be locked up f'r tearin' through th' sthreets," said Mr. Hennessy.

"Well, maybe," said Mr. Dooley. "But don't ye think a man that owns an autymobill is punished enough?" (72)

THE INTELLECTUAL LIFE:

"If ye had a boy wud ye sind him to colledge?" asked Mr. Hennessy.

"Well," said Mr. Dooley, "at th' age whin a boy is fit to be in colledge I wudden't have him around th' house." (111)

NATIONAL HOUSECLEANING:

"I think th' counthry is goin' to th' divvle," said Mr. Hennessey, sadly.

"Hinnissy," said Mr. Dooley, "if that's so I congratylate th' wurruld."

"How's that?" asked Mr. Hennessy.

"Well," said Mr. Dooley, "f'r nearly forty years I've seen this counthry goin' to th' divvle, an' I got aboord late. An' if it's been goin' that long an' at that rate, an' has got no nearer thin it is this pleasant Chris'mas, thin th' divvle is a divvle iv a ways further off thin I feared." (262)

BUSINESS AND POLITICAL HONESTY:

"It seems to me that th' on'y thing to do is to keep pollyticians an' business men apart. They seem to have a bad infloonce on each other. Whiniver I see an aldherman an' a banker walkin' down th' sthreet together I know th' Recordin' Angel will have to ordher another bottle iv ink." (281)

BANKS AND BANKING:

"Th' wurruld is full iv crooks," said Mr. Hennessy.

"It ain't that bad," said Mr. Dooley. "An', besides, let us thank Hivin they put in part iv their time cheatin' each other." (308)

Mr. Dooley Says (1910)

DIVORCE:

"I think," said Mr. Dooley, "if people wanted to be divorced I'd let thim, but I'd give th' parents into th' custody iv th' childher. They'd larn thim to behave." (13)

GLORY:

"Which wud ye rather be, famous or rich?" asked Mr. Hennessy.

"I'd like to be famous," said Mr. Dooley, "an' have money enough to buy off all threatenin' bi-ographers." (24)

43

EXPERT TESTIMONY:

"I'm glad that fellow got me off," said Mr. Hennessy, "but thim experts ar-re a bad lot. What's th' diff'rence between that kind iv testymony an' perjury?"

"Ye pay ye're money an' take ye're choice," said Mr. Dooley. (179)

THE JAPANESE SCARE:

"Sure thim little fellows wud niver tackle us," said Mr. Hennessy. "Th' likes iv thim!"

"Well," said Mr. Dooley," 'tis because they ar-re little ye've got to be polite to thim. A big man knows he don't have to fight, but whin a man is little an' knows he's little an' is thinkin' all th' time he's little an' feels that ivrybody else is thinkin' he's little, look out f'r him." (203)

Mr. Dooley at his Best (1938)

OLD AGE:

"How long wud you like to live," asked Mr. Hennessy.

"Well," said Mr. Dooley, "I wuddn't want to have me life prolonged till I become a nuisance. I'd like to live as long as life is bearable to me an' as long afther that as I am bearable to life, an' think I'd like a few years to think it over." (245)

Mr. Dooley On the Choice of Law (1963)

RECALL OF JUDGES:

"What is this English common law I read about?" asked Mr. Hennessy.

"It's th' law I left Ireland to get away fr'm," said Mr. Dooley. . . ." (175)

Miscellany

FOOTBALL:

"Why don't th' polis stop it?" asked Mr. Hennessy, testily.

"They can't," said Mr. Dooley. "They can't arrist a man f'r

assault onless he commits it to get food or money." (*Boston Globe,* Nov. 23, 1902)

ON ENGLAND AND GERMANY:

"D'ye think they'll have a war?" asked Mr. Hennessy. "I hope so."

"Ye can't tell," said Mr. Dooley. "They won't if they're not afraid iv each other. But ye can't tell what a proud nation will do whin it's scared to death." (*Boston Globe,* June 27, 1909)

On the Democratic Party:

"F'r Hinnissy, a man is not made a Raypublican or a Dimmycrat be platforms or candydates. A man's a Raypublican or he's a Dimmycrat, an' that's all ye can say about it onless he's an indepindent, an' thin he's a Raypublican."

"I suppose th' counthry will be safe with ayther candydate," said Mr. Hennessy.

"It will be," said Mr. Dooley. "It will be safe with ayther candydate, or with both, or with nayther." (*American Magazine*, July 1908, 304)

On Diplomacy:

"D'ye think republics are ongrateful?" asked Mr. Hennessy.

"I do," said Mr. Dooley. "That's why they continue to be republics." (*American Magazine,* June, 1908, 111)

VI. In Praise of Dooley.

Most of the Dooley essays could be read in five minutes (the magazine pieces tended to be longer), and the reader was first captured by the currency of the comment, then drawn along by Dunne's playful use of what he called Roscommon Irish, although he was the first to admit it was impure.[11] Dunne employed the common techniques of dialect writers: misspelling, puns, funny names. He used "dishpot" for despot, "autymobill" to make the point that automobiles were expensive, and a James Joycian mind could detect hidden meanings in the use of words.[12] He would make his point by repeating a phrase within a catalogue of items, such as suggesting reasons why people would be prompted to do evil, and using the phrase "fer th' money," a number of times; or he would introduce a personality as "a household wurrud" and then proceed to mispronounce his name as in "Mr. Dooley on the Democratic Party"[13] when commenting on Woodrow Wilson. Beyond his explanation of current events, his making human those who were high and mighty, his exposing the sham and hypocrisy that are byproducts of society, there was the genius of Finley Peter Dunne.

1. For example, *see* James C. Austin, Artemus Ward, 74 (N.Y. 1964).

2. Constance Rourke, American Humor, A Study of the National Character, 177 (N.Y., 1955).

3. Mr. Dooley at his Best, xxiii (from the Introduction of Finley Peter Dunne to Elmer Ellis, ed., N.Y., 1938).

4. This story is more fully told in Chapter 6 of Elmer Ellis, Mr. Dooley's America, 58-76 (N.Y., 1941).

5. ELMER ELLIS, MR. DOOLEY'S AMERICA, 288 (N.Y., 1941).

6. Preface, FINLEY PETER DUNNE, MR. DOOLEY IN PEACE AND IN WAR, vii-xiii (Boston, 1899). An unidentified newspaper clipping found in a second hand Mr. Dooley volume adds the following: "F.P. Dunne has gone to Europe, taking Dooley with him. Ireland, London, Paris and Rome are on the itinerary. Before sailing Mr. Dunne let out a few secrets. He said: 'There is no real Dooley. There lives, indeed, in Chicago, an old Irishman with a lovely brogue. Many years ago I heard him talk about Jay Gould, how he couldn't take his money with him when he died, etc., and that gave me the idea. I have not seen him for four years. My Dooley stories are, of course, purely fictitious. The old Irishman in Chicago is a very sensitive old man and he has been made almost crazy recently by the avalanche of clippings about Dooley that have descended upon him. He thinks it's libel and everything else, and doesn't appreciate the fun of it, at all, at all.' "

7. John V. Kelleher, *Mr. Dooley and the Same Old World,* 177 ATLANTIC MONTHLY, 119-20 (June 1945).

8. FRED C. KELLY, GEORGE ADE, 83 (Indianapolis, 1947).

9. MR. DOOLEY AT HIS BEST, xvii-xviii (Foreword, Elmer Ellis, ed., N.Y., 1938).

10. Lewis Gannett, *Books and Things,* New York Herald Tribune (Oct. 28, 1938). A clipping in the New York Herald Tribune morgue located at New York University.

11. "Mr. Dooley's Irish brogue made no pretense to be phonetically correct; it just went in for being funny. The author himself once described it to me as 'a language never heard on land or sea.' Certainly that word *jackuse* in 'The Dreyfus Case' — to my mind and eye one of the funniest yet invented — belongs to no known tongue." MAX EASTMAN, ENJOYMENT OF LAUGHTER, 133 (N.Y., 1936).

12. ". . . and Dunne was not averse to exploiting any of Dooley's humorous possibilities — of spelling 'Mickrobe' for 'microbe' and 'liar' for 'lira,' offering 'sang fraud' and 'bum vivants' for their originals, and having all kinds of general fun with proper names." MR. DOOLEY NOW AND FOREVER, IX (Louis M. Filler, ed., Stanford, 1954).

13. 64 AMERICAN MAGAZINE, 303 (July 1908).

Chapter 3

POLITICS

I. The Critics Appraise Dooley.

No book on Finley Peter Dunne and his creation, Mr. Dooley, would be complete without a chapter about politics. In fact, no book on American politics would be complete without some reference to Mr. Dooley. As Henry S. Commager has written, "Perhaps the most penetrating literary commentary of the changing nature of politics came not from any novelist but from Finley Peter Dunne, whose transcriptions of the wit and wisdom of 'Mr. Dooley' pricked every political bubble and exposed every political fraud of these transition years." [1]

Dunne's influence on the times cannot be exaggerated, and the following tribute by Kenneth S. Lynn is typical: "Finley Peter Dunne, one of the first and still the best of the urban humorists America has produced. . . . The extent to which Mark Sullivan relied on Mr. Dooley's remarks in his history of the United States at the turn of the century is only one proof that the philosopher of Archey Road was the most penetrating political commentator of the era." [2] His weekly comments, beginning in the *Chicago Post,* were not only read by the average citizen, but found their way into the inner sanctum of Cabinet meetings: "There was time for the President's [McKinley] teasing, for repartee spiced by the wit of Hay and Long; time to listen and laugh while Secretary Gage, trolling an Irish brogue through his Sophoclean whiskers, read out Mr. Dooley's latest sallies on the state of the nation." [3]

The success of Finley Peter Dunne cannot be measured by any political commentator before or after his time. No one was safe from his political barbs, no political theory was immune from caustic comment, and no sacred American institution could escape analysis. Strange to relate, no one complained; indeed, ". . . he became the barometer of public opinion who was read aloud in Washington at cabinet meetings, as Artemus Ward had once been read by Lincoln during the Civil War because he also reflected the feelings of the people . . . he even went so far as to say, 'The Supreme Court follows the election returns,' the last word of the political scepticism of the muckraking era." [4]

His comments on Senators Beveridge and Lodge, the perennial party-standard-bearer William Jennings Bryan, Presidents McKinley and Roosevelt, and earlier in Dunne's career, on local politicians and businessmen, ranged from their mental ineptness to their physical characteristics. He interpreted Senator Lodge's expansionism as, "Hands acrost th' sea an' into some wan's pocket." [5] Yet, at most, Theodore Roosevelt would take issue with Dunne in a carefully worded letter,[6] and there are no known unpleasant incidents as Mr. Dooley went about his way and "comforted the afflicted and afflicted the comfortable." [7]

Dunne himself looked back at his early essays and suspected "Mr. Dooley's irreverence would be considered treasonable [today]," [8] and Henry S. Canby voiced a similar opinion: "There are a dozen pieces in this little book whose equivalent could not have been published in any year since 1916 without landing the author in court or jail as a pacifist (Mr. Dooley a pacifist!), a pro-something or another, or a Red. . . . But where are the Dooleys now? . . . Mr. and Mrs. Hennessy are with us yet, millions strong; but where is Mr. Dooley?" [9]

II. The Influence of Mr. Dooley.

The respect tendered Mr. Dooley may well have been summarized in an exchange of correspondence between Henry Cabot Lodge and Theodore Roosevelt:

Dec. 7, 1899

My Dear Theodore:

... I see that Dooley has been making game of you, and as he once devoted a paper to me I naturally take pleasure in the misfortunes of my friends, although I am bound to say that I felt that, when I was made the subject of a Dooley paper, I had advanced far on the high road of fame. ...

Henry Cabot Lodge

———

Dec. 14, 1899

Dear Cabot

... Yes, I saw Dooley's article and enjoyed it immensely. It is really exceedingly bright. How he does get at any joint in the harness!

Theodore Roosevelt [10]

But Dooley, the "National wit and censor" (to borrow a chapter heading from Mr. Ellis' biography of Dunne), was too well-loved to be sued or berated. Mr. Dooley may have said things he should not have, but he was saying what everyone would have said if he could have put it into words — and had had the courage to do so. His reading public was the entire electorate from voter to ward heeler to senator to President, including expatriates such as Henry James and his adopted countrymen. Dunne was listened to respectfully because he lacked respect. Mr. Dooley was not a political commentator — no subject was too relevant or irrelevant for his irreverence — but politics lent itself more readily to disdain. It was a period of rugged individualism, robber barons, and human and land exploitation. While Dunne was not a muckraker,[11] he made it possible for Ida Tarbell,

Lincoln Steffens and others to expose the graft and the venality of the period. Dunne's popularity being what it was, a politician who attempted to bring him to task would find himself arguing with a mythical bartender on the one hand and bringing an unwanted public attention to himself on the other.

There have been other political pundits and American humorists who have been unafraid to hoist a politician on his own petard, but none had quite the same success as Dunne — perhaps because Dunne lacked vindictiveness. However, his topics were always relevant and were expressed clearly. Dialect it may have been, but everybody from an Anglo-Saxon to the most recent wave of immigrants could understand who he was talking about and realize that he knew what he was talking about. And above all, even above Mr. Dooley's integrity, there was the Dunne humor. Franklin P. Adams suggests that Dunne may be forgotten because of his reputation as a humorist,[12] but he has also written: "Reading this evening Mr. Finley Peter Dunne's musings on politicks I am greatly delighted at them, and discover politicks need not be dull, save only when made so, which is what most scriveners do. (Feb. 21, 1912 at 28). . . . For it seemeth to me he hath said all that could be said, and there is little of it that might not have been written yesterday. (May 26, 1921 at 284)"[13]

III. Mr. Dooley Today.

Dunne's political commentary must answer a more severe test than the fact that in his time, "Everybody read it, everybody quoted it, everybody waited for the next."[14] In the final analysis, Dunne's political comments, to be durable, must have relevance for other times. He has been quoted and admired by such contemporary politicians as Adlai Stevenson, Hubert H. Humphrey, John F. Kennedy, Lyndon Johnson, Eugene McCarthy; and political commentators Alistair Cooke, Arthur Krock, Max Lerner, William Safire, and Tom Wicker have all had occasion to refer to him. Mr. Dooley is also among the books selected for the White House Library.[15]

It is a rare anthology that neglects Mr. Dooley if the topic is politics or humor. He is included in Leonard C. Lewin's *A Treasury of American Political Humor.*[16] A reviewer of this book commented, ". . . excerpts from 'Mr. Dooley,' who is still funny; Mark Twain who is not; Will Rogers, also not."[17] And no critique of American political humor neglects Dunne. When Mort Sahl was the humorist of the hour, *Time* referred to the old master: "Finley Peter Dunne, whose Mr. Dooley is the all-time choice of many political connoisseurs, swaddled his man in an Irish dialect that magically permitted him to speak his mind. He once called John D. Rockefeller 'a kind iv society f'r th' prevention if croolty to money,' and had a skill at reworking slogans that has turned up again in Sahl."[18]

Any current assessment of Art Buchwald involves, invariably, a consideration of Dunne:

> "A few years ago, Paul Douglas, the former Senator from Illinois, said an interesting thing to me," Buchwald recalled. "He said that in each generation it seems as though the American people give a license to only one or two comedians or writers to make fun of politics and politicians. He mentioned Finley Peter Dunne, for instance, and Will Rogers, and he said that he thought that I had the license. And when you've got the license, you can get away with murder — be praised for writing things that another writer might be stoned in the streets for having written. . . ."[19]

Victor S. Navasky, reviewing a book by Dick Gregory, provides his list of American political humorists, which illustrates that, while critics have their own favorites, they invariably include Mr. Dooley: "Dick Gregory is not the first humorist to instruct Americans on how their government really works. Petroleum V. Nasby, Artemus Ward, Mark Twain, Ambrose Bierce, Finley Peter Dunne, Will Rogers, Mort Sahl, Russell Baker, Art Buchwald and Marvin Kitman are others who come immediately to mind." [20]

Jesse Bier's scholarly book on humor has an all-inclusive list of political humorists that reads as follows:

> Our comic as well as general preoccupation with militant politics from Freneau, Irving and Seba Smith through the southwesterners [A.B. Longstreet, J. J. Hooper, Joseph Baldwin, W. T. Thompson, T. B. Thorpe, George Washington Harris, H. C. Lewis], the literary comedians [including Lincoln himself, and James Russell Lowell, Charles Farrar Browne (Artemus Ward), David Ross Locke (Petroleum V. Nasby), Henry W. Shaw (Josh Billings), Harriet Beecher Stowe, Robert H. Newell, and R. J. Burdette in the North, George Horatio Derby (John Phoenix), Bret Harte, Billy Nye in the West, and Charles Henry Smith (Bill Arp) and Joel Chandler Harris in the South], and Dunne, to Norman Mailer and Art Buchwald, is both inheritance and original sin.[21]

To this list Norris W. Yates [22] adds John Kendrick Bangs, George Ade, Frank McKinney Hubbard (Abe Martin), and references to humorists such as Nathaniel Benchley and Dorothy Parker who only occasionally indulged in political humor.

All list Finley Peter Dunne; all quote frequently from his works. One can only conclude after a careful summarizing of the specialists in the fields of humor, history and political science that only a few are called to the ranks of political humor; of those called, most are unknown today; and, of them all, Finley Peter Dunne is by far the best.

IV. The Permanence of Mr. Dooley.

The claim for Dunne's preeminence in the field of political humor rests not on the opinion of specialists but on what he wrote and on its timelessness. The following extracts from the works of Finley Peter Dunne have been selected for their brevity (it would take large extracts, for instance, to investigate his attitude toward expansionism, an issue not strong in contemporary politics), popularity and currency. The litmus test of political humor is its relevance, and if the bright spot of Mr. Dooley's comments is how apropos his remarks on politics are to another generation, the dark spot is how little politics have changed since the turn of the century (or since the creation of social organizations). The quotes are arranged alphabetically by topic with an abbreviated source of the quote.

ALDERMAN:

Whiniver I see an aldherman an' a banker walkin' down th' sthreet together I know th' Recordin' Angel will have to ordher another bottle iv ink. (*Dissertations* 281)

AMBASSADOR:

An ambassadure is a man that is no more use abroad thin he wud be at home. A vice-prisidint iv a company that's bein' took in be a thrust, a lawyer that th' juries is onto, a Congressman that can't be reilicted. (*Dissertations* 88)

ANARCHIST:

If they was no newspapers they'd be few arnychists. (*Philosophy* 198)

ATTORNEY GENERAL:

On'y wan class is iligible [eligible] fr Attorney-gin'ral. To fill that job, a man's got to be a first-class thrust lawyer. (*Hearts* 145)

57

BANKER:

See ALDERMAN

BRIBERY:

Now, Hinnissy, that there man niver knowed he was bribed — th' first time. Th' second time he knew. He ast f'r it. (*Hearts* 29)

BUSINESSMEN AS POLITICIANS:

See also REFORM

"No, sir," said Mr. Dooley; "ye don't r-read th' pa-apers. Ivry year, whin th' public conscience is aroused as it niver was befure, me frinds on th' palajeems [Palladium] iv our liberties an' records iv our crimes calls f'r business men to swab out our govermint with business methods. We must turn it over to pathrites [patriots] who have made their pile in mercantile pursoots iv money wheriver they cud find it. We must injooce th' active, conscientious young usurers fr'm Wall Sthreet to take an inthrest in public affairs. Th' poolrooms is open. . . . Down with th' poolrooms, says I. But how? says you. Be ilictin' a business man mayor, says I. But who'll we get? says you. Who betther, says I, thin th' prisidint iv th' Westhren Union Tillygraft [sic] Comp'ny, who knows where th' poolrooms ar-re." (*Dissertations* 275)

CABINET:

If 'twas wan iv th' customs iv th' great raypublic iv ours, Jawn, f'r to appoint th' most competent men f'r th' places, he'd have a mighty small lot f'r to pick fr'm. But, seein' that on'y thim is iligible [eligible] that are unfit, he has th' divvle's own time selectin'. (*Hearts* 144)

CAMPAIGN:

It niver requires coercion to get a man to make a monkey iv himsilf in a prisidintial campaign. (*Peace* 184)

POLITICS

CANDIDATES:

"Speakin' iv pollyticks," said Mr. Hennessy, "who d'ye think'll be ilicted?"

"Afther lookin' th' candydates over," said Mr. Dooley, "an' studyin' their qualifications carefully I can't thruthfully say that I see a prisidintial possibility in sight." (*Will* 101)

Th' life iv a candydate is th' happiest there is. If I want annythin' pleasant said about me I have to say it mesilf. There's a hundherd thousan' freemen ready to say it to a candydate, an' say it sthrong. . . . He starts in with a pretty good opinyon iv himsilf, based on what his mother said iv him as a baby, but be th' time he's heerd th' first speech iv congratulation he begins to think he had a cold an' indiff'rent parent. . . .

If he hasn't done much to speak iv, his frinds rayport his small but handsome varchues [virtues]. (*Dissertations* 200, 201)

An' did ye iver notice how much th' candydates looks alike, an' how much both iv thim looks like Lydia Pinkham? Thim wondherful boardhin'-house smiles that our gifted leaders wears, did ye iver see annythin' so entrancin'? . . . Glory be, what a relief 'twill be f'r wan iv thim to raysume permanently th' savage or fam'ly breakfast face th' mornin' afther iliction! . . . 'Tis th' day afther iliction I'd like f'r to be a candydate, Hinnissy, no matther how it wint. (*Philosophy* 233, 234)

"I wondher," said Mr. Hennessy, "if us dimmycrats will iver ilict a prisidint again."

"We wud," said Mr. Dooley, "if we cud but get an illegible candydate."

"What's that?" asked Mr. Hennessy.

"An illegible candydate," said Mr. Dooley, "is a candydate that can't be read out iv th' party. . . .

"Ye might thry advertisin' in th' pa-apers. 'Wanted: A good, active, inergetic dimmycrat, sthrong iv lung an' limb;

59

must be in favor iv sound money, but not too sound, an' anti-impeeryalist but f'r holdin' onto what we've got, an inimy iv thrusts but a frind iv organized capital, a sympathizer with th' crushed an downthrodden people but not be anny means hostile to vested inthrests; must advocate sthrikes, gover'mint be injunction, free silver, sound money ... He must be akelly [equally] at home in Wall Sthreet an' th' stock yards, in th' parlors iv th' r-rich an' th' kitchens iv th' poor....'" (*Opinions* 93, 96, 97)

Church and State:

See also Preachers

Rellijon is a quare thing. Be itsilf it's all right. But sprinkle a little pollyticks into it an' dinnymite is bran flour compared with it. Alone it prepares a man f'r a betther life. Combined with pollyticks it hurries him to it. (*Will* 182, 183)

College:

Ye talk about ye'er colleges, Hinnissy, but pollyticks is th' poor man's college. A la-ad without enough book larnin' to r-read a meal-ticket, if ye give him tin years iv polly-tical life, has th' air iv a statesman an' th' manner iv a jook [duke], an' cud take anny job fr'm dalin' faro bank to r-runnin' th' threasury iv th' United States. His business brings him up again' th' best men iv th' com-munity, an' their customs an' ways iv speakin' an' thinkin' an robbin' sticks to him. (*Philosophy* 145, 146)

Congress:

See also Preachers

"Well, I see Congress has got to wurruk again," said Mr. Dooley.

"The Lord save us fr'm harm," said Mr. Hennessy. (*Observations* 49)

CONGRESSIONAL INVESTIGATION:
"Niver steal a dure-mat," said Mr. Dooley. "If ye do, ye'll be invistigated, hanged, an' maybe rayformed. Steal a bank, me boy, steal a bank." (*Hearts* 40)

CONGRESSMAN:
Th' on'y thing a Congressman isn't afraid iv is th' on'y thing I'd be afraid iv, an' that is iv bein' a Congressman. (*Says* 116)

CONSTITUTION:
'Tis funny about th' Constitution. It reads plain, but no wan understands it without an interpreter. (*Choice of Law* 171)
... th' constitootion iv th' United States is applicable on'y in such cases as it is applied to on account iv its applicability.... (*Philosophy* 105)

DEMOCRATIC PARTY:
Th' dimmycrats ar-re right an' the raypublicans has th' jobs. (*Philosophy* 122)
Whiniver a dimmycrat has to go to coort to win an iliction I get suspicious. (*Philosophy* 127)
Histhry always vindicates th' Dimmycrats, but niver in their lifetime. They see th' thruth first, but th' throuble is that nawthin' is iver officially thrue till a Raypublican sees it. (*Dissertations* 185-186)
"No, sir, th' dimmycratic party ain't on speakin' terms with itsilf. Whin ye see two men with white neckties go into a sthreet car an' set in opposite corners while wan mutthers 'Thraiter' an' th' other hisses 'Miscreent' ye can bet they're two dimmycratic leaders thryin' to reunite th' gran' ol' party." (*Opinions* 93)
Man an' boy I've seen th' dimmycratic party hangin' to th' ropes a score iv times. ... I've gone to sleep nights wondhrin' where I'd throw away me vote afther this an' whin I woke up there was that crazy-headed ol' loon iv a party with its hair sthreamin' in its eyes, an' an axe in its

61

hand, chasin' raypublicans into th' tall grass. 't is niver so good as whin 't is broke, whin rayspictable people speak iv it in whispers, an' whin it has no leaders an' on'y wan principal, to go in an' take it away fr'm th' other fellows. *(Opinions* 97, 98)

No wan can say what anny ten Dimmycrats will do whin they gather together f'r th' good iv th' counthry, in a hall. ... Ye may talk about ye'er heroes fr'm Leonydas ... but give me th' man who has voted th' Dimmycratic ticket in Vermont since th' war.... That's wan good thing about th' Dimmycratic party, it always has plenty iv candydates.... Th' Raypublicans have difficulty in selectin' a candydate f'r thimsilves because there's niver more thin wan, an' he's handed to thim....

"F'r, Hinnissy, a man is not made a Raypublican or a Dimmycrat be platforms of candydates. A man's a Raypublican or he's a Dimmycrat, an' that's all ye can say about it onless he's an indepindent, an' thin he's a Raypublican."

"I suppose th' counthry will be safe with ayther candydate," said Mr. Hennessy.

"It will be," said Mr. Dooley. "It will be safe with ayther candydate, or with both, or with nather." (*American Magazine,* July 1908, 301, 302, 304)

Diplomacy:

Di-plomacy has become a philanthropic pursoot like shop-keepin', but politicks, me lords, is still th' same ol' spoort iv highway robb'ry. (*Observations* 35)

Editors and Orators:

Orators an' iditors sildom do well in office. They have to express opinyons right off th' stove on ivry known subjick [subject] in language that ivry wan will remimber an' repeat, an' afther that they can't change without somebody diggin' up what they said. (*Will* 142)

ELECTIONS:

See also VOTING

Th' mornin' afther iliction, 't is Hinnissy to th' slag pile an' Dooley to th' beer pump an' Jawn D. Rockefellar to th' ile [oil] can, an' th' ol' flag floatin' over all iv us if th' wind is good an' th' man in charge has got up in time to hist [hoist] it. Foolish man, th' fun'rals don't stop f'r ilictions, or th' christenin's or th' weddin's. . . . Don't ye expict Hinnissy that anny throop iv angels will dhrop fr'm Hiven to chop ye'er wood on th' mornin' iv th' siventh iv Novimber if Bryan [William Jennings] is ilicted, an' don't ye lave Jawnny McKenna think that if th' raypublicans gets in, he'll have to put a sthrip iv ile-cloth on th' dure sill to keep pluthycrats [plutocrats] fr'm shovin' threasury notes undher th' dure [door]. (*Opinions* 110)

EQUAL PROTECTION OF THE LAW:

This home iv opporchunity where ivry man is th' equal iv ivry other man befure th' law if he isn't careful. (*Dissertations* 248)

FANATIC:

A fanatic is a man that does what he thinks th' Lord wud do if He knew th' facts iv th' case. (*Philosophy* 258)

GOVERNOR:

No man that bears a gredge [grudge] again' himsilf'll iver be governor iv a state. (*Philosophy* 18)

HONESTY IN POLITICS:

Ivry man ought to be honest to start with, but to give a man an office jus' because he's honest is like ilictin' him to Congress because he's a pathrite [patriot], because he don't bate his wife or because he always wears a right boot on th' right foot. A man ought to be honest to start with an afther that he ought to be crafty. A pollytician who's on'y honest is jus' th' same as bein' out in a winther storm without anny clothes on. (*Observations* 170)

INJUNCTION:

I care not who makes th' laws iv a nation if I can get out an injunction. (*Philosophy* 259)

LAWYER:

See also REFORM

"Another thing about rayform administhrations is they always think th' on'y man that ought to hold a job is a lawyer. Th' raison is that in th' coorse iv his thrainin' a lawyer larns enough about ivrything to make a good front on anny subject to annybody who doesn't know about it. So whin th' rayform administhration comes in th' mayor says: 'Who'll we make chief iv polis in place iv th' misguided ruffyan who has held th' job f'r twinty years?' 'Th' man f'r th' place,' says th' mayor's adviser, 'is Arthur Lightout,' he says. 'He's an ixcillent lawyer, Yale, '95, . . . he's been in th' milishy an' th' foorce needs a man who'll be afraid not to shoot in case iv public disturbance.'" (*Observations* 170, 171)

MAGAZINES:

"It looks to me," said Mr. Hennessy, "as though this counthry was goin' to th' divvle [devil]."

"Put down that magazine," said Mr. Dooley. (*Dissertations* 257)

OLD AGE:

Pollytics and bankin' is th' on'y two games where age has th' best iv it. Youth has betther things to attind to, an' more iv thim. (*Observations* 257)

OPINION:

Ye have a r-right to ye'er opinyon, an' ye'll hold it annyhow, whether ye have a r-right to it or not. (*Peace* 234)

PLATFORM MAKING:

" 'Why,' says Lafferty, 'ye ought to know th' histhry iv platforms,' he says. An' he give it to me, an' I'll give it to ye. Years ago, Hinnissy, manny years ago, they was a race between th' dimmycrats an' th' raypublicans f'r to see which shud have a choice iv principles. Th' dimmycrats lost. I dinnaw why. Mebbe they stopped to take a dhrink. Annyhow, they lost. Th' raypublicans come up an' they choose th' 'we commind' principles, an' they was nawthin' left f'r th' dimmycrats but th' 'we denounce an' deplores.' I dinnaw how it come about, but th' dimmycrats didn't like th' way th' thing shtud, an' so they fixed it up between thim that whichiver won at th' iliction shud commind an' congratulate, an' thim that lost shud denounce an' deplore. An' so it's been, on'y the dimmycrats has had so little chanct f'r to do annything but denounce an' deplore that they've almost lost th' use iv th' other wurruds. (*Philosophy* 100)

POLICE:

I believe in th' polis [police] foorce, though not in polismen. (*Hearts* 25)

POLITICIAN:

Th' man that sinds seeds to his constitooents lasts longer thin th' wan that sinds thim flowers iv iloquence.... (*Philosophy* 132, 133)

POLITICIAN AND BUSINESSMAN:

See also BUSINESSMEN AS POLITICIANS

A reg'lar pollytician can't give away an alley without blushin', but a business man who is in pollytics jus' to see that th' civil sarvice law gets thurly enfoorced, will give Lincoln Park an' th' public libr'y to th' beef thrust, charge an admission price to th' lake front an' make it a felony f'r annywan to buy stove polish outside iv his store, an' have it all put down to public improve-mints with a pitcher iv him in th' corner stone. (*Observations* 169)

POLITICIAN AND REFORMER:

See also REFORM

Rayformers, Hinnissy, is in favor iv suppressin' ivrything, but rale pollyticians believe in suppressin' nawthin' but ividince [evidence]. (*Opinions* 174)

POLITICS:

See also COLLEGE

"Tis a profissional spoort, like playin' base-ball f'r a livin' or wheelin' a thruck. Ye niver see an amachoor at annything that was as good as a profissional. . . . No, sir, pollytics ain't dhroppin' into tea, an' it ain't wurrukin' a scroll saw, or makin' a garden in a back yard. 'Tis gettin' up at six o'clock in th' mornin' an' r-rushin' off to wurruk, an' comin' home at night tired an' dusty. Double wages f'r overtime an' Sundahs. . . ."

"Yet ye say a pollytician oughtn't to get married," said Mr. Hennessy.

"Up to a certain point," said Mr. Dooley, "he must be marrid. Afther that — well, I on'y say that, though pollytics is a gran' career f'r a man, 'tis a tough wan f'r his wife." (*Philosophy* 142, 147)

"Politics," he says, "ain't bean bag. 'Tis man's game; an' women, childher, an' prohybitionists'd do well to keep out iv it." (*Peace* xiii)

"Th' two gr-eat American spoorts are a good deal alike — pollyticks an' base-ball. They're both played be pro-fissyonals, th' teams ar-re r-run be fellows that cudden't throw a base-ball or stuff a ballot-box to save their lives an' ar-re on'y intherested in countin' up th' gate receipts, an' here ar-re we settin' out in th' sun on th' bleachin' boords, payin' our good money f'r th' spoort, hot an' uncomfortable but happy, injying ivry good play, hootin' ivry bad wan, knowin' nawthin' about th' inside play an' not carin', but all jinin' in th' cry iv 'Kill th' empire.' [sic]. They're both grand games."

"Speakin' iv pollytics," said Mr. Hennessy, "who d'ye think'll be ilicted?"

"Afther lookin' th' candydates over," said Mr. Dooley, "an' studyin' their qualifications carefully I can't thruthfully say that I see a prisidintial possibility in sight." (*Boston Globe,* May 5, 1912)

If he'd been in pollyticks as long as I have an' was as active an' as prom'nent he wudn't have noticed th' insult. He'd know that in pollyticks th' worst men ar-re often libeled, so what can th' best expict?

It's a good thing, too, f'r it keeps sinsitive an' thin skinned men out iv public life an' dhrives thim into journalism. (*Choice of Law* 162, 163)

POVERTY:

Don't I think a poor man has a chanst in coort? Iv coorse he has. He has th' same chanst there that he has outside. He has a splendid, poor man's chanst. (*Choice of Law* 173)

PREACHERS IN CONGRESS:

'Tis a good thing preachers don't go to Congress. Whin they're ca'm [calm] they'd wipe out all th' laws an' whin they're excited, they'd wipe out all th' popylation. They're niver two jumps fr'm th' thumbscrew. 'T is quare th' best iv men at times shud feel like th' worst tow'rd those between. (*Opinions* 181, 182)

PRECEDENTS:

"Be hivins, Hinnissy, I want me advice up-to-date, an' whin Mack (President McKinley) an' Willum Jennings (Bryan) tells me what George Wash'nton an' Thomas Jefferson said, I says to thim: 'Gintlemen, they larned their thrade befure th' days iv open plumbin',' I says, 'Tell us what is wanted ye'ersilf or call in a journeyman who's wurrukin' card is dated this cinchry [century],' I says." (*Philosophy* 215)

PRESIDENT:

Th' proceedin's was opened with a prayer that Providence might r-remain undher th' protection iv th' administhration. (*Peace* 83)

If he hasn't done much to speak iv, his frinds rayport his small but handsome varchues [virtues]. . . . A man expicts to be ilicted Prisidint iv th' United States, Hinnissy, f'r th' fine qualities that th' r-rest iv us use on'y to keep out iv th' pinitinchry. (*Dissertations* 201)

68

"It's no sin to be a candydate f'r prisidint."

"No," said Mr. Dooley. " 'Tis sometimes a misfortune an' sometimes a joke." (*Philosophy* 180)

"Well," said Mr. Dooley, "a man is old enough to vote whin he can vote, he's old enough to wurruk whin he can wurruk. An' he's old enough to be prisidint whin he becomes prisidint. If he ain't, 't will age him." *(Opinions* 186)

. . . a man can be r-right an' be prisidint, but he can't be both at th' same time. (*Philosophy* 179)

PROFESSORS ON POLITICS:

" 'Me opinyon iv pollyticks, if ye shud ask me f'r it, is that we might as well give up th' experimint. A govermint founded be an ol' farmer like George Wash'nton an' a job-printer like Bin Franklin was bound to go down in roon [ruin]. It has abandoned all their ideels — which was a good thing — an' made worse wans. Look at Lincoln. There's a fellow ivrybody is always crackin' up. But what did he amount to? What did he do but carry on a war, free th' slaves, an' run this mis'rable counthry? But who asked him to free th' slaves? I didn't. A man utterly lackin' in principle an' sinse iv humor, he led a mob an' was conthrolled be it. An' who ar-re th' mob that direct this counthry? A lot iv coarse, rough people, who ar-re sawin' up lumber an' picklin' port, an' who niver had a thought iv th' Higher Life that makes men aspire to betther things an' indigestion. They ar-re ye're fathers an' mine, young gintlemen. Can I say worse thin that? An' to think iv th' likes iv thim runnin' this govermint! By Jove, if I had raymimbered las' Choosday that it was iliction day I'd have larned fr'm me milkman how to vote an' gone down to th' polls an' dhriven thim fr'm power. Well, there's wan consolation about it all: th' counthry won't last long.' " (*Dissertations* 109)

REFORM:

A man that'd expict to thrain lobsters to fly in a year is called a loonytic; but a man that thinks men can be tur-rned into angels be an iliction is called a rayformer an' remains at large. (*Philosophy* 261)

As a people, Hinnissy, we're th' greatest crusaders that iver was — f'r a short distance.... But th' throuble is th' crusade don't last afther th' first sprint. Th' crusaders drops out iv th' procission to take a dhrink or put a little money on th' ace an' be th' time th' end iv th' line iv march is reached th' boss crusader is alone in th' job an' his former followers is hurlin' bricks at him fr'm th' windows iv policy shops. (*Opinions* 154)

"... this counthry, while wan iv th' worst in th' wurruld, is about as good as th' next if it ain't a shade betther. But we're wan iv th' gr-reatest people in th' wurruld to clean house, an' th' way we like best to clean th' house is to burn it down. We come home at night an' find that th' dure has been left open an' a few mosquitoes or life-insurance prisidints have got in, an' we say: 'This is turr'ble. We must get rid iv these here pests.' An' we take an axe to thim. We desthroy a lot iv furniture an' kill th' canary bird, th' cat, th' cuckoo clock, an' a lot iv other harmless insects, but we'll fin'lly land th' mosquitoes.... But with this here nation iv ours somebody scents something wrong with th' scales at th' grocery-store an' whips out his gun, another man turns in a fire alarm, a third fellow sets fire to th' Presbyterian Church, a vigilance comity is formed an' hangs ivry foorth man; an' havin' started with Rockyfellar, who's tough an' don't mind bein' lynched, they fin'lly wind up with desthroyin' me because th' steam laundhry has sint me home somebody else's collars.

"It reminds me, Hinnissy, iv th' time I lived at a boardin'-house kept be a lady be th' name iv Doherty. She was a good woman, but her idee iv life was a combination iv pneumony an' love. She was niver still. Th' sight iv a spot

70

on th' wall where a gintleman boorder had laid his head afther dinner would give her nervous prostration. She was always polishin', scrubbin', sweepin', airin'. She had a plumber in to look at th' dhrains twice a week. Fifty-two times a year there was a rivolution in th' house that wud've made th' Czar iv Rooshya want to go home to rest. An' yet th' house was niver really clean. It looked as if it was to us. It was so clean that I always was ashamed to go into it onless I'd shaved. But Mrs. Doherty said no; it was like a pig-pen. 'I don't know what to do,' says she. 'I'm worn out, an' it seems impossible to keep this house clean.' 'What is th' throuble with it?' says she. 'Madam,' says me frind Gallagher, 'wud ye have me tell ye?' he says. 'I wud,' says she. 'Well,' says he, 'th' throuble with this house is that it is occypied entirely be human bein's,' he says. 'If 'twas a vacant house,' he says, 'it cud aisily be kept clean,' he says.

"An' there ye ar-re, Hinnissy. Th' noise ye hear is not th' first gun iv a rivolution. It's on'y th' people iv th' United States batin' a carpet. . . . Who is that yellin'? That's our ol' frind High Fi-nance bein' compelled to take his annual bath. . . ."

"I think th' counthry is goin' to th' divvle," said Mr. Hinnissy, sadly. . . .

"Well," said Mr. Dooley, "f'r nearly forty years I've seen this counthry goin' to th' divvle, an' I got aboord late. An' if it's been goin' that long an' at that rate, an' has got no nearer thin it is this pleasant Chris'mas, thin th' divvle is a divvle iv a ways further off thin I feared." (*Dissertations* 259-262)

"I don't like a rayformer," said Mr. Hennessy. "Or anny other raypublican," said Mr. Dooley. (*Observations* 172)

A rayformer thries to get into office on a flyin' machine. He succeeds now an' thin, but th' odds are a hundherd to wan on th' la-ad that tunnels through. (*Opinions* 177)

71

Th' enthusyasm iv this counthry, Hinnissy, always makes me think iv a bonfire on an ice-floe. It burns bright so long as ye feed it, an' it looks good, but it don't take hold, somehow, on th' ice. (*Philosophy* 75)

"... A rayfomer thinks he was ilicted because he was a rayformer, whin th' thruth iv th' matther is he was ilicted because no wan knew him. Ye can always ilict a man in this counthry on that platform. If I was runnin' f'r office, I'd change me name, an' have printed on me cards: 'Give him a chanst; he can't be worse.' " (*Observations* 167)

RELIGION:

See CHURCH AND STATE, PREACHERS

REPUBLICAN PARTY:

See also DEMOCRATIC PARTY, REFORM

"... th' convintion nomynates a man that ivrybody outside iv New York knew was goin' to be nommynated a year ago last Chris'mas, ivry body sings 'Th' Star-Spangled Banner' an' other Republican ballads, and thin goes to their peaceful an' highly oninthrestin' homes...." (*American Magazine* July 1908, 301)

REVOLUTION:

I'm sthrong f'r anny rivolution that ain't goin' to happen in me day.... I see gr-reat changes takin' place ivry day, but no change at all ivry fifty years. (*Dissertations* 271)

RIGHTS:

"But don't ask f'r rights. Take thim. An' don't let anny wan give thim to ye. A right that is handed to ye f'r nawthin' has somethin' th' matther with it. 'It's more than likely it's on'y a wrong turned inside out,' says I. 'I didn't fight f'r th' rights I'm told I injye, though to tell ye th' truth, I injye me wrongs more; but some wan did. Some time some fellow was prepared to lay down his life, or betther still, th' other fellows', f'r th' right to vote.' " (*Says* 38)

Woman's rights? What does a woman want iv rights whin she has priv'leges? Rights is th' last thing we get in this wurruld. They're th' nex' things to wrongs. They're wrongs tur-ned inside out. We have th' right to be sued f'r debt instead iv lettin' the bill run, which is a priv'lege. We have th' right to thrile be a jury iv our peers, a right to pay taxes an' a right to wurruk. None iv these things is anny good to me. They'se no fun in thim. All th' r-rights I injye I don't injye. I injye th' right to get money, but I niver have had anny money to spind. Th' consti-chooshion guarantees me th' right to life, but I die; to liberty, but if I thry bein' too free I'm locked up; an' to th' pursoot iv happiness, but happiness has th' right to run whin pursood, an' I've niver been able to three [tree] her yet. Here I am at iver-so-manny years iv age blown an' exhausted be th' chase, an' happiness is still able to do her hundhred yards in tin minyits flat whin I approach. I'd give all th' rights I read about for wan priv-lege. If I cud go to sleep th' minyit I go to bed I wudden't care who done me votin'. *(Observations* 253)

SENATE:

Th' Sinit is ruled be courtesy, like th' longshoreman's union. (*Dissertations* 119)

SPEECH MAKING:

I hope to read in th' pa-aper some day that Joe Cannon was arrested f'r usin' th' American flag to dicorate a speech on th' tariff, an' sintinced to two years solitary confinemint with Sinitor Bevridge [Beveridge]. (*Dissertations* 24)

SPORTS AND POLITICS:

See POLITICS

STATUTE OF LIMITATIONS:

Th' best citizens is thim that th' statue iv limitations was made f'r. (*Hearts* 37)

SUPREME COURT:

It niver gives a decision till th' crowd has dispersed an' th' players have packed their bats in th' bags an' started f'r home. . . .

"That is," said Mr. Dooley, "no matther whether th' constitution follows th' flag or not, th' supreme coort follows th' iliction returns." (*Opinions* 22, 26)

TRUSTS:

" 'Th' thrusts,' says he to himsilf, 'are heejous monsthers built up be th' inlightened intherprise iv th' men that have done so much to advance pro-gress in our beloved counthry,' he says. 'On wan hand I wud stamp thim undher fut; on th' other hand not so fast. What I want more thin th' bustin' iv th' thrusts is to see me fellow counthrymen happy an' continted. I wudden't have thim hate th' thrusts. Th' haggard face, th' droopin' eye, th' pallid complexion that marks th' inimy iv thrusts is not to me taste. Lave us be merry about it an' jovial an' affectionate. Lave us laugh an' sing th' octopus out iv existence. . . .' " (*Observations* 223, 224)

UNITED STATES:

"We're a gr-reat people," said Mr. Hennessy, earnestly.

"We ar-re," said Mr. Dooley. "We ar-re that. An' th' best iv it is, we know we ar-re." (*Peace* 9)

. . . this counthry, while wan iv th' worst in th' wurruld, is about as good as th' next if it ain't a shade betther. (*Dissertations* 259)

VICE-PRESIDENT:

He must be a good speaker, a pleasant man with th' ladies, a fair boxer an' rassler, something iv a liar, an' if he's a Raypublican campaignin' in Texas, an active sprinter. (*Dissertations* 117)

Th' prisidincy is th' highest office in th' gift iv th' people. Th' vice-prisidincy is th' next highest an' th' lowest. It isn't

74

a crime exactly. Ye can't be sint to jail f'r it, but it's a kind iv a disgrace. (*Dissertations* 115)

VOTING:

Thousan's iv men who wudden't have voted f'r him undher anny circumstances has declared that under no circumstances wud they now vote f'r him. (*Opinions* 207)

" 'Aint we intelligent enough?' says she.

'Ye'ar' too intelligent,' says I. 'But intilligence don't give ye a vote.'

'What does, thin,' says she. 'Well,' says I, 'enough iv ye at wan time wantin' it enough.' " (*Says* 32)

"Did an orator iver change ye'er vote?" asked Mr. Hennessy after thinking a moment.

"Always, me frind," said Mr. Dooley impressively; then with a convincing wave of his hand: "If he's a bad orator I vote again him instinctively, an' if he's a good wan who's swayed me soul I always do so as a kind iv an act of conthrition f'r lettin' me feelin's make a fool iv me." (*Wills* 142, 143)

Posterity don't begin to vote till afther th' polls close. (*Observations* 225)

"I'd give thim th' votes," said Mr. Dooley. "But," he added significantly, "I'd do th' countin'." (*Philosophy* 41)

Sure they ought to have wan place f'r a citizen to vote f'r his principles an' another to vote f'r his candydate. (Mr. Dooley on the Progress of the Campaign, *Boston Globe*, Oct. 21, 1900, 29)

V. Dunne and Dooley Compared in Politics.

One hesitates to conclude this chapter with Finley Peter Dunne's experiences in politics. His early years were spent learning to be a journalist, and an extremely able and affable one. Like a good reporter, then editor and publisher, he at first recognized the value of keeping politics at a distance. He had no ambitions to become a Hearst or Field, and he would have liked to hear the word "great" precede the word "publisher" in reference to his career in that capacity. If he had achieved that distinction it is doubtful that his name would come up in discussions of the Teapot Dome scandal.

In his early years, Dunne, an Irishman, was not about to listen to the siren calls of the Pullmans and Baers whose high sounding business integrity merely covered their greed and rapacity,[23] which sought more profits over the gnarled fingers and broken bodies of the working classes. While Dunne editorialized against graft and greed, and even outlined a platform for reform in a Chicago Council election of 1898, he saw reformers as businessmen who did not consider the welfare of the public. Better a few grafting policemen, than no police force; better a bit of bribery in office, than women and children evicted from their homes by honest reformers. If it were a question of choice, Finley Peter Dunne stood for those who had compassion for the poor, the disabled and the bewildered.

Dunne's only foray into politics proper came late in life. One can speculate that, if Dunne had politics in mind, his friendship with Theodore Roosevelt could have combined with his prominence to make him an eligible candidate for office or appointment. It was only when Dunne's popularity with his Mr. Dooley column had waned, when his publishing hopes had faded, that he suddenly had glimmers of being a power broker.

Dunne's venture into politics is described in his own words in his son's collection of his memoirs,[24] and his experience shows a naiveté about politics that was absent in Mr. Dooley. Dunne admits he had "helped in a small way to nominate Harding for the presidency," [25] and he later testified as a character witness for Harry Daugherty during the aftermath of the Teapot Dome oil grab. Dunne was in no way implicated, and it was an act of courage to testify for a notorious friend, if friend he was.

Dunne's political problems would never have beset Mr. Dooley. In his early essays Dunne has Mr. Dooley say some cruel things about appearing as a witness at a trial: "Mr. Dooley put down his newspaper with the remark: They cudden't get me into coort as a witness; no, sir, not if't was to hang me best frind.' " [26] And Mark Sullivan relates an anecdote about Dunne and Norman Hapgood. Dunne advised Hapgood against getting involved in litigation, as everyone would remember the incident however innocent he was, and no matter what the facts were: "Hapgood? Oh, yes, he was in jail one time for some kind of crime or other, something about forgery, I think it was." [27] Mr. Dooley's comments on the law have been covered elsewhere, and there were warning signals all over the horizon which Dunne closed his eyes to as he made his contribution to the Harding candidacy.

Mr. Dunne and Mr. Dooley may not have been Mr. Hyde and Dr. Jekyll, but they were not the same person. Mr. Dooley was a bartender to the end, proud of his competence in his profession and not above serving a beer with a collar. As has been noted in Chapter 1, Dunne's success brought wealth, fame and affluent friends. Dunne was welcome in all the clubs; and, while he disdained bores and those who could not hold their liquor (one anecdote has him helping a drunk to his feet in front of an exclusive club and suggesting that unless he picked another spot, he would be mistaken for a member), he found himself in the company of those, like Harry Daugherty, who were politicians with all the evil that word can connote (in those times, an Ohio politician had a particularly bad stigma). Dunne's Mr. Dooley probably saved a lot of people from the kind of unpleasant incident that befell Finley Peter Dunne himself.

In his last years, Dunne mellowed somewhat. He felt that
Al Smith, whom he admired, became too vindictive in his
later years. Dunne supported Franklin D. Roosevelt, and
one can see his recognition of Roosevelt's helping hand to
the poor of the Depression of the 1930's. Mr. Dooley had
found his way back to Mr. Dunne.

1. HENRY S. COMMAGER, THE AMERICAN MIND, 63 (New Haven, 1950).

2. KENNETH S. LYNN, THE COMIC TRADITION IN AMERICA, 403-404 (N.Y., 1958).

3. MARGARET LEECH, IN THE DAYS OF MCKINLEY, 384 (N.Y., 1959).

4. VAN WYCK BROOKS, THE CONFIDENT YEARS: 1885-1915 at 378-79 (N.Y., 1955).

5. FINLEY PETER DUNNE, MR. DOOLEY IN THE HEARTS OF HIS COUNTRYMEN, 225 (Boston, 1899). *See also* ELMER ELLIS, MR. DOOLEY'S AMERICA, 117 (N.Y., 1941).

6. ELMER ELLIS, MR. DOOLEY'S AMERICA, 146 (N.Y., 1941). *See also* PHILIP DUNNE, MR. DOOLEY REMEMBERS, 193 (Boston, 1963) for President Roosevelt's defense of Anglo-Saxonism.

7. PHILIP DUNNE, MR. DOOLEY REMEMBERS, 111 (Boston, 1963). This phrase appears originally in a Mr. Dooley essay, "Newspaper Publicity," as follows: "Th' newspaper does ivrything f'r us. It runs th' polis foorce an' th' banks, commands th' milishy, conthrols th' ligislachure, baptizes th' young, marries th' foolish, comforts th' afflicted, afflicts th' comfortable, buries th' dead an' roasts thim afttherward." Finley Peter Dunne, *Observations,* 240 (N.Y., 1902).

8. PHILIP DUNNE, MR. DOOLEY REMEMBERS, 209 (Boston, 1963).

9. H.S. CANBY, SEVEN YEARS' HARVEST, 56-59 (N.Y., 1936).

10. I SELECTIONS FROM THE CORRESPONDENCE OF THEODORE ROOSEVELT AND HENRY CABOT LODGE, 1884-1918 at 425-28 (N.Y., 1925).

11. For this term, and Dunne's literary contemporaries, see LOUIS FILLER, CRUSADERS FOR AMERICAN LIBERALISM (N.Y., 1961).

12. Franklin P. Adams, *Born Newspaperman, Born Wit,* New York Herald Tribune (Nov. 9, 1941). A clipping in the New York Herald Tribune morgue located at New York University.

13. FRANKLIN P. ADAMS, THE DIARY OF OUR OWN SAMUEL PEPYS, 1911-1934 (N.Y. 1935).

14. OWEN WISTER, ROOSEVELT, THE STORY OF A FRIENDSHIP, 1880-1919 at 113 (N.Y., 1930).

15. New York Times, 1 (Aug. 16, 1963).

16. LEONARD C. LEWIN, A TREASURY OF AMERICAN POLITICAL HUMOR (N.Y., 1964).

17. LIBRARY JOURNAL, 3751 (Oct. 1, 1964).

18. TIME, 42 (Aug. 15, 1960).

19. Thomas Meehan, *Cruise Director on the Titanic,* NEW YORK TIMES (Magazine), 11 (Jan. 2, 1972).

20. Book review of Dick Gregory, *Political Primer* (N.Y., 1972) in New York Times (Book Review), 5 (Feb. 6, 1972). It seems that every reviewer has his own list of humorists. Justin Kaplan, in reviewing two books on H. L. Mencken, has this observation: "More to the point, I think, may be Mencken's affinities with other curmudgeons, satirists, mavericks, village atheists and free wheelers who have adorned the American tradition — George Washington Plunkitt, Mr. Dooley, Harold L. Ickes, Westbrook Pegler." New York Times (Book Review) 1 at 27 (Sept. 7, 1980).

21. JESSE BIER, THE RISE AND FALL OF AMERICAN HUMOR, 466 (N.Y., 1968). The lists in parentheses are from pages 52 and 78.

22. NORRIS W. YATES, THE AMERICAN HUMORIST (N.Y., 1965).

23. For background information on Dunne's political views see, WILLIAM V. SHANNON, THE AMERICAN IRISH, 145-50 (N.Y., 1963); ELMER ELLIS, MR. DOOLEY'S AMERICA, 90 *et seq.* (N.Y., 1941); and PHILIP DUNNE, MR. DOOLEY REMEMBERS, 118 *et seq.* (Boston, 1963).

24. *See,* in general, note 23.

25. PHILIP DUNNE, MR. DOOLEY REMEMBERS, 119 (Boston, 1963).

26. FINLEY PETER DUNNE, OPINIONS, 117 (N.Y., 1901).

27. MARK SULLIVAN, THE EDUCATION OF AN AMERICAN, 213-14 (N.Y., 1938).

Chapter 4

HUMOR

There have been ample citations and quotations in previous chapters in connection with Finley Peter Dunne's reputation as a humorist. Critics and scholars, politicians and book reviewers, compilers and journalists have attested in abundance to his status as an American humorist. The emphasis, however, has been upon the pertinence of his political wit and insight to the turn of the century. Isolating Dunne's humor from his politics does not appear to be an easy matter, for it is certainly in the area of political humor that he has received the most attention. However, most of Dunne's writing is not political. Justice Oliver Wendell Holmes was known as The Great Dissenter, despite the fact that he was more often with the majority of his brethren on the Supreme Court; and, in the same manner, Dunne's political observations have obscured his nonpolitical humorous writing.

I. The Critics on Dooley.

Mark Sullivan's *Our Times* [1] is probably the source of the more prevalent quotations from Mr. Dooley. Sullivan offered paeans of praise to Mr. Dooley's humor and quoted from his magazine, newspaper and book essays to illustrate the human foibles that comprise the source of much of his humor. Dunne's extollers include the most respected of humorists. Stephen Leacock wrote:

> Indeed, the very joy we take in Mr. Dooley is based on the incongruity and contrast between his situation behind his basement bar, sunk in the very middle of a continent, and the width of the horizon that he sees from it.

81

But there is far more in the creation of Mr. Dooley than his peculiar political and international outlook. Mr. Dooley belongs to the humor of character, a far higher thing than the mere fun of words or incongruity of situation. . . . Mr. Dooley is one of the blossoms on this tree. . . . So too in Mr. Dooley there is something large, something ideal: Dooley, though he doesn't know it, lives in a world of wide vision and great men, a world as it should be; he walks with Pericles and Charlemagne: they would have recognized him at once.[2]

And E. B. White wrote that he was "a sharp and gifted humorist, who wrote no second-rate stuff. . . ."[3]

Compilers of humor, aside from political humor, invariably include Mr. Dooley among their selections. Louis Untermeyer, a frequent purveyor of humor, wrote:

. . . he invented the skeptical Mr. Dooley, who, in a series of Socratic dialogues, argued with his friend, the gullible Hennessy, about industry and art, politics and sports. When Dunne died in 1936 at the peak of his power [sic], critics of every persuasion mourned the loss of a man, who, without raising his fists or his voice, delivered so many blows against selfishness and stupidity. T.A. Daly called Dunne 'a kind of leprachaun' and Henry Seidel Canby praised the perfection of the 'marvelous little satires, with a twist at the end as incomparable as the last line of a sonnet.'[4]

Dunne is represented in collections of sports humor,[5] satire[6] and in humor selected by celebrities.[7] It is interesting to contemplate what Mr. Dunne would have thought of celebrities selecting humor, but the fact that Dunne was not a selector may be comment enough. In fact, Dunne frequently satirized the arbitrariness of this type of selection. He made fun of Dr. Charles Eliot's "Five Foot Shelf,"[8] and his comment on a Hall of Fame for great Americans was, "I r-read th' list today, Hinnissy, an' will ye believe me or will ye not, much as I know I cudden't recall more thin half th' names."[9] As to the world's greatest inventions he included the slot machine, "th' Croker machine an' th' sody fountain an' — crownin' wur-ruk iv our civilization — th' cash raygisther (register)."[10] It is interesting to note that while selections in anthologies vary widely, even to the extent of including the compiler himself, they invariably include a Mr. Dooley essay.

What are the ingredients of humor: Can it be explained? And if so can we apply the formula to Finley Peter Dunne? Max Eastman has attempted to define humor, and it is obvious that without the solvent of frequent examples the result would have been a hopeless bore of a book.[11] Elmer Ellis's biography of Dunne attempts to explain the universal qualities of the Mr. Dooley essays and their impact in satirizing issues and ridiculing institutions. But once again, his frequent quoting from the original is what makes it all plausible.

Humor can be explained in psychological terms (which this book will not attempt to do),[12] in literary terms (which this book will attempt to do), but best by example. In fact, when attempts are made to dissect humor, Finley Peter Dunne's Mr. Dooley is frequently called in as an expert witness. General books on humor can be informative and historical, but little more. There is no $E = mc^2$ for humor. In the light of this, frequent examples will be provided with the understanding that no particular loss will be experienced if the text is skipped.

II. Dialect.

Dunne employed every conceivable technique to get a laugh in his Mr. Dooley essays. No one today disputes that even the dialect (Mr. Dooley or Martin Dooley was

83

Roscommon Irish) was a ruse, and a most important one for Dunne to make his point:

> They [Mr. Dooley sketches] were not merely witty; the fun and the Irish dialect were a mask, a 'jester's license,' behind which Dunne, in a censurious age, could express his hatred of injustice, selfishness, pretentiousness, and stupidity. Dooley is the eternal skeptic, his friend Hennessy the eternal boob. Using dialect, Dunne could say what he pleased about the stuffed shirts of politics and industry.[13]

Of course the dialect was an ingenious front for Dunne to say things he would not say in his King's English essays. It was not Dunne speaking; it was an immigrant, ignorant Irish bartender. It must be understood that Mr. Dooley, with all his horse sense, his native wisdom, his cracker-box philosophy, his attacks on sham and hypocrisy, still spoke the language of the petty, narrow-minded, race-conscious Irishman — and there were many Irishmen who objected to Mr. Dooley,[14] just as today there are objections to the television character Archie Bunker and to the portrayals of Mafia characters. Dunne certainly was not stereotyping his own people; he could just best communicate with the character he created.

III. Race and Humor.

Dunne's attacks on prejudice were far in advance of the people who read him. At first blush, Mr. Dooley was a racist. Blacks were "nay-gurs" or "coons"; the German was a fat, unassimilated idiot; the "Jew man" was a usurer or a tailor; the Pole was a "Polack." He had particular venom for the White, Anglo-Saxon Protestant, or Wasp, as he is known today. A sizable collection could be made of Mr. Dooley's comments toward his own, the Irish, such as: "If all th' ol' men that swore they'd kilt sojers with a pike in '98 had been out fr'm under th' bed in thim days th' Irish parlyment'd be passin' laws in London City years gawn by." [15]

One can only surmise that many who read Mr. Dooley enjoyed his sallies at minorities without realizing that the joke was on them. For Mr. Dooley, unlike television's Archie Bunker of the 1970's, was not taken in by his own talk. As he said to Hennessy: "It's our conceit makes us supeeryor. Take it out iv us an' we ar-re about th' same as th' rest." [16] Dunne recognized that it is a fact of political life that people do not readily concede equality. One reads into Dunne that the most dread day aborning is that final blessed day when all racial, religious, and national barriers are eradicated, for it will reveal to all how unequal they really are. The human instinct for taking "legal" advantage is always present, and Dunne is not being prejudiced but practical when he has Mr. Dooley say of the American Way: ". . . this home iv opporchunity where ivry man is th' equal iv ivry other man befure th' law if he isn't careful." [17] This may be reading into Dunne more than he intended, but the point is, to use the vernacular, "he told it like it was" — and maybe like it still is.

IV. Satire.

Mr. Dooley dared to say what most suspected was behind the pious utterances of politicians, statesmen, professors, businessmen and all the elite and privileged in American society. When he satirized a political event that featured President McKinley, he observed that "Th' proceedin's was opened with a prayer that Providence might r-remain undher th' protection iv th' administhration;" [18] and he was saying some things about the President, his party and politics that politicians do not want people to be aware of. When William and Henry James were mentioned in awe by Mr. Dooley to Mr. Hennessy, Mr. Dooley realized that he has to make clear about whom he is talking: "I refer to th'

Matsachoosetts not th' Missoury Jameses." [19] Readers were amused and enlightened by hearing an ungrammatical, lower middle-class, naturalized citizen (I presume Mr. Dooley had his citizenship papers) parody, satirize and ridicule those who were in the mainstream of society. Not only did his remarks amuse a large audience of newspaper readers, but also those at whom they were aimed, such as Theodore Roosevelt, a prime target, as has been illustrated elsewhere.

Mr. Dooley was also read and enjoyed by Henry Adams,[20] Henry Cabot Lodge, Justice Holmes [21] and other prominent Americans of the period. Gilbert Seldes reports:

> I am convinced that nearly all of Mr. Dooley and nearly [all] of the later Lardner would stand without dialect. . . . Nearly everything serious in Dooley has the same relevance, and one reads about war experts and 'disqualifying the enemy' (in relation to the Spanish-American and Boer Wars) with a slightly dizzying sensation that this man has said everything that needs to be said twenty years in advance of his time. . . . There isn't a chance in the world that he will be forgotten, because he is recognized in England and we shall some day reimport his reputation. For he has the great advantage of being at the same time a humorist and a social historian, an everyday philosopher and the *homme moyen sensuel.*[22]

In addition to Seldes' remorse that Dunne has not retained his reputation as an immortal, it is interesting that Dunne's comments on the great contemporaries of his time have not been incorporated in their biographies. Biographies of Rockefeller, Carnegie, Taft, Wilson, and Bryan, to name a few who were roasted, do not include Dunne's evaluations (Theodore Roosevelt is the one exception). A compilation of Dunne's remarks on these men may not be the equivalent of Aubrey's *Brief Lives,* but one could suggest a reevaluation of many of the famed figures in American history and business. Some of Mr. Dooley's "biographical" comments can be located through the index to this book.

Despite Dunne's scourging of the hypocrisy of the elite, there is no indication that his Mr. Dooley was for equality in his bar (and we must remember that this bar was a microcosm of life in America). Mr. Dooley was not known for final solutions; if he had been, his value to future generations would have been limited. In his famous essay on the *cause célèbre* of Black educator Booker T. Washington's being invited to dine with President Theodore Roosevelt at the White House, Mr. Dooley indicated that, since he would lose business if Blacks patronized his bar, he would as soon they stayed out. On the other hand, his advice to those denied their rights has been taken to heart by both Blacks and women:

> But don't ask f'r rights. Take thim. An' don't let anny wan give thim to ye. A right that is handed to ye f'r nawthin' has somethin' th' matther with it. 'It's more than likely it's on'y a wrong turned inside out,' says I. 'I didn't fight f'r th' rights I'm told I injye, though to tell ye th' truth, I injye me wrongs more; but some wan did. Some time some fellow was prepared to lay down his life, or betther still, th' other fellows', f'r th' right to vote.' (*Says* 38)

In "The Race Question," Mr. Dooley parodies a Southerner speaking about the issue:

> 'Th' thruth iv th' matther is there is no race question ... [and then proceeds to show there is one]. Th' right way to settle it is to lave it where it is. We give th' naygur ivry r-right guaranteed by th' Constichoochion. We permit him to vote, only demandin' that he shall prove that his father an' mother were white. We let him

87

perform th' arjoos [arduous] manyul labor iv our fair land. We bury him or gather him as soovenirs. What more can be asked[?] But we insist that though this happy fellow-citizen may pass us our vittles, he shall not fork out our stamps. . . .' (*Dissertations* 189)

Dunne is just as critical of the Northerners:

"I'm not so much throubled about th' naygur whin he lives among his opprissors as I am whin he falls into th' hands iv his liberators." (*Philosophy* 217)

As for the Blacks getting help from the academic world, he has a college professor orate:

"Look at Lincoln. There's a fellow ivrybody is always crackin' up. But what did he amount to? What did he do but carry on a war, free th' slaves, an' ruin this mis'rable counthry? But who asked him to free th' slaves? I didn't. A man utterly lackin' in principle an' sinse iv humor, he led a mob an' was conthrolled be it." (*Dissertations* 109)

Finally, to indicate that no one was exempt from scorn, here are the words he puts into the mouth of a businessman:

"An' there's Lincoln. What a little business thrainin' wud've done f'r him! Look at th' roon [ruin] he brought on property be his carelessness. Millyons iv thim become worthless except as fuel f'r bonfires in th' Sunny Southland." (*Dissertations* 277-278)

As Louis Filler wrote:

He offered the Negro-hater the cold hand of Irish prejudice, and along with it arguments and information which showed up the base and disagreeable aspects of racism. Dooley's earthiness and sense of reality similarly separated him from the virginal and

88

fuzzy-minded equalitarian. So it was, too, with Dunne's references to the "Jew man," to the "Dutch," and to the other Americans.[23]

When Mr. Dooley was through, one would be hard put to find a qualified person to cast the first stone; but then, one can picture Mr. Dooley swabbing his bar or drawing a draft for Mr. Hennessy and summing up the matter with irrefutable logic:

> I don't suppose they have partitions up in th' other wurruld like th' kind they have in th' cars down south. They can't be anny Crow Hivin. I wondher how they keep up race supreemacy. Maybe they get on without it. (*Opinions* 209)

But if Mr. Dooley gave the back of his hand to other minorities, he was just as severe with his own people, the Irish: a quarrelsome, hard-drinking, temptation-ridden, clannish group who had as much trouble getting along with themselves as with others.[24] While Mr. Dooley constantly criticized the British, and their "Orange" cousins, he proceeded to undercut his position by remarking:

> Whin England purrishes, th' Irish'll die iv what Hogan calls ongwee [ennui], which is havin' no wan in th' weary wurruld ye don't love. (*Peace* 255)

If Mr. Dooley had one target above all others — one that brought out all his Irish and one that came across most viciously and effectively — it was the Anglo-Saxon or what is commonly known today as Wasps. The attitude of superiority on the part of a segment of those who arrived at these shores first rankled him. He parodied Henry Cabot Lodge's imperialistic or expansionist speeches into such slogans as: "Take up th' White man's burden an' hand it to th' coons," "Hands acrost th' sea an' into some wan's pocket," and "An open back dure an' a closed fr-ront door." [25] When the cry went up that immigration should be stopped lest America's Anglo-Saxon purity be diluted, Mr. Dooley in his essay on immigration suggested the only way to keep out the "offscourin" was to:

> Teach thim all about our institoochions befure they come. (*Observations* 54)

In one essay, not published in book form, Mr. Dooley said, "There are no Jews in New England, they can't make a livin' there." [26] The obvious implication is that in financial dealings even the Jews were no match with a blue blood Anglo-Saxon in his home territory. It is interesting to note that it is Mr. Hennessy, and not Mr. Dooley, whose judgment on the Dreyfus case is simply a matter of prejudice: "I don't know annything about it (the Dreyfus case), but I think he's guilty. He's a Jew." [27]

When it came to prejudice, Mr. Dooley was able to handle it by making fun of both sides and himself. He accused the one of not standing up for his rights, the other of having an inflated estimate of his worth based not on his inherent qualities but on those of a group; and, as for himself and the Irish, he saw nothing wrong in feeling superior if it brought advantages. Dunne seemed to be saying that civilization was a matter of competition and anyhow, the victory of one race over another would be a hollow one. Equality as a goal was a fine thing, but when achieved, it would only make the individual realize how unequal he really was, and leave him without the saving grace of having the excuse that he had not reached his true potential because he was Black, Irish, Jewish, female, or whatever current inequality crisis happened to be uppermost in the politics of the time.

In later life Dunne was convinced that life had become too serious for laughter; but the plight of minorities in America at the turn of the century was not a laughing matter. Lynching of a Black man was as much an atrocity as the horrors committed in a Nazi concentration camp. The weapons to defeat racism, pogroms and superimposed superiority are many and varied, but one is laughter. Dunne made the "superior races" ridiculous and thereby struck a blow for freedom. As he aged, and society looked different to him, he lost the knack.

V. Literary Devices.

While the dialect-monologue may have been the heart of the Mr. Dooley essay, it did somewhat obscure Dunne's intellectual skills. Although Dunne's formal education stopped at high school, he was far better read than many of our most renowned humorists. Like Artemus Ward, Mark Twain and other early humorists, he was nurtured as a journalist. Unlike them, he had a mother, and a future mother-in-law, who gave him a solid background in literature that constantly shows in his writings. Mr. Dooley was a very literate bartender. There are frequent references to Shakespeare, the Bible and Greek literature. One of the purposes of Father Kelly and Hogan in the essays was to credit them with some learning. Dunne's playful use of literature can be illustrated by his comment on the lot of men in marriage:

> We [men] first embrace, thin pity, thin endure.
> (*Dissertations* 43)

Dunne was obviously misquoting a passage from Alexander Pope: "We first endure, then pity, then embrace." [28] Pope was referring to vice, and one can only speculate how much Dunne was equating vice with marriage.

Although well read, Dunne was very cautious about advising people to read. Reading is allright, he has Mr. Dooley say, but "In modheration, an' afther th' chores is done." [29] And, when Mr. Dooley was asked if he had read the latest best seller, he replied that he would read it after he had completed the Bible and Shakespeare:[30]

91

"D'ye read thim all th' time?" she says.

"I niver read thim," says I. "I use thim f'r purposes iv defense. I have niver read them, but I'll niver read annything else till I have read thim," I says. "They stand between me an' all modhern lithrature." (*Observations* 7)

Of course dialect always tempts the user to attempt humor with misspellings and Dunne, along with Mark Twain and Artemus Ward, was no exception. In many instances the misspellings would be a play on words and provide an additional meaning. Some examples:

Bum vivant or bong vivant for bon vivant
Hurtage for heritage
Rile for royal
Dishpot for despot
Cue for queue
Joynts for giants
Mickrobe for (obviously an Irish) microbe
Lather iv fame for ladder of fame [31]

Possibly Dunne's best malapropism was misinterpreting Emile Zola's "J'accuse" as "jackass," which Mr. Dooley innocently says "is a hell of a mane [mean] thing to say to anny man . . ." let alone a contemptible judge.[32]

Names were a particular delight to Dunne. The ubiquitous Chauncey Depew becomes "Mr. Chansy Depot, care iv th' Grand Cintral Depew." A speaker extolling Woodrow Wilson's far-flung fame misspells his name each time he mentions it. And Admiral Dewey becomes "Cousin Dooley," so that Mr. Dooley can bring the issues closer to home. Roosevelt became "Rosenfelt," which may have given solace to those who were unhappy at having a cowboy in the White House, as Mark Hanna commented. The "Rosenfelt" did not bother the President, but he may not have been amused when Mr. Dooley wrote of the President's athletic tendencies: "I'd like to tell me frind Tiddy that they's a strenuse [strenuous] life an' a sthrenuseless life." [33]

Puns were an integral part of the Dooley repertoire. In discussing the problems of reentering the country, in his essay on the Custom House,[34] Dunne was not above weaving in some comments on "domestic duties." In discussing wealth, he wrote that "Th' cat was called Goold Bonds, because iv th' inthrest he dhrew." [35] One of his more atrocious puns has to do with music where he suggested to a singer: "why don't ye rent out some of y'er flats?" [36] Combining a pun with an adage, Mr. Dooley, in satirizing St. Patrick's Day observers, commented on a ludicrous figure on horseback that "pride goeth befure a fall." [37] Although Dunne went to great lengths to effect a play on words, it was not just the humor he was after but a telling way of making his point. One instance follows of his deflating civilization, literature, and inventive genius — and climaxing it with a play on words:

> "An' thin th' printin'-press was invinted. Gunpowdher was invinted th' same time, an' 't is a question I've often heerd discussed which has done more to ilivate th' human race." (*Observations* 5)

Jesse Bier [38] provides examples of Dunne's use of anticlimax and undercutting, which was one of Dunne's more effective devices. Dunne, like a good comedian, would save his punch line for last. He would begin with what would appear to be a truism, inflate the situation and climax it with a sentence of scorn or sarcasm. A classic example is his comment on professors,[39] one that academicians of humor have neglected for reasons known only to themselves:

> "Well, sir," said Mr. Dooley, "it must be a grand thing to be a college profissor."

93

"Not much to do," said Mr. Hennessy.

"But a gr-reat deal to say," said Mr. Dooley. "Ivry day th' minyit I pick up me pa-aper afther I've read th' criminal an' other pollytical news, th' spoortin' news, th' rale-estate advertisemints, th' invytations fr'm th' cultured foreign gent to meet an American lady iv some means, th' spoortin' news over again, thin th' iditoryals, I hasten to find out what th' colledge pro-fissor had to say yisterdah. I wish th' iditor wud put it in th' same column iv th' pa-aper ivry day. Thin he wudden't have to collect anny other funny column." (*Dissertations* 107)

Other examples are:

If I see a fellow with a chube [telescope] on his eye and hear him hollerin', 'Hooray, I've discovered a new planet,' I'll be th' last man in th' wurruld to brush th' fly off th' end iv th' telescope. (*Says* 132-133)

'No, sir,' says I, 'get as much amusement as ye can out iv ye'er infant,' says I. 'Teach him to love ye now,' I says, 'befure he knows. Afther a while he'll get onto ye an' it'll be too late.' (*Dissertations* 55)

The use of repetition was another effective technique for making a point. In a much quoted statement of Mr. Dooley's, Dunne uses this device to probe the prevalence of perversity in politics (alliteration was not used by Mr. Dooley):

It must be a good thing to be good or ivrybody wudden't be pretendin' he was. But I don't think they'se anny such thing as hypocrisy in th' wurruld. They can't be. If ye'd turn on th' gas in th' darkest heart ye'd find it had a good raison for th' worst things it done, a good varchous raison, like needin' th' money or punishin' th' wicked or tachin' people a lesson to be more careful, or

94

protectin' th' liberties iv mankind, or needin' th' money.
(*Observations* 267)

Dunne excelled in parody. Many instances have already
been given in this book, but his most famous, and much
quoted by historians and antitrust authorities, is the following on President Roosevelt:

> 'Th' thrusts,' says he to himsilf, 'are heejous monsthers
> built up be th' inlightened intherprise iv th' men that
> have done so much to advance pro-gress in our beloved
> counthry,' he says. 'On wan hand I wud stamp thim
> undher fut; on th' other hand not so fast. What I want
> more thin th' bustin' iv th' thrusts is to see me fellow
> counthrymen happy an' continted. I wudden't have
> thim hate th' thrusts. Th' haggard face, th' droopin' eye,
> th' pallid complexion that marks th' inemy iv thrusts is
> not to me taste. Lave us be merry about it an jovial an'
> affectionate. Lave us laugh an' sing th' octopus out iv
> existence. (*Observations* 223-224)

But all of Dunne's techniques — malapropisms,
misquotations,[40] "Dooleymorphisms",[41] the tall tale, clichés
— had a purpose. Dunne was not just trying to be a comic.
He had a message to impart to the world, and it grieved him
that he could only do it through Mr. Dooley. Unlike
Artemus Ward and Will Rogers, Dunne was not a
performer. Possibly one reason that Ward and Rogers, and
even Mark Twain, are often not funny in print is that they
had to be seen to be enjoyed. Mr. Dooley performs on paper,
and his content is every bit as serious as Huckleberry Finn's
musings.

VI. Dunne and Dooley Compared in Humor.

Elmer Ellis in his biography of Dunne provides anecdotes
of Dunne's humor in his own life, the most famous being his

suggestion that if President Roosevelt must take a trip in a newly constructed submarine he should take the Vice-President with him, the implication being that Mr. Fairbanks would not be an ideal President should Teddy suffer a mishap.[42] Dunne was also a much sought after club member, although Philip Dunne's [43] anecdotes about his father being bored with bores and fatheads are not in a class with Mr. Dunne as Mr. Dooley. The classic anecdote in Ellis has to do with Dunne's relationship with Mark Twain. The two were observed in New York City and gawked at by a large crowd. Dunne's suggestion that the crowd considered him to be the object of their attention took the egotistical Twain by surprise.[44] Dunne and Twain apparently got on well, exchanged quips, shot pool in Twain's home, and indulged in a practical joke or two. Dunne was a member of Twain's Damned Human Race Luncheon Club, which appropriately enough never organized a luncheon.[45]

Unlike Mr. Dooley, Dunne was not active personally in matters of politics, race relations and other topics of the day. And certainly his private opinions are his own. In his early days he had a few things to say about reform as an editor, and in his days on the *American* he associated with the major muckrackers of the day, if he was not considered one of them. Philip Dunne records his attitude toward the exclusion of Jews from New York Clubs.[46] It is quite obvious that Dunne would not exclude people from his friendship for reasons of race, religion or creed. It is even understandable that Dunne did not take too active a role in the betterment of the human race as his forte was more to point out human foibles than to correct them. Humorists are probably much too self-conscious to be reformers.

His early political editorials in the Chicago newspapers did not noticeably affect Chicago politics in his day; his political foray for Harding's nomination, as we have seen, turned into an embarassment, and his involvement with a

Russian revolutionist turned into what Dunne himself might have called an "opéra bouffe." Dunne was a member of a literary group (which included Mark Twain) that invited Maxim Gorki to the United States to raise funds for Russian revolutionaries who were fighting the oppression of the Tsar. Gorki arrived in New York City on April 11, 1906 and registered at an exclusive hotel with a woman not his wife (she was for all practical purposes his common-law wife). Yellow journalists reported this fact, Gorki was asked to leave the hotel, the scheduled dinner was never held, and Mr. Dunne and his would-be fellow hosts were not known to have opposed this calamitous ending of a cause, which, if furthered, might have changed the history of our times.[47] Mr. Dunne was destined to make his contribution to American society through the medium of Mr. Dooley.

VII. Examples of Dooley's Humor.

Throughout this chapter, an attempt has been made to point out the various facets of Dunne's humor. To summarize, there is the dialect, the ingrained skepticism, the use of paradox (e.g. the frequent suggestion that the poor and rich alike are beset with similar problems or that all of society's ills are due to widows and orphans), misuse of cliches and aphorisms, irony, the anticlimax, puns, orthographic humor, malapropisms, misquotations, tall tales, parodies, undercutting and repetition. Analysis dulls effect, and to make up for this deficiency, this chapter will conclude with a number of quotations unmarred by analysis, that have not previously been used in this volume. They can be used as examples of his techniques, or more to the point, enjoyed as humor.

One caveat is necessary. Dunne is quotable to the extent that one neglects the whole for the parts. But this does a disservice to the art of Finley Peter Dunne. The selections, while effective in themselves, are but part of the mosaic of the entire essay. As has been the practice in this volume, citations to the original are provided for those who prefer visiting the Sistine Chapel rather than viewing "details" in an art book.

ADVOCACY, ART OF:

If a lawyer thinks his client is innocint he talks to th' jury about th' crime. But if he knows where th' pris'ner hid th' plunder, he unfurls th' flag, throws out a few remarks about th' flowers an' th' bur-rds, an' asks th' twelve good men an' thrue not to break up a happy Christmas, but to sind this man home to his wife an' childher, an' Gawd will bless thim if they ar-re iver caught in th' same perdicymint. *(Dissertations 23)*

ALCOHOL:

'It ought to be th' reward iv action, not th' cause iv it,' he says. 'It's f'r th' end iv th' day, not th' beginnin',' he says. *(Philosophy 152)*

ATHLETE:

An athlete was always a man that was not sthrong enough f'r wurruk. Fractions dhruv him fr'm school an' th' vagrancy laws dhruv him to baseball. *(Opinions 81)*

BACHELOR:

A marrid man gets th' money, Hinnissy, but a bachelor man gets th' sleep. *(Philosophy 241)*

BLUE LAWS:

'Ye can't make laws f'r this community that wud suit a New England village,' he says, 'where,' he says, 'th' people ar-re too uncivilized to be immoral,' he says. *(Opinions 157)*

BRAVERY:

I don't know what wud make me fight nowadays. I know lots iv things that wud make me want to fight, but I've larned to repress me desires. (*Observations* 153)

BUNCO (SCHEME):

Ye can be too honest to be bunkoed, but niver too smart. (*Dissertations* 307)

CRIMINAL LAW:

In England a man is presoomed to be innocent till he's proved guilty an' they take it f'r granted he's guilty. In this counthry a man is presoomed to be guilty ontil he's proved guilty an' afther that he's presoomed to be innocent. (*Will* 212)

DOCTORS:

I wondher why ye can always read a doctor's bill an' ye niver can read his purscription. (*Says* 93-94)

EDITORS:

"D'ye know I'd like to be an iditor," said Mr. Dooley.

"It must be a hard job," said Mr. Hennessy. "Ye have to know so much."

" 'T is a hard job," said Mr. Dooley, "but 't is a fascinatin' wan. They'se nawthin' so hard as mindin' ye'er own business an' an iditor niver has to do that." (*Opinions* 55)

EDUCATION:

I don't think it makes anny difference 'wan way or th' other how free ye make idjacation. Men that wants it 'll have it be hook an' be crook, an' thim that don't ra-aly want it niver will get it. Ye can lade a man up to th' university, but ye can't make him think. (*Opinions* 149)

But I believe 'tis as Father Kelly says: 'Childher shudden't be sint to school to larn, but to larn how to larn. I don't care what ye larn thim so long as 'tis onpleasant to thim.' (*Philosophy* 249)

MR. DOOLEY AND MR. DUNNE

EQUALITY:

'Behold, th' land iv freedom' he says, 'where ivry man's as good as ivry other man,' he says, 'on'y th' other man don't know it,' he says. (*Opinions* 162)

HISTORY:

Th' further ye get away fr'm anny peeryod th' betther ye can write about it. Ye are not subject to interruptions be people that were there. (*Wills* 105-6)

Ye can't spile (spoil) histhry be makin' it unthrue. (*Will* 58)

I know histhry isn't thrue, Hinnessy, because it ain't like what I see ivry day in Halsted Sthreet. If any wan comes along with a histhry iv Greece or Rome that'll show me th' people fightin', gettin' dhrunk, makin' love, gettin' married, owin' th' grocery man an' bein' without hard-coal, I'll believe they was a Greece or Rome, but not befure. Historyans is like doctors. They are always lookin' f'r symptoms. Those iv them that writes about their own times examines th' tongue an' feels th' pulse an' makes a wrong dygnosis. Th' other kind iv histhry is a post-mortem examination. It tell ye what a counthry died iv. But I'd like to know what it lived iv. (*Observations* 271)

IMPERIALISM:

We import juke, hemp, cigar wrappers, sugar, an' fairy tales fr'm th' Ph'lippeens, an' export six-inch shells an' th' like. (*Peace* 46)

INVENTIONS:

An' th' invintions, — th' steam-injine an' th' printin'-press an' th' cotton-gin an' the gin sour an' th' bicycle an' th' flyin'-machine an' th' nickel-in-th'-slot machine an' th' Croker machine an' th' sody fountain an' — crownin' wur-ruk iv our civilization — th' cash raygisther. (*Peace* 173)

An' th' name I'll put down fourth is th' fellow that invinted suspinders. I've often talked to ye about him. He's wan iv me gr-reatest heroes. I don't know his name, but ivry time I look down at me legs an' see they're properly dhraped I think kindly iv this janius [genius]. (*Wills* 23)

JURY:

Thank th' Lord, whin th' case is all over, the jury'll pitch th' tistimony out iv th' window, an' consider three questions: 'Did Lootgert look as though he'd kill his wife? Did his wife look as though she ought to be kilt? Isn't it time we wint to supper?' (*Peace* 145)

In due time twelve men iv intilligence who have r-read th' pa-apers an' can't remember what they've r-read, or who can't r-read, or ar-re out iv wurruk, ar-re injooced to sarve, an' th' awful wheels iv justice begins to go around. (*Wills* 216)

LARCENY:

A good manny people r-read th' ol' sayin' 'Larceny is th' sincerest form iv flatthry.' (*Philosophy* 262)

LAW:

'I want a law,' he says, 'that mesilf an' all other good citizens can rayspict,' he says. (*Philosophy* 126)

MORMON:

A Mormon, Hinnissy, is a man that has th' bad taste an' th' rellijion to do what a good manny other men ar-re restrained fr'm doin' be conscientious scruples an' th' polis. (*Philosophy* 111)

NEWS:

They ain't anny news in bein' good. (*Philosophy* 174)

No wan cares to hear what Hogan calls: 'Th' short an' simple scandals iv th' poor.' (*Opinion* 122)

101

NEWSPAPERS:

If men cud on'y enjye th' wealth an' position th' newspapers give thim whin they're undher arrest! Don't anny but prominent clubmen iver elope or embezzle? (*Philosophy* 261)

POLICEMEN:

A polisman goes afther vice as an officer iv th' law an' comes away as a philosopher. (*Opinions* 154)

PRAYERS:

'Hogan,' [Father Kelly] says, 'I'll go into th' battle with a prayer book in wan hand an' a soord in th' other,' he says; 'an,' if th' wurruk calls f'r two hands, 'tis not th' soord I'll dhrop,' he says. 'Don't ye believe in prayer?' says Hogan. 'I do,' says th' good man; 'but,' he says, 'a healthy person ought,' he says, 'to be ashamed,' he says, 'to ask f'r help in a fight,' he says. (*Peace* 50)

PROFANITY:

But it don't do to use pro-fanity th' way ye wud ordin'ry wurruds. No, sir. Ye've got to save it up an' invist it at th' right time or get nawthin' fr'm it. It's betther thin a doctor f'r a stubbed toe but it niver cured a broken leg. It's a kind iv a first aid to th' injured. It seems to deaden th' pain. . . . But if ye hurl it broadcast, if ivry time ye open ye'er mouth a hot wan lapes out, th' time will come whin ye'll want to say something scorchin' an' ye'll have nawthin' to say that ye haven't said f'r fun. I'd as soon think iv swearin' f'r pleasure as iv lindin' money f'r pleasure. . . .

But th' best thing about a little judicyous swearin' is that it keeps th' temper. 'Twas intinded as a compromise be-tween runnin' away an' fightin'. (*Observations* 227-28)

RECREATION:

... a rich man's raycreation is a poor man's wurruk. (*Observations* 179)

STRIKE:

A sthrike is a wurrukin' man's vacation ... sthrikes come in th' summer time an' lockouts in th' winter. .... 'Tis a sthrange thing whin we come to think iv it that th' less money a man gets fr his wurruk, th' more nicissry it is to th' wurruld that he shud go on wurrukin'. (*Says* 78, 79, 85)

TRUTH:

What we call thruth an' pass around fr'm hand to hand is on'y a kind iv a currency that we use fr convenience. There are a good manny countherfeiters an' a lot iv th' countherfeits must be in circulation. (*Dissertations* 231)

WAR:

Some day, Hinnissy, justice'll be done me, an' th' likes iv me; an', whin th' story iv a gr-reat battle is written, they'll print th' kilt, th' wounded, th' missin', an' th' seryously disturbed. An' thim that have bore thimsilves well an' bravely an' paid th' taxes an' faced th' deadly newspa-apers without flinchin' 'll be advanced six pints an' given a chanst to tur-rn jack fr th' game. (*Peace* 54)

I can see in me mind th' day whin explosives'll be so explosive an' guns'll shoot so far that on'y th' folks that stay at home'll be kilt, an' life insurance agents'll be advisin' people to go into th' ar-rmy. ... (*Philosophy* 68)

WOMEN:

Whin a woman discovers she has a soul, Hinnissy, 'tis time she was sint to a rest-cure. It niver comes till late in life, an' ye can't tell what she'll do about it. She may join a woman's club, an' she may go on th' stage. Tis sthrange how manny ladies with wan leg in th' grave wud like to see th' other in th' front row iv th' chorus. (*Dissertations* 13)

MR. DOOLEY AND MR. DUNNE

1. (N.Y., 1926). Consulting the index to this set, one can find dozens of references to Mr. Dooley. In consulting indexes for references to Mr. Dooley one should check under Dunne, Dooley, Mr. Dooley; on occasion the indexer neglects to index references to Mr. Dooley. Mr. Dooley has been cited by the Supreme Court (A.F.L. v. American Sash Door, 335 U.S. 538, at 557 (1949), and was referred to in a play about Justice Holmes (Lavery, The *Magnificent Yankee*). Frequently, he is quoted without benefit of citation.

2. STEPHEN LEACOCK, THE GREATEST PAGES OF HUMOR. . . ., 173-74 (N.Y., 1936).

3. A SUBTREASURY OF AMERICAN HUMOR, xv (E. B. White and K. S. White, eds. N.Y., 1941).

4. A TREASURY OF LAUGHTER, 215 (Louis Untermeyer, ed., N.Y., 1946).

5. A TREASURY OF SPORTS HUMOR (Dave Stanley, ed., N.Y., 1946).

6. AMERICAN SATIRE IN PROSE AND VERSE (Henry C. Carlisle, Jr., ed., N.Y., 1962).

7. HUMOR BY VOTE (Hewitt H. Howland, ed., N.Y., 1933).

8. FINLEY PETER DUNNE, MR. DOOLEY SAYS, 135 (N.Y., 1910).

9. FINLEY PETER DUNNE, OPINIONS, 111 (N.Y., 1901).

10. FINLEY PETER DUNNE, MR. DOOLEY IN PEACE AND IN WAR, 173 (Boston, 1899). The Croker machine, of course, was a reference to political machines, in this case, Tammany Hall. In the same volume Mr. Dooley rates suspenders high on the invention list as they freed man's hands for work (page 23).

11. MAX EASTMAN, ENJOYMENT OF LAUGHTER (N.Y., 1936).

12. *See* the Eastman book, note 32 *infra,* and the Bier book in the bibliography for explanations and citations to Freud, *et al.*

13. TWENTIETH CENTURY AUTHORS (Stanley S. Kunitz and Howard Haycraft, eds., N.Y., 1942).

14. ELMER ELLIS, MR. DOOLEY'S AMERICA, 182 (N.Y., 1941).

15. *The Day of the Fire,* Chicago Evening Post, 9 (Oct. 14, 1893).

16. FINLEY PETER DUNNE, MR. DOOLEY SAYS, 58 (N.Y., 1910).

17. FINLEY PETER DUNNE, DISSERTATIONS BY MR. DOOLEY, 248 (N.Y., 1906).

18. FINLEY PETER DUNNE, MR. DOOLEY IN PEACE AND IN WAR, 83 (Boston, 1899).

19. *Mr. Dooley on Philosophers,* AMERICAN MAGAZINE, 540 (March, 1908). *See also,* as to a meeting between Henry James, a reader of Mr. Dooley, and Finley Peter Dunne, ELMER ELLIS, MR. DOOLEY'S AMERICA, 200 (N.Y., 1941).

20. W.C. FORD, II LETTERS OF HENRY ADAMS, 254, 366 (Boston, 1938).

21. Mark DeWolfe Howe, Holmes-Laski Letters, 102, 221 (Cambridge, 1953).

22. Gilbert Seldes, The 7 Lively Arts, 123 (N.Y., 1957). Seldes qualifies his remarks as to Dunne's immortality when reflecting on this, his earlier opinion.

23. Louis Filler, Mr. Dooley: Now and Forever, xiv (Stanford, Cal., 1954).

24. *See* William V. Shannon, The American Irish, 145 (N.Y., 1963).

25. Finley Peter Dunne, Mr. Dooley in the Hearts of his Countrymen, 225 (Boston, 1899). *See also* Elmer Ellis, Mr. Dooley's America, 117 (N.Y., 1941).

26. *A Dissertation on the Jews,* Boston Globe, 45 (Nov. 16, 1902). It should be noted that many of Dunne's Mr. Dooley essays do not appear in book form. See Elmer Ellis, Mr. Dooley's America, 305 (N.Y., 1941). There are slight variations, on occasion, when the essays appear in book form. Mr. Ellis suggests that a good many of his harshest verdicts were not included in the eight books Dunne published.

27. Finley Peter Dunne, Mr. Dooley in Peace and in War, 234 (Boston, 1899).

28. Essay on Man, line 220.

29. Finley Peter Dunne, Observations of Mr. Dooley, 11 (N.Y., 1902).

30. For examples of Dunne's use of Shakespeare, see Norris W. Yates, The American Humorist, 94 (N.Y., 1964); Jesse Bier, The Rise and Fall of American Humor (N.Y., 1968); Elmer Ellis, Mr. Dooley's America, 308 (N.Y., 1941).

31. *See also* Jesse Bier, The Rise and Fall of American Humor, 188 (N.Y., 1968).

32. Finley Peter Dunne, Mr. Dooley in Peace and in War, 236 (Boston, 1899). *See also* Max Eastman, Enjoyment of Laughter, 133 (N.Y., 1936).

33. Finley Peter Dunne, Mr. Dooley's Philosophy, 262 (N.Y., 1900).

34. Finley Peter Dunne, Opinions, 165 (N.Y., 1901).

35. Finley Peter Dunne, Mr. Dooley in Peace and in War, 76 (Boston, 1899).

36. *Mr. Dooley on Music,* Boston Globe (Magazine), 5 (March 24, 1907).

37. Finley Peter Dunne, Mr. Dooley on Making a Will and Other Necessary Evils, 194 (N.Y., 1919).

38. Jesse Bier, The Rise and Fall of American Humor, 19, 185 (N.Y., 1968).

39. Dunne had an anti-intellectual streak in him that showed particularly in his attitude toward the academic world.

40. ELMER ELLIS, MR. DOOLEY'S AMERICA, 308 (N.Y., 1941).

41. *See* JESSE BIER, THE RISE AND FALL OF AMERICAN HUMOR, 188 (N.Y., 1968). Mr. Bier also discusses Dunne's technical proficiency throughout this volume. Check the entries in the index.

42. ELMER ELLIS, MR. DOOLEY'S AMERICA, 219 (N.Y., 1941). *But see* Mr. Dooley's comments on vice-presidents in the politics chapter to this book.

43. MR. DOOLEY REMEMBERS, 232-33 (Philip Dunne, ed., Boston, 1963).

44. ELMER ELLIS, MR. DOOLEY'S AMERICA, 195-96 (N.Y., 1941). *See also* MR. DOOLEY REMEMBERS, 250-51 (Philip Dunne, ed., Boston, 1963). It should be remembered that Mr. Ellis had access to the memoir printed by Philip Dunne.

45. II MARK TWAIN-HOWELLS LETTERS, 828, 842 (Henry N. Smith and William M. Gibson, eds., Cambridge, 1960).

46. MR. DOOLEY REMEMBERS, 36 *et seq.* (Philip Dunne, ed., Boston, 1963).

47. JERRY ALLEN, THE ADVENTURES OF MARK TWAIN, 290 (Boston, 1954).

Chapter 5

WILL THE REAL MR. DOOLEY—MR. DUNNE STAND UP

I. Home Life of Dunne and Dooley.

Before evaluating and analyzing the corpus of Mr. Dunne's work, it may be enlightening to compare him with his alter ego. Compared to Mr. Dooley, a hardworking and poorly rewarded bartender, Mr. Dunne was a bon vivant. Dunne was not averse to leisurely hours at the club and homes away from home, while Mr. Dooley would reduce playing golf to a ridiculous experience and country living to an experience in torture (" 'I hope,' says I, [going to a loft to sleep] 'I'm not discommodin' th' pigeons,' I says. 'There ain't anny pigeons here,' says he. 'What's that?' says I. 'That's a mosquito,' says he.").

Where Mr. Dooley put in long hours on his feet behind his bar, Mr. Dunne never picked up a glass except in anger or thirst. Mr. Dooley remained a bachelor for reasons which he was constantly reminding his public of, while Mr. Dunne had the misfortune to have his Mr. Dooley articles on the joys of bachelorhood reprinted on the eve of his marriage. Mr. Dunne married an Anglo-Saxon, which Mr. Dooley would have considered somewhat of a crime. Mr. Dooley had been a precinct captain and was proud of his political record; Dunne had nothing but apologies for his political doings. Mr. Dunne was wealthy at a comparatively young age and maintained the appearance of wealth for the rest of his life. He spent money lavishly and enjoyed the fruits of capitalist enterprise, including a one-half million dollar inheritance from a friend. Mr. Dooley never knew wealth. When he came over from Ireland he was told the sidewalks were paved with gold, but all he ever hit with the pickaxe involuntarily put in his unwilling hands was rock. He was quite satisfied with the humble rewards of tending a bar. I suspect that Mr. Dooley and Mr. Dunne were alike on matters of religion. Both loved the Roman Catholic Church in their own way (when someone had the temerity to ask Mr. Dunne if he was Roman Catholic, he was told that he was Chicago Catholic), which was nobody else's business.

The contrasts and similarities between Dunne and Dooley, between theory and practice, between leisure and work, between the American Dream as dreamt and as lived are what provided that marvelous spell of creativity that gave Mr. Dooley to the world and the world to Mr. Dunne.

II. Appraisal of Mr. Dooley.

Final conclusions about the timelessness of Dunne are varied. There are critics who feel his work is dated, the dialect is too difficult, the humor label too fatal.

Elmer Ellis concludes his biography of Dunne by speculating on the value of his work:

> Whether it will last or not depends upon the world itself. If it continues to accept the values which Dunne cherished — personal integrity, plain speaking, catholic tolerance, compassion for the weak, good humor, and salty wit — if it continues to treasure these, then Peter Dunne will surely continue to be read.[1]

Louis Filler is this generation's apostle of the Dooley creed. His perceptive prefaces to his two collections of Dunne's essays objectively sum up the creative efforts of Finley Peter Dunne as editor, essayist, and above all, as the creator of Mr. Dooley. Filler's verdict:

> ... he had reared a monument of human nature, with good will, day-in-and-day out concern for American affairs, to which we can turn for refreshment and illumination. He and Mr. Dooley had come to grips with the whole spectrum of our troubles and joys.[2]

108

In 1963 four books were published on Finley Peter Dunne with "Mr. Dooley" in every title.[3] In 1969, a reprint of Elmer Ellis' fine collection, *Mr. Dooley At His Best* was published. University Microfilms lists a number of the Mr. Dooley books available in Xerox copies. Possibly the fact that most of the Dunne material is in the public domain has something to do with this spate of publishing. It is more likely that Mr. Dooley has a diehard coterie of believers who will support his continued publication. They will agree with the statement of J.C. Furnas in his review of the four 1963 publications:

> Dooley, a creature of Dunne's fancy but as real as Huckleberry Finn for all that, said little that failed to strike home. In all American humor from Benjamin Franklin to Nichols & May only the best of Mark Twain and the best of Ring Lardner are of the same order of nimble joy.[4]

However, the pervasive influence of Dunne is not to be explained by conclusions of literary critics but by the use made of the Mr. Dooley device and the revolution in communications of the post-Dunne period. Let me first take up what I consider to be imitation Mr. Dooley.

III. Imitation Mr. Dooley.

The extent to which Mr. Dooley has been imitated is a measure of his value and this will soon be explored. It is the existence of doubtful Mr. Dooleys that has not previously been examined in any study of Finley Peter Dunne. Imitations of Mr. Dooley are one thing, unidentified Mr. Dooleys are another.

An example of Mr. Dooley that has been quoted as the product of Finley Peter Dunne's pen but that is not in keeping with his "Roscommon" Irish style, nor does it appear in any of his books or biographies, or have the double edge of the usual Dooley comment, is the following frequently quoted statement:

> 'What's all this in the papers about the open shop?' asked Mr. Hennessey.
>
> 'Why don't ye know?' said Mr. Dooley. 'Really, I'm surprised at yer ignorance, Hinnissey. What is th' open shop? Sure tis wheer they kape the doors open to accommodate th' constant stream of min comin' in t' take jobs cheaper than the min that has th' jobs. . . .'
>
> 'But,' said Mr. Hennessey, 'these open-shop min ye menshun say they are f'r unions if properly conducted.'
>
> 'Sure,' said Mr. Dooley, 'if properly conducted. An' there we are; an' how would they have thim conducted? No strikes, no rules, no contracts, no scales, hardly iny wages an' damn few members.'[5]

Not only has this quote appeared in labor texts, it was repeated by the eminent economist Paul Samuelson.[6] It appears in none of the Mr. Dooley books published, nor in a fairly extensive perusal of his unpublished material. No source is offered for it, and one can only surmise that it belongs to a union supporter who recognized the impact of the Dooley name appended to his thoughts.

It is interesting to compare this possibly spurious Mr. Dooley with Finley Peter Dunne's Mr. Dooley essay called, "The Labor Troubles." Its conclusions show more concern for those oppressed by both labor and management:

> 'They ought to get together,' said Mr. Hennessy. 'How cud they get anny closer together thin their prisint clinch?' asked Mr. Dooley. 'They're so close together now that those that ar-re between thim ar-re crushed to death.' (*Dissertations* 64)

An instance of tampering with Mr. Dooley results in a canard on corporation lawyers. The original reads:

A law, Hinnissy, that might look like a wall to you or me wud look like a thriumphal arch to th' expeeryenced eye iv a lawyer.[7]

Unlike the previous example, this item by the addition of one word, not Mr. Dooley's, has an entirely different connotation. In one instance it shows up as the following:

All of the language of the law is such, as Mr. Dooley once put it, that a statute which reads like a stone wall to the layman becomes, for the corporation lawyer, a triumphal arch.[8]

It is not the damage to the corporation lawyer that makes this type of infringement a crime of great magnitude as much as the abusing of another's reputation to support a position that a propagandist cannot substantiate in any other way. Plagiarism is simply stealing another's words; the practice of attributing to an author words or meanings that are not his is plagiarism that deserves not just civil but criminal sanctions. The net result is that the misquotation or wrongly attributed quotation becomes compounded by repetition to the discredit of the innocent and defenseless author.[9] In both instances, a proper regard for the author would have required a search for the original, and if not found, then the use of the material with proper precautions to the reader.

The specific lesson to be learned from this is the value of the Mr. Dooley label. The general lesson is that anyone who would indulge in this deviousness is at most, immoral; at best, misleading; and, at the very least, an exponent of poor scholarship.

Philip Dunne, the son of Mr. Dooley, is critical of people who use Mr. Dooley to say what they think Mr. Dunne would have said were he alive today. He does not cite any examples, but in a way, he himself has been guilty of the same crime. In promoting his book, *Mr. Dooley Remembers,* Philip Dunne told of President John F. Kennedy's admiration for Mr. Dooley, particularly in the following quote:

> "It was a great one," Dunne recounted yesterday. "It goes something like this, without the Irish brogue: When a triumphal arch is built, people do well to make it out of bricks so that they'll have something to throw at the hero when they get tired of him." [10]

This quote does not appear in any of Mr. Dunne's books, nor does it appear in Philip Dunne's book, or in any of Elmer Ellis's material, and it has not showed up in any of my research into unpublished Dunne material.

What does appear is the following account by Mark Sullivan:

> When a grateful raypublic Mr. Hinnessy, builds an ar-rch to its conquering hero, it should be made of brick, so that we can have something convanyient to hurl after him when he has passed by. *That quotation is from memory.* [Italics supplied] [11]

Did Finley Peter Dunne ever actually make such a comment about triumphal arches? If so, there is no trace of it in his writing.

Another theory is possible and that is that Dunne might have *said* it. From his early days at the Whitechapel Club, to his golfing outings with important and influential people, to his membership in literary and businessmen clubs, Dunne was a much sought after raconteur and wit. Elmer Ellis provides many examples of Dunne's impromptu wit. In person, and as Mr. Dooley, Dunne was a sharp and observant man. Possibly Dunne may have said it to his friend, Mark Sullivan.

An example of Dunne's off-the-cuff comments getting into print can be seen in frequent references to Mr. Dooley by the late Dean Roscoe Pound of the Harvard Law School.

> Referring to the words of Mr. Dooley about the function of the probate court on page 22 of the September-October 1957 issue of *Case and Comment,* I would say that the saying so far as I know was not published in any of Mr. Dunn's writings [sic — Dean Pound was in his 80's at the time of this letter], but is something I heard him say at a luncheon at the Press Club in Chicago in the winter of 1907-1908. As I remember, he said, "Hinnissy, it is the function of the probate coort to see to it that iv'ry mimber of the bar gets a fair chanst at phat the dicased could not take with him." He used to say many things of this kind offhand. Mr. Kramer used to tell many of them that never reached publication but were a delight to his friends.[12]

Dean Pound has also quoted a Dooleyism that has amused a number of people in the legal world, but is also not in published form: It doesn't mane [mean] what it says, it manes what it manes.[13]

Another example of what I believe to be spurious or unfounded Dunne, but sounds more like a paraphrase of the original than an attempt to be original, was given in a speech by Senator Humphrey before the Arkansas State Democratic Convention on September 18, 1964:

> Mr. Dooley once saw his friend Hennessey shining up a set of brass knuckles and asked where he was going. 'To a Democratic unity meeting,' said Hennessey, 'I always go prepared.' [14]

Questionable Dunne is one thing, imitation another. And literature would be somewhat diminished if envious writers, who properly label their activity, did not take liberties with the ingenious creation of Mr. Dooley.

The imitations take a variety of forms and hopefully send the true Dooley admirer back to the original. One variety of imitation will build around a borrowed phrase from Mr. Dooley.[15] There are numerous samples of authors and editors simply adopting the Mr. Dooley setting and then espousing their own ideas.[16] Ethically, the author should indicate, as is usually the case, that he owes apologies to Mr. Dunne for borrowing Mr. Dooley from him. As Mr. Dooley once said, "Larceny is th' sincerest form of flattery."

Mr. Dooley has not only been imitated, he has been copied. George Creel indicates that his "Uncle Henry" character was good for ten years,[17] and the "Discourses of Keidansky," a Jewish Mr. Dooley,[18] apparently had some vogue. James Joyce may have given some immortality to Mr. Dooley with his anti-war poem called "Dooleysprudence." [19] And finally, Mr. Dooley was the song hit of a musical comedy ("A Chinese Honeymoon," performed in 1902), with Mr. Dunne given a special ovation on its opening night.[20]

All this suggests that Mr. Dooley has gone beyond his original promise. He is not just in the public domain; he is more like an industry spinning off new literary ideas. As with inventions, general ideas are not copyrightable and, like aspirin, can be dispensed under any label.

Paradoxically, Finley Peter Dunne, despite the fact that he did well economically, was plagued with plagiarism. His first efforts were "borrowed" by other newspapers until he was properly syndicated. He was pirated by an English publisher in a volume entitled *What Dooley Says* (1899), and Mr. Dunne paid his respects to these pirates by a vengeful dedication printed in *Mr. Dooley in the Hearts of his Countrymen.* It is unfortunate that Mr. Dunne cannot provide us with his observations about all the attention paid to his creation thirty-five years after his death.

IV. Mr. Dooley as Theater.

The Mr. Dooley technique has been extensively borrowed on radio and television.

> Fred Allen never borrowed Dunne's barroom format, as Ed "Archie" Gardner did for "Duffy's Tavern" and as Jackie Gleason appropriated it for TV later, but he was the strict inheritor of Dunne's scathing Irish wit, which Gardner tried to use in a much lower key, but which Gleason, for all his noisy buffoonery, never would attempt at all.[21]

Obviously, Dunne's influence still prevails, but the question remains whether he will endure in the original.

Perenially at election time Mr. Dooley is quoted. His observations on life, women, international affairs, law, sports, and journalism are frequently found in newspapers, magazines and books. Max Morath, in a one man show, "An Evening with Max Morath at the Turn of the Century,"[22] included with his scintillating jazz a presentable format of Mr. Dooley's pertinent comments on the period.

It was reported that a play, "Mr. Dooley," was headed for Broadway,[23] and literary commentators have attempted to waken producers to Mr. Dooley's potential.

116

They seem eminently stageable also. *The New Woman* and other dramatical essays could provide interludes with Dooley not only behind his bar lecturing and bamboozling Hennessy, but out on Archey Road fighting with Dorsey, and one might transpose scenes to actual courtroom settings and Democratic rally halls. Updated international and Asian references might give another topical dimension to the political satire. An Holbrookian impersonation of Dooley and an overall conception like that of The Thurber Carnival suggest an inevitable production in the near future.[24]

John V. Kelleher's article offered his method of remodeling Dooley for a modern audience.[25] Mr. Kelleher's appreciation of Mr. Dooley (Dunne unfortunately always takes second billing) is probably the best analysis of the spirit that Mr. Dooley passed to millions of readers. He captures Mr. Dooley in song, in pathos and in his inimitable style. To Kelleher, Dooley is everyman. He is the Irish struggling for acceptance in American life, he is David preparing his slingshot (possibly the closest to Dunne's style today is the Israeli author, Ephraim Kishon), he is the light in the darkened room. Kelleher suggested that the late Barry Fitzgerald put Mr. Dooley on record, and he even suggested a script, although his entire article, sparkling with Dooleyisms and bright comment, would make an excellent recording in itself.

The point these gentlemen are making is that with radio and television the dialect problem, which so many critics emphasize, is minimized. If Mark Twain and Will Rogers can be interpreted on stage and on television, a revival of Mr. Dooley can not be far behind. On May 1, 1972, the author of this book was master of ceremonies at a banquet

117

held for the New York University Law Review. Mr. Dooley's comments on oratory were well received although this author is not an actor.

An evening with Mr. Dooley has potential if it avoids the pitfalls of general collections of Mr. Dooley material. The early Louis Filler book and the Manchester collection are faulty for this purpose because they are arrangements of Dunne material in the order of publication of Dunne's books. The original Dunne material is not indexed and is haphazard in topic. The later Filler book is far too broad in arrangement; Ellis's collection is somewhat topical but leaves out too much material. Specialized collections such as Lewin on politics and Bander on law have practicality for a segment of a show. Presenting Dunne in vignettes, gatherings on one topic from all his essays, has, in this author's estimate, excellent potential. At the conclusion of this chapter, Mr. Dooley's comments on life from his various essays are offered as a sample script for the reader to judge.

At the minimum, Dunne deserves a new edition of his works. It should contain a comprehensive index, additional volumes to cover the unpublished material, annotations where necessary, and a glossary.

There will always be cells of Mr. Dooley followers, whatever the verdict of history, and as Mr. Dooley said about himself, "f'r mesilf I'm still uncharted."

V. Script for Mr. Dooley on Life.

"How can I know anything, whin I haven't puzzled out what I am mesilf. I am Dooley, ye say, but ye'r on'y a casual observer. Ye don't care annything about me details. Ye look at me with a gin'ral eye. Nawthin that happens to me really hurts ye. Ye say, 'I'll go over to see Dooley,' sometimes, but more often ye say, 'I'll go over to Dooley's.' I'm a house to ye, wan iv a thousand that looks like a row iv model wurrukin' men's cottages. I'm a post to hitch ye'er silences to. I'm always about th' same to ye. But to me I'm a millyon Dooleys an' all iv thim sthrangers to ME. I niver know

119

which wan iv thim is comin' in. I'm like a hotel keeper with on'y wan bed an' a millyon guests, who come wan at a time an' tumble each other out. I set up late at night an' pass th' bottle with a gay an' careless Dooley that hasn't a sorrow in th' wurruld, an' suddenly I look up an' see settin' acrost from me a gloomy wretch that fires th' dhrink out iv th' window an' chases me to bed. I'm just gettin' used to him whin another Dooley comes in, a cross, cantankerous, crazy fellow that insists on eatin' breakfast with me. An' so it goes. I know more about mesilf than annybody knows an' I know nawthin'. Though I'd make a map fr'm mem'ry an' gossip iv anny other man, f'r mesilf I'm still uncharted." (*Says* 130, 131)

"A man has more fun wishin' f'r th' things he hasn't got thin injyin' th' things he has got. Life, Hinnissy, is like a Pullman dinin'-car; a fine bill iv fare but nawthin' to eat. Ye go in fresh an' hungry, tuck ye'er napkin in ye'er collar, an' square away at th' list iv groceries that th' black man hands ye. What 'll ye have first? Ye think ye'd like to be famous, an' ye ordher a dish iv fame an' bid th' waither make it good an' hot. He's gone an age, an' whin he comes back ye'er appytite is departed. Ye taste th' ordher, an' says ye: 'Why, it's cold an' full iv broken glass.' 'That's th' way we always sarve Fame on this car,' says th' [waiter]. 'Don't ye think ye'd like money f'r th' second coorse? Misther Rockyfellar over there has had forty-two helpin's,' says he. 'It don't seem to agree with him,' says ye, 'but ye may bring me some,' ye say. Away he goes, an' stays till ye're bald an' ye'er teeth fall out an' ye set dhrummin' on th' table an' lookin' out at th' scenery. By-an'-by he comes back with ye-er ordher, but jus' as he's goin' to hand it to ye Rockyfellar grabs th' plate. 'What kind iv a car is this?' says ye. 'Don't I get anny-thing to eat? Can't ye give me a little happiness?' 'I wudden't ricommend th' happiness,' says th' waither. 'It's canned, an' it kilt th' las' man that thried it.' 'Well, gracious,' says ye.

120

'I've got to have something. Give me a little good health, an' I'll thry to make a meal out iv that.' 'Sorry, sir,' says th' black man, 'but we're all out iv good health. Besides,' he says, takin' ye gently be th' ar-rm, 'we're comin' into th' deepo [depot] an' ye'll have to get out,' he says." (*Dissertations* 35, 36)

". . . Wan iv th' sthrangest things about life is that it will go on in onfav'rable circumstances an' go out whin ivrything is aisy [easy]. A man can live an' have a good time, no matther what happens to him that don't kill him. I lived here durin' th' cholery [cholera]. I didn't like it, but they was on'y wan other thing to do, an' I didn't care f'r that. If ye're livin' in a town that's bein' bombarded ye don't like it at first, but afther awhile ye begin to accommydate ye'ersilf to it, an' by-an'-by, whin a shell dhrops while ye're argyin' about th' tariff, ye step aside, an' if ye're still there afther th' smoke is cleared away ye resume th' argymint. Ye have to make new frinds, but so ye do in Chicago. A man iv me age loses more frinds in a year, an' is in more danger thin a definder iv Port Arthur [Russo-Japanese War] at twinty-wan. Bustin' shells is on'y wan iv th' chances iv life, like pnoomony an' argyin' with a polisman." (*Dissertations* 289, 290)

". . . 'Idjacation [education],' he says, 'is something that a man has to fight f'r an' pull out iv its hole be th' hair iv its head,' he says. 'That's th' reason it's so precious,' he says. 'They'se so little iv it, an' it's so hard to get,' he says. 'They'se anny quantity iv gab that looks like it, but it ain't th' rale thing,' he says. 'Th' wurruld is full iv people wearin' false joolry iv that kind,' he says, 'but afther they've had it f'r a long time, it tur-rns green an' blue, an' some day whin they thry to get something on it, th' pawnbroker throws thim out. No, sir, idjacation means throuble an' wurruk an' worry. . . .' "

"I don't think it makes anny difference wan way or th' other how free ye make idjacation. Men that wants it 'll have it be hook an' be crook, an' thim that don't ra-aly want it niver will get it. Ye can lade a man up to th' university, but ye can't make him think...." (*Opinions* 148-149)

"I've been up to th' top iv th' very highest buildin' in town, Hinnissy, an' I wasn't anny nearer Hivin thin if I was in th' sthreet. Th' stars was as far away as iver. An' down beneath is a lot iv us run over, haulin' little sthrips iv ir'n to pile up in little buildin's that ar-re called sky-scrapers but not be th' sky; wurrukin' night an' day to make a masheen [machine] that'll carry us fr'm wan jack-rabbit colony to another an' yellin', 'Pro-gress!' Pro-gress, oho! I can see th' stars winkin' at each other an' sayin': 'Ain't they funny! Don't they think they're playin' hell!' "

"I want to see sky-scrapin' men. But I won't. We're about th' same hight as we always was, th' same hight an' build, composed iv th' same inflammable an' perishyable mateeryal, an exthra hazardous risk, unimproved an' li'ble to collapse. We do make pro-gress but it's th' same kind Julyus Caesar made an' ivry wan has made befure or since an' in this age iv masheenery we're still burrid be hand." (*Observations* 218)

"... th' wan great object iv ivry man's life is to get tired enough to sleep." (*Observations* 179)

"I'll tell ye," said Mr. Dooley. "I tell ye ivrything an' I'll tell ye this. In th' first place 'tis a gr-reat mistake to think that annywan ra-aly wants to rayform [reform]. Ye niver heerd iv a man rayformin' himsilf. He'll rayform other people gladly. He likes to do it. But a healthy man'll niver rayform while he has th' strenth. A man doesn't rayform till his will has been impaired so he hasn't power to resist what th' pa-apers calls th' blandishments iv th' timpter." (*Observations* 167)

"No, sir, whin I come to think iv it, I'll not deny th' pleasure iv bein' sick. It's th' on'y way some people has iv callin' attintion to thimsilves an' bein' talked about. If I tell Hogan ye're well he don't care. But if I say ye're sick he's got inthrest enough in ye at laste [least] to ask: 'What's th' matther with him?' Ivry sick man is a hero if not to th' wurruld or aven to th' fam'ly, at laste to himsilf. An' 'tis th' proper business iv th' doctor to make him feel like wan. A patient in th' hands iv a doctor is like a hero in th' hands iv a story writer. He's goin' to suffer a good dale [deal], but he's goin' to come out all right in th' end." (*Will* 126, 127)

123

MR. DOOLEY AND MR. DUNNE

1. ELMER ELLIS, MR. DOOLEY'S AMERICA, 310 (N.Y., 1941).

2. THE WORLD OF MR. DOOLEY, 18 (Louis Filler, ed., N.Y., 1962).

3. Check the bibliography for books by Edward J. Bander, Philip Dunne, Louis Filler and Robert Hutchinson. *See* the New York Times (Book Review), 3 (Dec. 22, 1963).

4. J.C. Furnas, *An Irish Saloon Keeper as Real as Huck Finn,* New York Times (Book Review), 3 (Dec. 22, 1963).

5. ALEINE AUSTIN, THE LABOR STORY: A POPULAR HISTORY OF AMERICAN LABOR, 1786-1949, 158-59 (N.Y., 1949). *See also* PHILIP S. FONER, HISTORY OF THE LABOR MOVEMENT IN THE UNITED STATES, 57 (N.Y., 1947).

6. Paul Samuelson, *The Case Against Goldwater's Economics,* New York Times (Magazine), 28 (Oct. 25, 1964). In the current edition of Professor Samuelson's ECONOMICS 126 (11th ed. 1980), he "attributes" this imitation to Finley Peter Dunne without substantiation.

7. MR. DOOLEY ON THE CHOICE OF LAW, 64 (Edward J. Bander, ed., Charlottesville, Va., 1963). This essay originally appeared in 62 AMERICAN MAGAZINE, (Oct., 1906), and the Boston Globe (Magazine), 5 (Nov. 4, 1906).

8. FRED RODELL, WOE UNTO YOU, LAWYERS, 8 (N.Y., 1939). It is also quoted in CASE & COMMENT, 63 (Nov.-Dec., 1959). This is not to say that Dunne was kind to corporation lawyers. *See* MR. DOOLEY ON THE CHOICE OF LAW, 35 (Edward J. Bander, ed., Charlottesville, Va., 1963).

9. The corporation canard has reached across an ocean. *See* 1 TASMANIAN UNIV. L. REV., 542 (1961).

10. Jean M. White, *Dooley's Bricks Still Make Mark,* Washington Post (Nov. 4, 1963).

11. MARK SULLIVAN, I OUR TIMES, 340 (N.Y., 1926).

12. Letter to the author (Oct. 21, 1957).

13. 66 HARVARD L. REV., 42 (1952).

14. Letter from Senator Humphrey to the author (Oct. 2, 1964). For my guess as to origin of this quote, *see* the definitions in Chapter III for *Democratic Party.*
To compound this confusion, witness an article by James Reston attributing a Dooley quote to President Truman, and a Humphrey paraphrase of a Dooley quote (quoted in my text), characterizing Senator Humphrey's debating technique with Senator McGovern: "Well, as Harry Truman or somebody else once said, 'politics ain't beanball [sic].' It is a brass-knuckles business, and maybe one of Humphrey's wild swings will connect, but it is still ironic and a little sad to watch Humphrey, of all people, trying to rescue himself in California by implying that McGovern is soft on the poor and soft on Communism." James Reston, "Let George Do It?", New York Times, 41 (May 31, 1972). Strangely

enough, "Politics ain't beanbag," is common to the editorial page of the New York Times. See William Safire, 'Government Ain't Machinery,' New York Times, 36 (Jan. 5, 1971); and Tom Wicker, "Mr. Mills Plays It Rough," § 4 New York Times, 13 (March 14, 1971). It seems that humor is bean bag.

15. Richard Starnes, *Mr. Dooley and the GOP,* New York World Telegram, 23 (July 21, 1964). The item begins with Mr. Dooley's statement, "Polytiks ain't bean bag," and Mr. Starnes follows with his imitation. The author of this book has also used this style: "No, Hinnissy, some people take a job — as oive said befure — an' some people take a chance," Villager, 16 (Greenwich Village, N.Y.C., July 1, 1965). Another example is reviving the memory of a Mr. Dooley target and then applying it to current affairs, as illustrated by Roscoe Fleming, *Mr. Dooley comments on Civil Defense, Teddy Rosenfelt, and Battle iv San Juan,* Cong. Rec. A1279 (Feb. 8, 1956). (This is the only source located that is available in print. Mr. Fleming, according to Rep. Byron G. Rogers of Colorado, was "a capable and well-known writer of the West." (Same citation.))

16. The following are a sampling of imitations of this variety: Charles F. Porter and Charles E. Rush, *Mr. Jooley on the Library School,* Library Journal, 142 (April 1908); Paul Sarnoff, *Mr. Dooley on Money and Banking,* 151 Bankers Magazine, 103 (Aug. 1968); James M. Marsh, *Mr. Dooley Discovers a Unanimous Dissent,* 7 The Shingle, 191 (Aug. 1968); *Mr. Dooley on the Case System* (an anonymous item in the collection of Harvard University); *Mr. Dooley on the World Championship* [chess], 10

AMERICAN CHESS BULLETIN, 244 (Nov. 1913); *Automation, Mr. Dooley*, LIFE, 41 (March 3, 1961); *Massachusetts*, NEW REPUBLIC, 6 (Oct. 1, 1962); John B. Mannion, *The Pope and Mr. Dooley on Jazz Masses*, COMMONWEAL, 416 (Jan. 20, 1967). The author of this book has also attempted Mr. Dooley imitations but will only supply citations on written request. One can notice that there are no political or social boundaries to Mr. Dooley from the above citations.

17. "Heaven knows the pieces were miles removed from the brilliance of Mr. Dooley...." GEORGE CREEL, REBEL AT LARGE, 267 (N.Y., 1947).

18. *See* New York Times, 71 (April 5, 1964).

19. *See* RICHARD ELLMAN, 2 JAMES JOYCE, 436-38 (N.Y., 1959), and THE CRITICAL WRITINGS OF JAMES JOYCE, 246 (Ellsworth Mason and Richard Ellman, eds., N.Y., 1959).

20. ELMER ELLIS, MR. DOOLEY'S AMERICA, 183-84 (N.Y., 1941).

21. JESSE BIER, THE RISE AND FALL OF AMERICAN HUMOR, 273 (N.Y., 1968). As noted earlier, Mr. Dooley was read at cabinet meetings of President McKinley, and a good many people who quote him orally delight in attempting the Irish dialect. One such reader was Robert Frost:

"Another extremely important sidelight is provided in this letter by Cox's reference to Robert Frost's reading aloud and with obvious relish (during the year 1911-1912) from the writings of Finley Peter Dunne. Throughout the remainder of his life, Robert Frost was very fond of Dunne's Irish saloon keeper, Mr. Dooley, who comically criticized events, leaders and aspects of the social scene in a rich brogue. At this phase of his life, Robert Frost was beginning to emulate Dooley's comical fault-finding of the national scene." LAWRANCE THOMPSON, ROBERT FROST, THE EARLY YEARS 1874-1915 at 577 (N.Y., 1966).

22. New York Times, 35 (Feb. 18, 1969). Al Vecchione, who produced the television filming for the Democratic National Convention in 1976, included a script based on Mr. Dooley comments with Edward Asner portraying Mr. Dooley. It was not an artistic success through no fault of Mr. Dooley. *See,* in general, *Democrats Focusing Convention for TV,* New York Post, 4 (June 14, 1976).

23. Boston American (Jan. 2, 1957).

24. JESSE BIER, THE RISE AND FALL OF AMERICAN HUMOR, 185, n.5 (N.Y., 1968). Since the publication of Mr. Bier's book there have been portrayals of Will Rogers, H.L. Mencken, Frederick Douglass, and the author some years ago attended a stage performance of the words of Justice Oliver Wendell Holmes. Since the "Thurber Carnival" Broadway had a

successful run of "You're a Good Man, Charley Brown," based on incidents from the comic strip, Peanuts.

25. John V. Kelleher, *Mr. Dooley and the Same Old World,* 177 ATLANTIC 119 (June 1946).

SELECTED BIBLIOGRAPHY

The great bulk of Dunne's writing has not been collected. His early items in the *Chicago Post* are available on microfilm. They were unsigned but all the Colonel McNeery and Mr. Dooley items were written by Dunne. With syndication Dunne appeared in the *Boston Globe,* the *New York Times* and other newspapers. Mr. Dooley essays appeared in leading magazines of the period including *Harper's Weekly, Century, Cosmopolitan* and *Ladies Home Journal.* Dunne wrote both Mr. Dooley essays and regular essays ("In the Interpreter's House") for *American Magazine.* Some of his Mr. Dooley essays also appeared in *Hearst's Magazine.* On occasion an early Mr. Dooley piece would be reprinted, and the Bell Syndicate reprinted some Mr. Dooley pieces in 1923. In 1925 *Liberty* signed Mr. Dunne to do a new series of Mr. Dooley articles that on occasion had flashes of the old brilliance ("On the Income Tax" and "Mr. Dooley Reviews a Book [on Col. House]"). The Appendix section to this volume contains the only attempt to list all the Mr. Dooley essays.

Primary Sources

Bander, Edward J., ed., *Mr. Dooley on the Choice of Law* (Charlottesville, Va.: Michie, 1963). A collection of Mr. Dunne's items that in one way or another relate to law. Contains a capable preface by the compiler and an introduction by Dean Roscoe Pound. Also a list of "words and phrases" and a "glossary-index."

Dunne, Finley Peter, *Dissertations by Mr. Dooley* (N.Y.: Harper, 1906).

_____, *Mr. Dooley in Peace and in War* (Boston: Small, Maynard, 1898), *reprinted by* Scholarly Press in 1968.

_____, *Mr. Dooley in the Hearts of his Countrymen* (Boston: Small, Maynard, 1899), *reprinted by* Scholarly Press in 1968 and Greenwood Press in 1969.

_____, *Mr. Dooley on Making a Will and Other Necessary Evils* (N.Y.: Scribner, 1919).

_____, *Mr. Dooley on Timely Topics of the Day — On Life Insurance Investigation, On Business and Political Honesty, On National Housecleaning* (N.Y.: Colliers, 1905), a *reprinting of* the November 4, 18 and Christmas issues of *Collier's National Weekly.*

_____, *Mr. Dooley Says* (N.Y.: C. Scribner's Sons, 1910).

_____, "Mr. Dooley's Friends: Teddy Roosevelt and Mark Twain," 212, *Atlantic,* 77 (Sept. 1963). Compiled from *Mr. Dooley Remembers.* Selections of *Mr. Dooley Remembers* also appeared in the *Boston Globe* beginning with the Oct. 11, 1964 issue. This material was also available to Elmer Ellis in his biography of Dunne.

—————, *Mr. Dooley's Opinions* (N.Y.: R.H. Russell, 1901).

—————, *Mr. Dooley's Philosophy* (N.Y.: R.H. Russell, 1900). Harper and Bros. brought out a reprint of this volume that did not include the essay, "President's Message."

—————, *Observations by Mr. Dooley,* (N.Y.: Harper, 1906).

—————, *What Dooley Says* (Chicago: Kazmar & Co., 1899). An unauthorized collection of Mr. Dooley items. *See* Ellis's *Mr. Dooley's America,* 132-33.

Dunne, Philip, *Mr. Dooley Remembers, the Informal Memoirs of Finley Peter Dunne,* (Boston: Little, Brown, 1963). The memoirs of Dunne, plus commentary by Philip Dunne and a selection of the Mr. Dooley essays and aphorisms "translated into English." There are those who believe Mr. Dooley is just as effective without the dialect, but something is lost in the translation.

Ellis, Elmer, ed., *Mr. Dooley at his Best* (N.Y.: Charles Scribner's Sons, 1938). An excellent collection arranged by such topics as: politics, Theodore Roosevelt, athletics, literary criticism, women, education, etc. Foreword by F. P. Adams.

Filler, Louis, ed., *Mr. Dooley Now and Forever ...,* (Stanford: Academic Reprints, 1954). Selections from most of the Mr. Dooley books. Perceptive introduction.

—————, *The World of Mr. Dooley* (N.Y.: Collier, 1962). A good introduction followed by chapters on the Irish, politics, wars and heroes, reform, foreign matters, philosophy and miscellaneous. Includes six pieces of Dunne's non-dialect prose taken from *American Magazine.*

PRIMARY SOURCES

Hutchinson, Robert, ed., *Mr. Dooley on Ivrything and Ivrybody* (N.Y.: Dover Publications, 1963). A good introduction, and some essays are footnoted to accent the event Mr. Dooley was discussing. Arranged in the order of the essays in the first six books of Mr. Dooley.

Schaaf, Barbara C., *Mr. Dooley's Chicago* (N.Y.: Doubleday, 1977). Includes a number of early Mr. Dooley essays that have not previously been published in book form. The commentary provides information on the events and personalities that provided the impetus for many of Mr. Dooley's forays.

Secondary Sources

Adams, Franklin P., "Mr. Dooley," 94 *New Republic* (May 4, 1938). An affectionate epitaph to the creator of Mr. Dooley.

Adams, J. Donald, "Speaking of Books," *New York Times (Book Review),* 2 (Oct. 28, 1962). The author suggests that humor does not last and that Benchley is in and Dunne is done.

Ade, George, "When Good Fellows Got Together," 82 *Hearst's International Magazine,* 98 ff. (Feb. 1927). Discusses Dunne and Whitechapel Club.

Anon, Review: Mr. Dooley Remembers, *Time,* 64 (Dec. 27, 1963). A sensible review of the book and Mr. Dunne.

Bander, Edward J., "The Dooley Process of Law," 62 *Case and Comment,* 20 (Sept.-Oct. 1957).

_____, "Mr. Dooley and the Chicago Bar," 54 *Illinois Bar Journal,* 318 (Dec. 1965).

_____, "Mr. Dooley and the Law," 36 *New York State Bar Journal,* 336 (August 1964).

_____. " 'N th' Law Did Mr. Dooley Rib," *Boston Sunday Globe,* 1 (Aug. 12, 1962).

_____, "Speakin iv Pollyticks," *New York Times,* 12 (Sept. 17, 1972).

Bier, Jesse, *The Rise and Fall of American Humor,* (N.Y.: Holt, Rinehart and Winston, 1968). From Philip Freneau to Lenny Bruce with frequent and perceptive references to Dunne. A selective bibliography that indicates that humor is even more difficult to write about than write.

135

Britt, Albert, *Turn of the Century* (Barre, Mass.: Barre Publishers, 1966). A newspaperman of the period finds Dunne required reading for the turn of the century (p. 35), but in recounting Dunne's attack on the Payne-Aldrich Tariff measure, he misses Mr. Dooley's pun on the word, "divvy divvy." (See *Mr. Dooley Says,* p. 144 ff. for the original).

Brockway, Wallace and Winer, Bart Keith, eds., *Homespun America* (N.Y.: Simon and Schuster, 1958). 30 pages of Dooleyisms.

Brogan, Denis W., *American Themes.* (N.Y.: Harper, 1947). A generous appraisal of Dunne by a noted British writer (pp. 47-50).

Canby, Henry S., "Mr. Dooley and Mr. Hennessy," 14 *Saturday Review of Literature,* 3 (May 9, 1936).

_____, *Seven Years' Harvest* (N.Y.: Farrar & Rinehart, 1936). A literary cornucopia with much praise for Mr. Dooley.

Carlisle, Henry C. Jr., ed., *American Satire in Prose and Verse* (N.Y.: Random House, 1962). An interesting collection from Ben Franklin to Joseph Heller with two by Dooley.

Carrigan, Jim R., Review: Bander, "Mr. Dooley on the Choice of Law," 57 *Law Library Journal,* 93 (1964). Comments on the relevancy of Mr. Dooley.

Cosgrove, Cornelius, "Mr. Dooley and the Reformers," 6 *American History Illustrated,* 23 (Oct. 1971). A fair presentation of Dunne's attitude toward reform with frequent references to Mr. Dooley.

Coyle, Lee, *George Ade* (N.Y.: Twayne, 1964). Capable biography that includes references to Dunne and to the period to which he belongs.

SECONDARY SOURCES

Dodd, John W., *American Memoir* (N.Y.: Popular Library, 1961). The chapter on satire includes a selection from Mr. Dooley on progressive education. The book is based on a television series by Professor Dodd.

Dudden, Arthur P., ed., *The Assault of Laughter: A Treasury of American Political Humor* (N.Y.: Yoseloff, 1962). A standard collection with twenty-one items by F.P. Dunne.

Ellis, Elmer, *Mr. Dooley's America: A Life of Finley Peter Dunne* (N.Y.: Knopf, 1941). The only biography of Dunne, *reprinted by* Archon Press in 1969.

Fadiman, Clifton, ed., *The American Treasury, 1455-1955* (N.Y.: Harper, 1955). Mr. Dooley is well represented in this broad range of American literature.

Filler, Louis, "Finley Peter Dunne," *Dictionary of American Biography*. A succinct biography of Dunne and the significance of Mr. Dooley.

Furnas, J.C., *The Americans; A Social History of the United States* 1587-1914 (N.Y.: G.P. Putnam's Sons, 1969). A social historian who knows the value of Mr. Dooley.

_____, "An Irish Salon Keeper as Real as Huck Finn," *New York Times (Book Review),* 3 (Jan. 26, 1964). A composite review of "Mr. Dooley Remembers," "The World of Mr. Dooley," "Mr. Dooley on Ivrything and Ivrybody" and "Mr. Dooley on the Choice of Law."

_____, "Speaking of Books," *New York Times (Book Review),* 2 (June 26, 1960). Emphasizes Mr. Dooley's political ripostes and comments on his deadly punning.

Hampden, Michael D., Review: Bander, Mr. Dooley on the Choice of Law, 38 *Harvard Law Record,* 11 (April 9, 1964).

Harbaugh, William H., *Power and Responsibility* (N.Y.: Farrar, Straus, 1961). An example of the use made of Mr. Dooley by historians and social scientists.

Howells, W. D., "Work of Finley Peter Dunne," 176 *North American Review,* 743 (May 1903). An early recognition of the permanence of Dunne.

Howland, Hewitt H., *Humor by Vote . . .,* (N.Y.: The Laugh Club, 1933). Selections by some people I never heard of, of some people I never heard of — Mr. Dunne is the only humorist represented by more than one selection.

Keeffe, Arthur John, Review: Bander, Mr. Dooley on the Choice of Law, 14 *Catholic University Law Review,* 137 (1965). Mr. Keeffe has done more to keep the Mr. Dooley essays alive through reviews and his column in the *American Bar Association Journal* than any other man of law.

Kelleher, J.V., "Mr. Dooley and the Same Old World," 177 *Atlantic,* 119 (June 1946). My selection for the best essay on Mr. Dooley.

Kelly, Fred C., *George Ade: Warmhearted Satirist* (Indianapolis: Bobbs-Merrill, 1947). Valuable for the light it throws on the Chicago literati of the period, including Mr. Dunne.

King, Willard L., *Melville Weston Fuller* (N.Y.: Macmillan, 1950). Interesting background on the origin of the famous Dooleyism that "th' Supreme Coort follows th' iliction returns." (pp. 237 ff.).

Leacock, Stephen, *The Greatest Pages of American Humor . . .,* (Garden City: Doubleday, 1936). A recognized humorist pays his respects to Mr. Dooley.

Lewin, Leonard, ed., *A Treasury of American Political Humor* (N.Y.: Dial, 1964). A wide ranging collection of political humor with five good selections from the pen of Finley Peter Dunne.

Lynn, Kenneth ed., *The Comic Tradition in America* (N.Y.: Doubleday, 1958). A personal selection of humor with five entries for Mr. Dooley.

McCarthy, John, ed., *The Home Book of Irish Humor* (N.Y.: Dodd, Mead & Co., 1968). Includes Mr. Dooley.

McPhaul, John J., *Deadlines and Monkeyshines; the Fabled World of Chicago Journalism* (Englewood Cliffs, N.J.: Prentice-Hall, 1962). A blend of fact and journalism with some interesting copy on Mr. Dunne.

Masson, Thomas, *Our American Humorists* (N.Y.: Moffat, Yard & Co., 1922).

Million, Elmer M., Review: Bander, Mr. Dooley on the Choice of Law, *New York Law Journal,* 4 (March 13, 1964). A composite review of books on Mr. Dooley with emphasis on the law and imitation Mr. Dooley essays.

Morris, Lloyd, *Postscript to Yesterday* (N.Y.: Random House, 1947). Very perceptive comments on Dunne. *See* pages 285, 292, 293, 323.

Murphy, Edward F., comp. "Of Dimmycrats, Raypublicans, Etc.," *New York Times (Magazine),* 107 (Sept. 9, 1962). A page of quotations from Mr. Dooley.

Poore, Charles, Review: Dunne, P., Mr. Dooley Remembers, *New York Times,* 23 (Nov. 21, 1963). The author approves of Dunne with the dialect removed. But see the review of J.C. Furnas which takes an opposite view (Jan. 26, 1964).

Ripley, John W., "Another Look at the Rev. Mr. Charles M. Sheldon's Christian Daily Newspaper," 31 *Kansas Historical Quarterly,* 25 (Spring 1965). Provides the historical background to a Mr. Dooley satire ("Christian Journalism" in *Mr. Dooley's Philosophy,* p. 169) that was mysteriously removed from the Topeka Public Library.

Rourke, Constance, *American Humor, A Study of the National Character* (N.Y.: Doubleday, 1931). The one book they all go back to. Some comment on Mr. Dooley without acknowledgment to Mr. Dunne.

Sayre, Paul, *The Life of Roscoe Pound* (Iowa City: College of Law Committee, 1948). A great law teacher and dean, who, like many other teachers, frequently quoted Mr. Dooley to his classes.

Schutz, Charles E., *Political Humor From Aristophanes to Sam Ervin* (Cranbury, N.Y.: Associated University Presses, 1977).

Seldes, Gilbert, *The 7 Lively Arts* (N.Y.: Sagamore Press, 1957). A survey of the arts with a lively comment on Mr. Dooley's place in American literature.

Shannon, William V., *The American Irish* (N.Y.: Macmillan, 1963). An interesting discussion of Mr. Dunne's art and politics.

Spiller, R.E., et al., *Literary History of the United States* (N.Y.: Macmillan, 1955). The selections and comments are an indication that Mr. Dunne belongs in the mainstream of American literature.

Stanley, David, ed., *A Treasury of Sports Humor* (N.Y.: Lantern Press, 1946). One by Dunne ("On Athletics"), in the company of William Saroyan, Ring Lardner, Damon Runyon and lesser beings.

Sullivan, Mark, *Our Times . . . 1900-1925* (N.Y.: Scribner's, 1926). 5 vols. A social history of the period with extensive references to Mr. Dooley's pithy comments on the period.

Untermeyer, Louis, ed., *Great Humor: Including Wit, Whimsy, and Satire from the Remote Past to the Present* (N.Y.: McGraw-Hill, 1972).

—————, *A Treasury of Laughter* (N.Y.: Simon and Schuster, 1946). A potpourri with Mr. Dooley on "Alcohol as Food," and on "Expert Testimony."

White, E.B. and White, K.S., eds., *A Subtreasury of American Humor* (N.Y.: Modern Library, 1948, c. 1941). Includes selections from the Mr. Dooley essays as well as praise for Dunne.

Wind, Herbert W., ed., *The Realm of Sport* (N.Y.: Simon & Schuster, 1966). "Some rare, some classic, some funny" and Mr. Dooley on American football.

Yates, Norris W., *The American Humorist, Conscience of the Twentieth Century* (Ames, Iowa: Iowa State University Press, 1964). A good chapter on Dunne, and an excellent source book on humorists from George Ade to E.B. White. On page 370 the author cites "The 'Mr. Dooley' Papers" which I have been unable to locate.

Addenda

Bander, Edward J. "Mr. Dooley, on Dimmycrats Chasin' iv th' Raypublicans," *New York Times,* 19 (Nov. 4, 1980).

Gibson, William M., *Theodore Roosevelt Among the Humorists: W.D. Howells, Mark Twain, and Mr. Dooley* (Knoxville Univ. of Tenn. Press, 1980) The author analyzes Mr. Dooley's influence on a President's decisions.

APPENDIX

A Chronological Listing of Finley Peter Dunne's Mr. Dooley Essays.

The quotations and comments are provided for literary and historical background. In most instances, where the Boston Globe is included as a source, the quotations and comments are based on a reading of the Globe entry. There are instances where the Mr. Dooley items have been edited for inclusion in the collections of Mr. Dooley.

1. Leave Grover Alone

    Col. McNeery criticizes report that Cleveland has cancer.

    Chicago Evening Post, September 2, 1893

2. Days of the Home Rule

    Col. McNeery and Irish Home Rule.

    Chicago Evening Post, September 9, 1893

3. It Doesn't Suit Mac

    On a World Religious Congress.

    Chicago Evening Post, September 16, 1893

4. He Stayed in his Bed

    Train robbery.

    Chicago Evening Post, September 23, 1893

5. Col. McNeery's Away

    Finley Peter Dunne prepares his audience for Mr. Dooley.

    Chicago Evening Post, September 30, 1893

6. John McKenna visits his old Friend Martin Dooley Up in Archey Road

    First Mr. Dooley column. Mr. Dooley commends a tenor

for his rendition of some fine Irish ballads only to find out he is a German.

Mr. Dooley's Chicago, p. 74;
Chicago Evening Post, Oct. 7, 1893

7. The Day of the Fire

"There seems to be a dam sight more reminiscences than they was fire. 'Twast that way always. I mind now it used to be a sayin' thru Connock that if all th' ol' men that swore they'd kill sojers with a pike in '98 had been out fr'm undher th' bed in thim days th' Irish parlyment'd be passin' laws in London city years gawn by." (Mr. Dooley describes Archey Road at the time of the fire. The fire did not spread to Archey Road, and it was a year before Dooley got around to check on its effect. To Dooley, to celebrate a fire was like "gettin' up a holiday f'r th' chollery. . . .")

Mr. Dooley's Chicago, p. 330;
Chicago Evening Post, October 14, 1893

8. Dooley Advises Cleveland — Points for Grover

Mr. Dooley tells "Big Steve" to use patronage to tame the Senate and makes his point with the O'Brien-Googin encounter in local politics.

Mr. Dooley's Chicago, p. 225;
Chicago Evening Post, October 21, 1893

9. Dooley Isn't Sorry

The closing of the fair.

Chicago Evening Post, October 28, 1893

10. In Every Other Land

The Irish Away from home.

Chicago Evening Post, November 4, 1893

144

11. Mr. Dooley Explains the Republican Victory

Cleveland's renegging on a campaign promise to "Willum Joyce" to be Ambassador to the Court of St. James (within dynamiting distance of the Queen) is what defeated the Democrats.

Mr. Dooley's Chicago, p. 230;
Chicago Evening Post, November 11, 1893

12. Mr. Dooley Held Up

Chicago Evening Post, November 18, 1893

13. Dooley at the Game

Mr. Dooley on sports.

Chicago Evening Post, December 2, 1893

14. Women's Influence in Politics — Behind the Throne

Mr. Dooley discusses his activities as precinct captain. He feels women will not support a bald man because they have no hold on him. He also feels that a woman decides who her man will vote for.

Mr. Dooley's Chicago, p. 271;
Chicago Evening Post, December 9, 1893

15. Mr. Dooley's Mail

Political mail.

Chicago Evening Post, December 16, 1893

16. Christmas in Ireland

Mr. Dooley recalls the old country.

Mr. Dooley's Chicago, p. 189;
Chicago Evening Post, December 23, 1893

17. Mr. Dooley's Trials

An acquittal of a local tough results in a difference of opinion at Dooley's bar.

Mr. Dooley's Chicago, p. 79;
Chicago Evening Post, March 10, 1894

18. On Bicycles

Sarsfield Dennehy introduces the bicycle to Archey Road. Mr. Dennehy gives the ax to the bicycle.

Mr. Dooley's Chicago, p. 154;
Chicago Evening Post, May 19, 1894

19. Dooley and the War

Mr. Dooley never goes to a Decoration Day parade. Mr. Dooley reminisces on the day Fort Sumter was fired on and Duggan and others joined the army.

Mr. Dooley's Chicago, p. 320;
Chicago Evening Post, June 2, 1894

20. Anarchism

An anarchist, with a beard like a coconut, amuses Dooley and puts Matt Doolan to sleep. Marriage ends his proseletyzing for the proletarians and Doolan comments " 'tis on'y another victhry iv th' rulin' classes.' "

Hearts, p. 165;
Mr. Dooley's Chicago, p. 109;
Chicago Evening Post, June 9, 1894 (The Ruling Class)

21. The Pullman Strike

Mr. Dooley vents his disapproval of Mr. Pullman.

Mr. Dooley's Chicago, p. 341;
Chicago Evening Post, July 7, 1894

22. The Freedom Picnic

    (Mr. Dooley says that picnics have replaced dynamiting). "Be hivins, if Ireland cud be freed be a picnic, it'd not on'y be free to-day, but an impire, begorra..." "What's that all got to do with freeing Ireland?" asked Mr. McKenna. "Well, 'tis no worse off thin it was befure, annyhow," said Mr. Dooley.

    Hearts, p. 92;
    Mr. Dooley's Chicago, p. 181;
    Chicago Evening Post, August 18, 1894 (On Irish Picnics)

23. On George M. Pullman

    Mr. Dooley envies Pullman's "dayvilopin' th' whiskers iv a goat without displayin' anny other iv th' good qualities iv th' craythur...." Mr. Pullman refuses to help the needy, and Dooley envies him because he has no feelings for sorrow: "Whin Gawd quarried his heart a happy man was made."

    Mr. Dooley's Chicago, p. 345;
    Chicago Evening Post, August 25, 1894

24. Populism on Archey Road

    The farmer element on Archey Road.

    Mr. Dooley's Chicago, p. 113;
    Chicago Evening Post, September 15, 1894

25. A Christening in Archey Road

    The naming of Hogan's tenth child Augustus instead of Mike brings early ageing on the father.

    Mr. Dooley's Chicago, p. 83;
    What Dooley Says, p. 134;
    Chicago Evening Post, November 11, 1894

26. On Football

Immaculate "Conciption" takes on Father Kelly's church. Grogan sees one of his clan running away from a Mayoman and took a pickaxe to the other team. His antics brought out the paddy wagon and ruined Father Kelly's chance for victory.

Mr. Dooley's Chicago, p. 158;
Chicago Evening Post, December 1, 1894

27. Courtship in Archey Road

"For an impetchoos an' darin' people th' Irish is th' mos' cowardly whin it comes to mathrimony that iver I heerd tell iv." Father Kelly brings Honoriah and Danny together.

Mr. Dooley's Chicago, p. 87;
What Dooley Says, p. 129;
Chicago Evening Post, December 8, 1894

28. The Emigration of Mr. Dooley

Mr. Dooley describes his first working experiences in America.

Mr. Dooley's Chicago, p. 185;
Chicago Evening Post, December 22, 1894

29. Mr. Dooley at the Fair

Mr. Dooley's Chicago, p. 193;
Chicago Evening Post, December 29, 1894

30. The Wanderers

(A "Tipp'rary" man's baby dies during a raging storm at sea before it reaches the land of hope.)

Hutchinson, p. 81;
Filler, Now and Forever, p. 92;

Hearts, p. 139;
What Dooley Says, p. 111 (A Storm on the Atlantic);
Mr. Dooley's Chicago, p. 198;
Chicago Evening Post, Feb. 16, 1895

31. Molly Gives a "Vowdyville"

Molly Donahue creates a salon in her house to keep up with the Hogans. Her husband, Terence, is appalled when the fetching Mademoiselle Turee appears on stage and breaks up the soiree.

What Dooley Says, p. 214;
Mr. Dooley's Chicago, p. 275;
Chicago Evening Post, February 22, 1895

32. The Parlor Saloon

Temperance reform introduces the non-alcoholic saloon featuring "Temp'rance dhrinks." Someone spikes the malted milk and the great experiment ends in a riot.

Mr. Dooley's Chicago, p. 91;
What Dooley Says, p. 115;
Chicago Evening Post, February 23, 1895

33. The Woman's Bible

Women want the Bible rewritten. They protest the bad rap given to Eve and the fact scripture is quoted against them. Mr. McKenna wants to know if the new Bible will bring about the new woman. "Jawn," said Mr. Dooley severely, "This ain't goin' to be an almanac. It's a Bible I've been tellin' ye about."

What Dooley Says, p. 232;
Mr. Dooley's Chicago, p. 282;
Chicago Evening Post, May 18, 1895

34. Irish Invasion of Canada

The Fenians' abortive raid into Canada. Mr. Dooley's Uncle Mike returns soured on modern warfare.

Hearts, p. 158 (A Bit of History);
Mr. Dooley's Chicago, p. 202;
Chicago Evening Post, June 15, 1895

35. Hennessy Umpires a Baseball Game

Hennessy makes the mistake of agreeing to umpire a game. Mr. Dooley concludes, "As Shakespeare says, 'Ol' min f'r th' council, young min f'r th' ward.'"

Mr. Dooley's Chicago, p. 164;
Chicago Evening Post, June 22, 1895

36. The Illinois Central Catechism

Mr. Dooley resents a railroad acting as if it created Lake Michigan.

Mr. Dooley's Chicago, p. 95;
Chicago Evening Post, August 10, 1895

37. Flying the Flag

The Lutherans object to a law making it mandatory for their schools to fly the American flag and Dooley is sympathetic. "Most iv th' great pathriotic orators iv th' da-ay is railroad lawyers." Mr. Dooley concludes with a discussion of the Lutheran vote.

Mr. Dooley's Chicago, p. 348;
Chicago Evening Post, August 17, 1895

38. Meat Packers and Sewer Stealing

Mr. Dooley tries to explain why a rich meat packer would steal water from a community.

Mr. Dooley's Chicago, p. 351;
Chicago Evening Post, September 7, 1895

39. On Yachting

Charges and counter charges in the America's Cup yacht race of 1895, and the O'Brien-Dorsey scow race of 1875.

Mr. Dooley's Chicago, p. 169;
Chicago Evening Post, September 14, 1895

40. Thanksgiving

"Macchew Hagan," a proud Irishman, refuses charity for the entire year that he is out of work. "An' to think iv a man givin' thanks to Hivin f'r bein' allowed to wurruk! "

What Dooley Says, p. 97;
Mr. Dooley's Chicago, p. 206;
Chicago Evening Post, November 30, 1895

41. How a Bill is Passed

Mr. Dooley describes the futility of reformers trying to prevent boodlers from passing legislation to line their pockets.

Mr. Dooley's Chicago, p. 121;
Chicago Evening Post, February 11, 1896

42. Mr. Hennessy on the Demonetization of Silver

Mr. Hennessy lectures Mr. McKenna and Mr. Dooley on the crime of '73.

Mr. Dooley's Chicago, p. 128;
Chicago Evening Post, June 4, 1896

43. Mr. Dooley Discusses the Conventions

Mr. Dooley agrees that the Democrats are down, but suggests to McKenna that the worst thing for a politician or a fighter is to take pity on an opponent.

Mr. Dooley's Chicago, p. 237;
Chicago Evening Post, June 27, 1896

44. On the Game of Golf

Mr. Dooley can tell the score in golf by reading the list of invited guests.

Mr. Dooley's Chicago, p. 172;
Chicago Evening Post, September 12, 1896
Peace and War, p. 249

45. The Bryan Nomination

Mr. Dooley predicts that Bryan won't do well in his ward, and questions the sanity of Bryan supporters.

Mr. Dooley's Chicago, p. 241;
Chicago Evening Post, September 26, 1896

46. On the Pollsters

Mr. Dooley discounts straw votes and statisticians. They consider any deviation from their analysis as the work of anarchists or the results of coercion.

Mr. Dooley's Chicago, p. 246;
Chicago Evening Post, October 3, 1896

47. Political Parades

"It niver requires coercion to get a man to make a monkey iv himsilf in a prisidintial campaign."

Mr. Dooley's Chicago, p. 251;
Chicago Evening Post, October 10, 1896;
Hutchinson, p. 34;
Peace and War, p. 181

48. On Too Much Exposure

Mr. Dooley predicts that Bryan's reputation will fall when Chicagoans see him in the flesh. Voters "vote f'r a statue ... Th' more people sees a candidate f'r

Prisidint, th' less votes he gets." Dooley likes the way Hanna is secreting McKinley.

Mr. Dooley's Chicago, p. 255;
Chicago Evening Post, October 17, 1896

49. Campaigns as Wars

All campaigns are alike the Wednesday after election.

Mr. Dooley's Chicago, p. 259;
Chicago Evening Post, October 31, 1896

50. Football and Thanksgiving

Mr. Dooley describes the first football game, circa 1608. Cotton Mather is portrayed running downfield "breakin' collar bones an' ribs an' th' tin commandmints as he wint."

Mr. Dooley's Chicago, p. 161;
Chicago Evening Post, November 28, 1896

51. Organized Charity

Mr. Dooley questions whether anything more need be asked than whether a person is hungry. He tells the story of Mother Clancy, a strange woman, who dies of starvation while Dougherty is checking on her moral character.

Mr. Dooley's Chicago, p. 209;
Chicago Evening Post, December 5, 1896

52. The Poor

Mr. Dooley admits to 65. "Yis, I know th' wur-ruk iv relief is goin' on, but what th' la-ads need is th' relief iv wurruk.... To think that a man can square himsilf with his conscience be givin' wan thousan' dollars to a polisman an' tellin' him to disthribute it! " Mr. Dooley says it is the poor who help the poor and tells the story of Father Kelly aiding Clancy, the atheist.

What Dooley Says, p. 30;
Mr. Dooley's Chicago, p. 213;
Chicago Evening Post, January 30, 1897

53. Bryan as Reporter

Mr. Dooley criticizes Bryan in his role as journalist. He, too, should write about Cleveland kissing his wife, as all the other real reporters did.

Mr. Dooley's Chicago, p. 263;
Chicago Evening Post, March 4, 1897

54. Mr. Dooley's Platform for Mayor

A sample pledge: "I believe in fair assissmints provided th' rale estate boord an' th' capitalists don't have to pay thim. Th' min that ar-re buildin' up this gr-reat an' growin' city iv ours sh'd not be worrid be havin' to pay taxes."

Mr. Dooley's Chicago, p. 132;
Chicago Evening Post, March 27, 1897

55. The Bridge

A "Polacker" is appointed to man the red bridge, a job traditionally assigned to the Irish. Mr. Dooley laments the passing of Irish political power, and reminisces about the time Clancy opened the bridge to prevent the law from getting at the lads "fr'm the mills;" and of the time his Uncle Mike satisfied his grudge against Doherty by refusing to open the bridge and tied up all traffic on the river.

Mr. Dooley's Chicago, p. 217;
Chicago Evening Post, May 15, 1897

56. Yerkes and Lincoln
Mr. Dooley's Chicago, p. 138;
Chicago Evening Post, June 5, 1897

57. On Old Time Journalism

Mr. Dooley recounts Storey's *Times:* "If they wasn't a hangin' on th' front page some little lad iv a rayporther'd lose his job." Mr. Dooley finds the current papers far too tame. "It wasn't rispictable in thim days to have ye'er name in th' paper . . . Now I see har-rd wurrukin' men thrampin' down to th' newspaper offices with . . ."

Mr. Dooley's Chicago, p. 357;
Chicago Evening Post, June 26, 1897

58. The Unveiling of a Monument to General John A. Logan, July 21, 1897

Mr. Dooley is distressed that Hennessy would go downtown for the likes of Logan. He admired Logan as the type of fighter who, if his enemies and friends were unequal, would add or subtract a few to keep the contest alive. And anyways, things always look better in the papers. Monuments are bigger, crowds are larger.

Mr. Dooley's Chicago, p. 361;
Chicago Evening Post, July 24, 1897

59. Chicago as a Vacationland

Mr. Dooley vividly describes Chicago as an environmentalist's nightmare, but insists that the pure air and healthy food of the country would destroy a Chicagoan.

Mr. Dooley's Chicago, p. 98;
Chicago Evening Post, September 4, 1897

60. The American Revolutionist

Mr. Dooley knows the lads that advocate dynamiting our society. He knows they are harmless and "Thank th' Lord we'er a windy people an' can let out our bad sintimints be wurrud iv mouth."

Mr. Dooley's Chicago, p. 117;
Chicago Evening Post, September 25, 1897

61. Celebrating the Chicago Fire of Oct. 7, 1871

Mr. Dooley says that you might as well celebrate the day that Yerkes came to Chicago. He discusses the panic, the poor, the relief, but refuses to be drawn into the celebration.

Mr. Dooley's Chicago, p. 334;
Chicago Evening Post, October 9, 1897

62. On Municipal Ownership

Mr. Dooley has his doubts about making entrepreneurs out of politicians.

Mr. Dooley's Chicago, p. 142;
Chicago Evening Post, October 16, 1897

63. On the County "Dems"

Mr. Dooley describes a County Democracy Marching Club spectacle. He suggests the best of Chicago would be a match for the best of New York.

Mr. Dooley's Chicago, p. 146;
Chicago Evening Post, October 30, 1897

64. The Education of "Jawnny Powers"

Johnny Powers graduates from the petty thievery of "Law Avnoo" to those "that'd steal th' whole West Side iv Chicago an' thin fix a gr-rand jury to get away with it." When Hennessy suggests something should be done to reform the reformers, Mr. Dooley advocates a Hull

House for "th' banks an' th' boord iv thrade an' th' stock exchange. I'd have ladin' citizens come in an' larn be contact with poor an' honest people th' advantage iv a life they've on'y heard iv."

Mr. Dooley's Chicago, p. 125;
Chicago Evening Post, January 15, 1898

65. On the Copperheads

During the war Mr. Dooley "was at me post iv jooty, dalin' out encouragement at two f'r a quarter. . . ." Mr. Dooley had Copperhead sympathies at first. A copperhead on principle he accepted. "A man that's wrong on principle I can stand." But a man who does things for money alone should get the money first or he chances dying in the attempt.

Mr. Dooley's Chicago, p. 326;
Chicago Journal, March 12, 1898

66. The Donahue Family at War

Donahue feels indemnity against Spain rather than war would be a better solution. He is outvoted by the women in the family.

Mr. Dooley's Chicago, p. 287;
Chicago Journal, March 26, 1898

67. McKinley and Military Genius

Being dressed to kill is more important than being able to kill in McKinley's army.

Best, p. 41;
Hutchinson, p. 9;
Peace and War, p. 25 (On Some Army Appointments);
Boston Globe, May 29, 1898

68. Dooley Tells Hennessey How the Army Went to Cuba
    "We're a gr-reat people," said Mr. Hennessey earnestly.
    "We ar-re," said Mr. Dooley. "We ar-re that. An' th' best iv it is we know we ar-re."
    Best, p. 37;
    Hutchinson, p. 3;
    Peace and War, p. 6 (On War Preparations);
    Boston Globe, June 12, 1898

69. Dooley's Plan of Invasion
    Jackasses at the front; jackasses at the rear.
    Best, p. 38;
    Hutchinson, p. 5;
    Now and Forever, p. 16;
    Peace and War, p. 14 (Of Mules and Others);
    Boston Globe, June 26, 1898

70. Dooley Gives a Friendly Warning to "Prince Hinnery"
    The German propensity for battle.
    Boston Globe, July 17, 1898

71. Dooley Reads Hennessey a Letter from the Front
    Enlisted man Terry Donahue finds that the Cubans have to work the rolling mills just like the Americans.
    Peace and War, p. 58;
    Boston Globe, July 24, 1898

72. Dooley Tells Hennessey About our Cuban Allies
    American work ethic not exportable.
    Best, p. 54;
    Hutchinson, p. 20;
    Peace and War, p. 63;
    Boston Globe, July 31, 1898

73. On Porther Ricky

"Gin'ral Miles gran' picnic an' moonlight excursion. . . . A proud people that can switch as quick as thim la-ads have nawthin' to larn in th' way iv what Hogan calls th' 'signs iv governmint,' even fr'm th' supreme court."

Best, p. 55;
Hutchinson, p. 12;
Peace and War, p. 34 (On General Miles's Moonlight Excursion);
Boston Globe, August 7, 1898

74. Mr. Dooley is an Anglo-Saxon

"Some day, Hogan, justice'll be done me, an' th' likes iv me, an' whin th' story iv a gr-reat battle is written they'll print th' kilt, th' wounded, th' missin' an' the seryously disturbed. An' thim that have bore thimsilves well an' bravely an' paid th' taxes an' faced th' deadly newspa-apers without flinchin' 'll be advanced six pints an' given a chanst to tur-rn jack f'r th' game. . . . An Anglo-Saxon, Hinnissy, is a Garman that's forgot who was his parents."

Hutchinson, p. 18;
Best, p. 127;
Now and Forever, p. 41;
Peace and War, p. 53;
Boston Globe, August 14, 1898

75. Dooley and Dewey

(Admiral Dewey's exploits). " 'Tis a tur-rble thing to be a man iv high sperrits, an' not to know whin th' other fellow's licked."

Peace and War, p. 39 (On Admiral Dewey's Activity);
Boston Globe, August 21, 1898

76. Mr. Dooley and Mr. Alger

". . . what me frind, Gin'ral Sherman meant [was that] war was hell whin 'twas over." Mr. Alger's letter to Chauncey Depew.

Peace and War, p. 73 (On a Letter to Mr. Depew); Boston Globe, August 28, 1898

77. On the Dreyfus Case

"Ye have a r-right to ye'er opinyon, an' ye'll hold it annyhow, whether ye have a r-right to it or not. Like most iv ye'er fellow-citizens, ye start impartial. Ye don't know annything about th' case. . . . 'Let us pro-ceed,' says th' impartial an' fair-minded judge, 'to th' thrile iv th' haynious monsther Cap'n Dhry-fuss,' he says. Up jumps Zola, an' says he in Frinch: 'Jackuse,' he says, which is a hell of a mane thing to say to anny man."

Best, p. 136;
Now and Forever, p. 60;
Hutchinson, p. 52;
Choice of Law, p. 19;
Peace and War, p. 234;
Boston Globe, September 4, 1898

78. On Anarchists

The hard life of a king. " 'Tis no good prayin' again arnychists, Hinnissy. Arnychists is sewer gas."

Peace and War, p. 229;
Boston Globe, September 18, 1898

79. Mr. Dooley and the Horse Doctor

Peace and War, p. 77 (On the President's Cat); Boston Globe, September 25, 1898

80. On the Spanish Wake

    Boston Globe, October 2, 1898

81. On the Indian War

    "But, annyhow, he's doomed, as Hogan says; th' onward march iv th' white civilization with morgedges an' other modhern improvements is slowly but surely, as Hogan says, chasin' him out..."

    Peace and War, p. 245;
    Boston Globe, October 9, 1898

82. On the Hero in Politics

    "Here's th' pitchers iv candydates I pulled down from th' windy, an' jus' knowin' they're here makes me that nervous f'r th' contints iv th' cash dhrawer I'm afraid to tur'rn me back f'r a minyit.... I was sayin', Hinnissy, whin a man gets to be my age he ducks pol-itical meetin's an' r-reads th' pa-apers an' weighs th' iv'dence an' th' argymints, pro-argymints an' con-argymints, an' makes up his mind ca'mly an' votes th' dimmycratic ticket... Ye know Plunkett — a good man if they was no gr-rand juries."

    Peace and War, p. 87;
    Boston Globe, October 16, 1898

83. President Dooley and President Mack

    (President McKinley is in town and he is welcome at Dooley's bar). "I may go to me grave without gettin' an eye on th' wan man beside meself that don't know what th' furrin' (foreign) policy iv th' United States is goin' to be." (McKinley attends a banquet). "Th' proceedin's was opened with a prayer that Providence might r-remain undher th' protection iv th' administration."

    Best, p. 77;

161

Now and Forever, p. 41;
Hutchinson, p. 24;
Peace and War, p. 81 (On a Speech by President McKinley);
Boston Globe, October 23, 1898

84. On the French Character

(On the fickle French, the rapacious English, the vengeful Irish, the subdued African, and Captain Dreyfus). "Whin England purrishes th' Irish 'll die iv what Hogan calls ongwee, which is havin' no wan in th' weary wurruld ye don't love."

Peace and War, p. 255;
Boston Globe, October 30, 1898

85. On the Duties of a Son

Boston Globe, November 6, 1898

86. On the Party out of Power

"No, Hinnissy, th' dimmycratic party is not doomed to victhry."

Boston Globe, November 13, 1898

87. On a Recent Poem by Mr. Rudyard Kipling

Hutchinson, p. 57;
Hearts, p. 13;
Boston Globe, November 20, 1898

88. On the Matter of Territorial Expansion

Philippine expansion.

Boston Globe, December 4, 1898

89. The Philosopher Sees "Cyrano de Bergerac"

Hutchinson, p. 99;

Hearts, p. 228;
Boston Globe, December 11, 1898

90. On the Wisdom of Hanging Aldermen

". . . 'Tis har-rd to hang an aldherman, annyhow. Ye'd
have to suspind most iv thim be th' waist. . . . I believe
in th' polis foorce, though not in polismen. . . . Now,
Hinnissy, that there man niver knowed he was bribed
— th' first time. Th' second time he knew. He ast f'r it.
An' I wudden't hang Dochney. . . . I wudden't if I was
sthrong enough. But some day I'm going to let me temper r-run away with me an' get a comity together an' go
out an' hang ivry dam widdy an' orphan between th'
rollin' mills an' the foundlin's home. If it wasn't f'r thim
raypachious crathers they'd be no boodle annywhere."

Hutchinson, p. 59;
Hearts, p. 23;
Boston Globe, December 18, 1898

91. On the Recent Performances of Lieut. Hobson

" 'Tis th' way th' good Lord has iv makin' us cow'rds
continted with our lot that he niver med a brave man
yet that wasn't half a fool."

Hearts, p. 216;
Boston Globe, December 25, 1898

92. On Gen. Shafter's Hay Fleet

Hutchinson, p. 95;
Hearts, p. 210;
Boston Globe, January 1, 1899

93. On the Fashion of Literary Lion Hunting

". . . 'Th' vileness iv th' press iv America,' he says, 'is
beyond annything I know,' he says. 'Manny and

163

manny's th' time th' privacy iv me r-room has been
invaded be rayporthers, an' th' secrets iv me ar-rt an'
me life wrinched fr'm me, an' thin they didn't print
more thin half iv what I said,' he says.'"

Mr. Dooley's Chicago, p. 102;
Chicago Journal, January 7, 1899;
Boston Globe, January 8, 1899

94. Another Discourse on the Expansion Question

On the Philippines.

Best, p. 63;
Now and Forever, p. 66;
Hearts, p. 3 (Expansion);
Boston Globe, January 29, 1899

95. On the Subject of Trusts

Mr. Dooley's Chicago, p. 367;
Chicago Journal, February 4, 1899;
Boston Globe, February 5, 1899

95A. On a Hero Who Worked Overtime ("Aggynaldo")
The Philippines. The perils of patriotism.

Hearts, p. 8;
Boston Globe, February 12, 1899

96. On the Visit of Lord Charles Beresford

Mr. Dooley muses about the Anglo-American alliance
(or White Man's Burden Thrajeedy Company) and
wonders if the cement will hold.

Now and Forever, p. 72;
Hearts, p. 18;
Boston Globe, February 19, 1899

97. On Admiral Dewey's Attitude Toward a Presidential Nomination

Boston Globe, March 5, 1899

98. On the Decline of National Feeling

("Hinnery Cabin Lodge" and "Joseph Choate" embrace their British brethren). "Hands acrost th' sea an' into some wan's pocket. . . ."

Best, p. 127;
Hutchinson, p. 97;
Hearts, p. 222;
Boston Globe, March 12, 1899

99. On the Profits of Patriotism in Cuba

Boston Globe, March 19, 1899

100. On a Recent Visit to Jekyl Island

McKinley, Hanna and Reed on vacation.

Hearts, p. 119;
Boston Globe, March 26, 1899

101. On the "Union of Two Great Fortunes."

Mr. Dooley is cynical about the "bonds iv mathrimony."

Now and Forever, p. 97;
Hutchinson, p. 101;
Hearts, p. 234;
Boston Globe, April 9, 1899

102. Mr. Dooley at Close Quarters with the Dreyfus Case

The trial.

Harpers Weekly, September 23, 1899;
Hearts, p. 240;
Boston Globe, September 17, 1899

103. On the Mysteries of the Dreyfus Case

More on the trial.

Hearts, p. 249;
Harpers Weekly, September 30, 1899;
Boston Globe, September 24, 1899

104. On the Siege of Jules Guerin

Anti-semitism in France.

Harpers Weekly, October 7, 1899;
Hearts, p. 259;
Boston Globe, October 1, 1899

105. Hinnissy's Friend at Close Quarters with the Dreyfus Case

On the forgeries at the trial.

Harpers Weekly, October 14, 1899 (Bertillon & Co.);
Hearts, p. 268;
Boston Globe, October 8, 1899

106. Mr. Dooley's Advice to the Court

(Mr. Dooley takes the stand in the Dreyfus case). ". . . I come fr'm a land where injustice is unknown, where iv'ry man is akel (equal) befure th' law, but some are better thin others behind it . . . ."

Harpers Weekly, October 21, 1899;
Hearts, p. 276;
Boston Globe, October 15, 1899

107. On Anglo-American Sports (Olympics)

The "common Hurtage" of the English and Americans.

Harpers Weekly, October 28, 1899;
Philosophy, p. 201;
Boston Globe, October 22, 1899

108. On the Transvaal

(The British and the Boers. Mr. Dooley's solution): "I'd give thim th' votes," said Mr. Dooley. "But," he added, significantly, "I'd do th' countin'."

Now and Forever, p. 111;
Philosophy, p. 35;
Harpers Weekly, November 4, 1899;
Boston Globe, October 29, 1899

109. On War and War Makers

"I'll niver go down again to see sojers go off to th' war. But ye'll see me at th' depot with a brass band whin th' men that causes war starts f'r th' scene iv carnage." (The conflicts in the Philippines and South Africa).

Best, p. 67;
Harpers Weekly, November 11, 1899;
Philosophy, p. 43;
Boston Globe, November 5, 1899

110. On Polygamy

(The hue and cry that followed a Mormon running for Congress). "A Mormon, Hinnissy, is a man that has th' bad taste an' th' rellijion to do what a good manny other men ar-re restrained fr'm doin' be conscientious scruples an' th' polis."

Philosophy, p. 109;
Harpers Weekly, November 18, 1899;
Boston Globe, November 12, 1899

111. Mr. Dooley Reviews a Book

(Mr. Dooley suggests that Theodore Roosevelt's book on his role in the Spanish-American War be called): "Alone in Cubia." (Also, paraphrasing T.R.): " 'On th' thransport goin' to Cubia,' he says, 'I wud stand beside

wan iv these r-rough men threatin' him as an akel,
which he was in ivirything but birth, education, rank
an' courage, . . .' " (Also): "No man that bears a gredge
again' himsilf 'll iver be governor iv a state."

Mr. Dooley Remembers, p. 272 (not in dialect);
Best, p. 99;
Hutchinson, p. 104;
Now and Forever, p. 104;
Philosophy, p. 13;
Boston Globe, November 19, 1899;
Harpers Weekly, November 25, 1899

112. On Public Fickleness

The effervescence of war news.

Hutchinson, p. 130;
Philosophy, p. 115;
Harpers Weekly, December 2, 1899;
Boston Globe, November 26, 1899

113. Mr. Dooley Visits the Donahues

Mr. Dooley is described in detail. He strolls to the
Donahues and is greeted respectfully by all the
shopkeepers and citizens of Bridgeport. They discourse
on that middleclass status symbol — the piano.

Mr. Dooley's Chicago, p. 290;
Ladies' Home Journal, December 1899, Jan. 1900

114. On the Gratitude of the Public

A fickle public turns on Admiral Dewey.

Philosophy, p. 135;
Harpers Weekly, December 9, 1899;
Boston Globe, December 3, 1899

115. On the President's Message

Boiler plate for a President's speech writer. McKinley tells his cabinet how to compose a Message.

Philosophy, p. 103 (1900 ed.);
Harpers Weekly, December 23, 1899;
Boston Globe, December 17, 1899

116. On Underestimating your Enemy

(The war in South Africa). "I tell ye, Hinnissy, ye can't beat a man that fights f'r his home an' counthry in a stovepipe hat."

Hutchinson, p. 113;
Philosophy, p. 49;
Harpers Weekly, December 30, 1899;
Boston Globe, December 24, 1899

117. Preface

"Politics," he says, "ain't bean bag."

Best, p. 6;
Hutchinson, p. 1;
Peace and War, p. xiii

118. On Diplomacy

Diplomacy is like a shell game and only professionals need apply.

Peace and War, p. 1

119. On Fitz-Hugh Lee

Portrait of a general. "They ain't such a lot iv dirr'rence between th' bravest man in the wurruld an' th' cow'rdliest."

Peace and War, p. 10

120. On His Cousin George

Admiral Dewey's Philippine activities.

Best, p. 42;
Hutchinson, p. 7;
Now and Forever, p. 22;
Peace and War, p. 20

121. On Strategy

Admiral Dewey ("Cousin George" to Mr. Dooley) has no
time for the effete Strategy Board in Washington.

Best, p. 46;
Hutchinson, p. 11;
Peace and War, p. 30

122. [This number reserved.]

123. On the Philippines

How the press confuses the public about the
Philippines. "We import juke, hemp, cigar wrappers,
sugar, an' fairy tales fr'm th' Ph'lippeens, an' export
six-inch shells an' th' like."

Best, p. 59;
Hutchinson, p. 14;
Now and Forever, p. 31;
Peace and War, p. 46

124. On Prayers for Victory

Mr. Dooley facetiously compares the prayers of both
sides in the battle over the Philippines with the tools of
war. "'Hogan,' [says Father Kelly], 'I'll go into th'
battle with a prayer book in wan hand an' a soord in th'

other,' he says; 'an,' if th' wurruk calls f'r two hands, 'tis not th' soord I'll dhrop,' he says. 'Don't ye believe in prayer?' says Hogan. 'I do,' says th' good man; 'but,' he says, 'a healthy person ought,' he says, 'to be ashamed,' he says, 'to ask f'r help in a fight,' he says."

Best, p. 45;
Hutchinson, p. 16;
Now and Forever, p. 35;
Peace and War, p. 48

125. On the Destruction of Cervera's Fleet

Best, p. 49;
Hutchinson, p. 22;
Peace and War, p. 68

126. On New Year's Resolutions

Mr. Dooley decides that he cannot love his enemies; ". . . life'd not be worth livin' if we didn't keep our inimies."

Best, p. 7;
Hutchinson, p. 26;
Peace and War, p. 95

127. On Gold Seeking

"Me experyence with goold minin' is it's always in th' nex' county." Mr. Dooley tells Hennessy what a mean old curmudgeon he would become if he ever struck gold. "I don't want ye iver to speak to me whin ye get rich, Hinnissy." "I won't," said Mr. Hennessy.

Best, p. 27;
Hutchinson, p. 28;
Peace and War, p. 100

128. On Books

Mr. Dooley says that newspapers will never hurt an
uneducated man. He is not sure but that book learning
is a poor substitute for life. He says to Father Kelly, "If
ye want to show thim what life is, tell thim to look
around thim. There's more life on a Saturdah night in
th' Ar-rchy Road thin in all th' books fr'm Shakespeare
to th' rayport iv th' drainage thrustees.... Father
Kelly says, 'Books is f'r thim that can't injye thimsilves
in anny other way,' he says. 'If ye're in good health an'
ar-re atin' three squares a day, an' not ayether sad or
very much in love with ye'er lot, but just lookin' on an'
not carin' a' — he said rush — 'not carin' a rush, ye don't
need books,' he says.... 'Well,' says I, 'whin I was
growin' up, half th' congregation heard mass with their
prayer books tur-rned upside down, an' they were as
pious as anny. Th' Apostles' Creed niver was as
con-vincin' to me afther I larned to r-read it as it was
whin I cudden't read it, but believed it!..."

Best, p. 187;
Hutchinson, p. 30;
Peace and War, p. 105

129. On Reform Candidates

How reform candidates fare against professionals. The
reform candidate was "out f'r th' good iv th' community.
Flannigan was out f'r Flannigan an' th' stuff."

Peace and War, p. 111

130. On Paternal Duty

Mr. Dooley illustrates the perils of doting on children
by recounting the story of "Dan'l O'Connell Ahearn."

Peace and War, p. 118

131. On Criminals

"Who'll tell what makes wan man a thief an' another man a saint?" The heart-rending tale of a psychopath.

Hutchinson, p. 32;
What Dooley Says, p. 189 (Petey Scanlon);
Choice of Law, p. 12;
Peace and War, p. 124

132. On a Plot

The plot to blow up Queen Victoria and the Czar. Mr. Dooley follows the conspirator Tynan.

Peace and War, p. 130

133. On the New Woman

Mr. Donahue threatens to become the "new man" and mother and daughter realize the error of their militant ways.

Hutchinson, p. 34;
Peace and War, p. 136

134. On Expert Testimony

The Lootgert case. "Thank th' Lord, whin th' case is all over, th' jury'll pitch th' tistimony out iv th' window, an' consider three questions: 'Did Lootgert look as though he'd kill his wife? Did his wife look as though she ought to be kilt? Isn't it time we wint to supper?' "

Choice of Law, p. 16;
Peace and War, p. 141

135. On the Popularity of Firemen

"Did anny wan iver see a fireman with his coat on or a polisman with his off?" Clancy's last fire.

Best, p. 272;

Hutchinson, p. 36;
Peace and War, p. 146

136. On the Game of Football

"Th' Christyan Brothers" and "Saint Aloysius" have a less than brotherly love go at one another.

Hutchinson, p. 38;
Peace and War, p. 152

137. On the Necessity of Modesty Among the Rich

The story of Willum Edmond Fitzgeral Dorsey, Justice iv th' peace, mimber iv Parlymint, an' landlord. When the famine came, Dorsey foreclosed on his tenants on the one hand, and partied every night on the other. He was murdered by a hungry peasant, "an' a jury iv shopkeepers hanged Shaughnessy so fast it med even th' judge smile."

Peace and War, p. 158

138. On the Power of Love

"It's th' business iv men to fight, an' th' business iv their wives fr to make thim fight. . . . 'Afther all,' Father Kelly says, 'an' undher all, we're mere brutes; an' it on'y takes two lads more brutal than th' rest fr to expose th' sthreak in th' best iv us. Foorce rules th' wurruld, an' th' churches is empty whin th' blood begins to flow,' he says." The Corbett-Fitzsimmons fight.

Mr. Dooley Remembers, p. 285 (non dialect);
Best, p. 163;
Hutchinson, p. 41;
Peace and War, p. 165

139. On the Victorian Era

The Jubilee of Queen Victoria. Mr. Dooley, the same

174

age as the Queen, recounts all that has happened since he came to the States. "... I've seen th' shackles dropped fr'm th' slave, so's he cud be lynched in Ohio. ... An' th' invintions, ... th' cottn-gin an' th' gin sour ... th' nickel-in-th'-slot machine an' th' Croker machine an' th' sody fountain an' — crownin' wur-ruk iv our civilization — th' cash raygisther...." Mr. Hennessy asks, "What have ye had to do with all these things?" "Well," said Mr. Dooley, "I had as much to do with thim as th' queen."

Hutchinson, p. 42;
Now and Forever, p. 54;
Peace and War, p. 170

140. On the Currency Question

"Whiskey is th' standard iv value. It niver fluctuates; an' that's funny, too, seein' that so much iv it goes down."

Peace and War, p. 175

141. [This number reserved.]

142. On Charity

Mr. Dooley's cynicism toward charity is cut short when it is revealed that his heart is softer than his words. "I knowed a society wanst to vote a monyment to a man an' refuse to help his fam'ly, all in wan night."

Peace and War, p. 187

143. On Nansen

Thoughts on Nansen, the North Pole, the walrus, and the reason for arctic explorations.

Peace and War, p. 192

144. On a Populist Convention

The Populist Party.

Peace and War, p. 197

145. On a Family Reunion

Ill-advised, says Mr. Dooley, as he recounts one of his own.

Best, p. 19;
Hutchinson, p. 46;
Peace and War, p. 202

146. On a Famous Wedding

The infamous wedding of "The Jook iv Marlburrow" and the "Ganderbilks" daughter. The price of marrying into poor royalty.

Peace and War, p. 208

147. On a Quarrel Between England and Germany

Mr. Dooley reduces the prospect of the Irish and Germans getting together to free the Irish from the English to local conditions.

Peace and War, p. 213

148. On Oratory in Politics

Smith O'Brien Dorgan pits his oratorical skill against Bill O'Brien. Bill "niver med wan speech. No wan knew whether he was f'r a tariff or again wan, . . . he wint to th' picnics, . . . 'Well,' says Dorgan, 'I can't undherstand it,' he says. 'I med as manny as three thousan' speeches.' he says. 'Well,' says Willum J. O'Brien, 'that was my majority,' he says."
Best, p. 122;

Hutchinson, p. 49;
Peace and War, p. 218

149. On Christmas Gifts

All Mr. Dooley wants for Christmas is the auditorium. "I've wanted that to play with f'r manny years."

Peace and War, p. 223

150. On the Decadence of Greece

Mr. Dooley explains why the Greeks are not the valiant warriors of old by analogizing it to the tenth precinct. " 'Tis histhry," says Mr. Dooley.

Peace and War, p. 239

151. [This number reserved.]

152. The Grip

Microbes ("Mickrobes" to Mr. Dooley) have laid Mr. Dooley low.

Hutchinson, p. 62;
What Dooley Says, p. 101;
Hearts, p. 30

153. Lexow

(Mr. Dooley says the best citizens make up the reform committees.) "Th' best citizens is thim that th' statue iv limitations was made f'r. . . . Jawn," said Mr. Dooley. "Yes," responded Mr. McKenna. "Niver steal a dure-mat," said Mr. Dooley. "If ye do, ye'll be invistigated, hanged, an' maybe rayformed. Steal a bank, me boy, steal a bank."

Now and Forever, p. 78;
What Dooley Says, p. 194 (Reformers);
Hearts, p. 35

154. Their Excellencies, the Police

A cameo on the police ordering a curfew.

Hearts, p. 41

155. Shaughnessy

A vignette of one of life's heroes: a man who has outlived his wife, buried all his children, but his daughter, who has married and left the hearth.

Mr. Dooley Remembers, p. 276 (non dialect);
Best, p. 13;
Hutchinson, p. 63;
What Dooley Says, p. 36;
Hearts, p. 45

156. Times Past

Old time elections of stuffing ballots, riots, and politicians, like Duggan, who forget who elected them.

Best, p. 111;
Hutchinson, p. 65;
Hearts, p. 50

157. The Skirts of Chance

"Jawn McKenna" fails to beat Mr. Dooley's slot machine.

Hutchinson, p. 67;
What Dooley Says, p. 79 (The Nickel-in-the slot machine);
Hearts, p. 56

158. A Brand from the Burning

(Flanagan's rise from brawler to ward boss and real estate man). "D'ye mind, Jawn, that th' r-rale estate

178

business includes near ivrything fr'm vagrancy to manslaughter?"

Hutchinson, p. 71;
Hearts, p. 60

159. When the Trust is at Work

The high cost of living for the poor. ". . . an' ivry cint a pound manes a new art musoom or a new church, to take th' edge off hunger."

Hutchinson, p. 69;
Hearts, p. 61

160. A Winter Night

Mr. Dooley gives a wooden coin to a hobo who frequents a rival bar.

Best, p. 10;
Hutchinson, p. 74;
Hearts, p. 72

161. The Blue and the Gray

Mr. Dooley believes that real soldiers do not march in parades or make a show of themselves at cemeteries or demean their former enemies.

Hutchinson, p. 75;
Now and Forever, p. 85;
What Dooley Says, p. 64 (Decoration Day);
Hearts, p. 76

162. The Tragedy of the Agitator

Dorgan's son joins the army and returns home to quell his father's strike activities.

Hearts, p. 82

163. Boyne Water and Bad Blood

Should the Orange be permitted to have a parade on
July 12? Mr. Dooley tells about one such event.

Hearts, p. 85

164. The Idle Apprentice

The story of Carey, the thief, and Clancy, the cop. They
destroy one another morally and physically.

Best, p. 289;
Hutchinson, p. 77;
Hearts, p. 96

165. The O'Briens Forever

The Democratic Convention is attended by Dooley and
Hennessy. Hennessy mistakes a local O'Brien for
William Jennings Bryan.

Hearts, p. 101

166. A Candidate's Pillory

(Inane interviewing of presidential candidates). "Ivry
day a rayporther comes to th' house with a list iv
questions. 'What are ye'er views on th' issue iv eatin'
custard pie with a sponge?' . . . Thin, if he don't answer,
ivry wan says he's a thrimmer . . . ."

Hearts, p. 107

167. The Day After the Victory

Everybody is convinced he supported the winning
candidate.

Hearts, p. 113

168. Slavin Contra Wagner

On listening to a friend's child play the piano, Mr. Dooley feels like taking it up.

Hutchinson, p. 79;
What Dooley Says, (Miss Molly's Piano);
Hearts, p. 125

169. Grand Opera

It's politics as usual as Dooley, Cassidy, O'Regan, et al do not let Rigoletto interfere with their first love.

What Dooley Says, p. 149 (At the Opera);
Hearts, p. 130

170. The Church Fair

Flaherty makes sure only the church can be a winner.

What Dooley Says, p. 179;
Hearts, p. 135

171. Making a Cabinet

"If 'twas wan iv th' customs iv th' great raypublic iv ours, Jawn, f'r to appoint th' most competent men f'r th' places, he'd have a mighty small lot f'r to pick fr'm. But, seein' that on'y thim is iligible that are unfit, he has th' devvle's own time selectin'."

Hutchinson, p. 83;
Choice of Law, p. 151;
Hearts, p. 143

172. Old Age

Hennessy foolishly tries ice skating at his advanced age. "'Martin,' says he, 'I've been a sinful man in me time; but I niver had th' like iv that f'r a pinance,' he says."

What Dooley Says, p. 9 (Skating);
Hearts, p. 149

173. The Divided Skirt

Molly Donahue shocks the community by wearing pants and riding a bicycle.

Hutchinson, p. 85;
What Dooley Says, p. 204;
Hearts, p. 154

174. The Optimist

Tim Clancy is not bothered by the heat.

Hutchinson, p. 86;
Hearts, p. 170

175. Prosperity

(Mr. Dooley analyzes the portents of prosperity). "Th' newspapers is run be a lot iv gazabos that thinks wurruk is th' ambition iv mankind. Most iv th' People I know 'd be happiest layin' on a lounge with a can near by, or stretchin' thimsilves f'r another nap at eight in th' mornin'."

Hutchinson, p. 88;
Hearts, p. 175

176. The Great Hot Spell

Mr. Dooley spins a yarn about the time the heat melted the street car tracks to while away a hot spell.

What Dooley Says, p. 47;
Hearts, p. 180

177. Keeping Lent

(Mr. Dooley's father's losing battle to abstain from smoking during Lent. Mr. Dooley succumbs to a hot toddy without a battle. Father Kelly recognizes that): "Starvation don't always mean salvation."

Hutchinson, p. 90;

What Dooley Says, p. 14;
Hearts, p. 185

178. The Quick and the Dead

Mr. Dooley says that if he had the funeral he deserved he would have too much pride to come back as a ghost. Did O'Grady's ghost disappear because of a bottle of holy water or because any bottle would do?

Hutchinson, p. 92;
What Dooley Says, p. 138 (Ghosts);
Hearts, p. 190

179. The Soft Spot

(A tragedy in St. Louis has Mr. Dooley talking about Peter O'Brien, the cruel landlord whose one good deed may have saved his soul). "... beneath ivry man's outside coat there lies some good feelin'. We ain't as bad as we make ourselves out."

What Dooley Says, p. 163 (Peter O'Broyn);
Hearts, p. 196

180. The Irishman Abroad

Mr. Dooley ticks off the Irish who have done great things abroad and speculates on the glory of Ireland if they had stayed home.

Hearts, p. 202

181. The Serenade

(On women): "It is thim that divides our sorrows an' doubles our joys,..." (Felix Pendergast's abortive attempt to woo Molly Donahue with his cornet).

What Dooley Says, p. 224 (Felix's Lost Chord);
Hearts, p. 206

182. Education

Mr. Dooley discourses on charity. "The money most
people pay in charity is no more thin six per cent on
what they steal, anyhow." "I regard it as th' hite of
civility when a man asks me f'r money instead of takin'
it away fr'm me." Sobieski is killed stealing coal
because he could not understand English and did not
understand a railroad cop who yelled, "Halt."

Now and Forever, p. 4;
What Dooley Says, p. 24

183. After St. Patrick's Day

Mr. Dooley has nostalgia for the old parades.

What Dooley Says, p. 40

184. A Primary Election

Republican primaries are not acceptable on Archey
Road. "Sure, Politics ain't bean bags. 'Tis a man's game,
an' women, childher, cripples an' prohybitionists'd do
well to keep out iv it."

What Dooley Says, p. 44

185. Suicide

Story of two Germans. Young one squanders old one's
money, and latter commits suicide by drowning. Young
one "dhrowns" his grief at a bar.

What Dooley Says, p. 54

186. A Good Man

Inaugurating an alderman. Mr. Dooley sketches his
career. How he put down the ward boss who divided the
loot unevenly.

What Dooley Says, p. 59

187. Law and Lawyers

Mr. Dooley is sued by Maddigan, loses the suit (actually a vest), and wants to do away with all lawyers.

Choice of Law, p. 27;
What Dooley Says, p. 69

188. In Society

A County Democrats' Ball reminds Dooley of his frivolous days.

What Dooley Says, p. 74

189. On Love

Malachi Dorgan's daughter marries Cornelius Coogan.

What Dooley Says, p. 84

190. Cassidy on a Bicycle

Mr. Cassidy runs into a lamp post.

What Dooley Says, p. 89

191. The Monroe Doctrine

The Monroe Doctrine is invoked against any incursion on the soil of Venezuela.

Now and Forever, p. 11;
What Dooley Says, p. 93

192. Trilby

Mr. Dooley reviews the evil eye.

What Dooley Says, p. 106

193. Of the Blood Royal

Tracing genealogy leads more to bad blood than royal blood in Dooley's ward.

What Dooley Says, p. 120

194. On Hennessy's Wedding

Hennessy's marriage to Odalia Ann O'Leary.

What Dooley Says, p. 125

195. Christmas

A bachelor at Xmas time.

What Dooley Says, p. 144

196. Reform

"Willum J. O'Broyn" is nominated at a reform meeting that ends in a riot.

What Dooley Says, p. 153

197. Jury Service

What goes on in the jury room.

Choice of Law, p. 30;
What Dooley Says, p. 158

198. Commencement Exercises

Hennessy's son graduates and Mr. Dooley describes the program of student efforts.

What Dooley Says, p. 169

199. Fishing

Mr. Dooley hooks Hennessy's ear. He also tells about the one that got away. Clancy tells Dooley that under the game laws he had a right to Hennessy's ear.

What Dooley Says, p. 174

200. France

History a la Dooley.

What Dooley Says, p. 184

APPENDIX

201. At a Raffle

A diamond raffle ends in a scuffle with the diamond falling on a stove top and melting.

What Dooley Says, p. 200

202. Amateurs Theatricals

Parents think their children should be heroes in plays.

What Dooley Says, p. 208

203. Mary Tries to Vote

Mary Donahue tries to register to vote.

What Dooley Says, p. 220

204. Hinnery Irving

Mr. Dooley reviews the Merchant of Venice with Irving playing Shylock.

What Dooley Says, p. 222

205. Mr. Dooley's Farewell to the Chicago River

A paean for the river.

Mr. Dooley's Chicago, p. 372;
Chicago Journal, January 13, 1900

206. On Young Oratory

(Mr. Dooley analyzes Senator Beveridge's florid speech on the Philippines). "T'was a speech ye cud waltz to . . . Th' man that sinds seeds to his constitooents lasts longer than th' wan that sinds thim flowers iv iloquence, . . ."

Philosophy, p. 129;
Boston Globe, January 21, 1900

207. On the American Abroad

Mr. Dooley faults William Waldorf Astor for being ashamed of the country of his birth. He discusses original sin and makes an allegory of what life is in America.

Hutchinson, p. 106;
Philosophy, p. 19;
Boston Globe, January 28, 1900

208. Women in Politics — Voting Qualifications

The role of politics in Archey Road. The newspaper and trolley car have turned what was once a man's game to a woman's concern. The Donahues discuss the matter. Molly Donahue and the suffragettes show up to vote. Mr. Donahue challenges their vote on the grounds of insanity. The female Donahues' votes are thrown out: Molly was too young, Mrs. Donahue too messy.

Mr. Dooley's Chicago, p. 299;
Ladies' Home Journal, February 1900

209. On the Customs of Kentucky

A gun fight in Kentucky.

Philosophy, p. 181;
Boston Globe, February 4, 1900

210. On the Servant Girl Problem

(The perennial servant problem). " 'No,' says I, 'they'se no naytionality now livin' in this counthry that're nathral bor-rn servants,' I says."

Best, p. 246;
Hutchinson, p. 110;
Philosophy, p. 27;
Boston Globe, February 11, 1900

211. On the Politics of Kentucky

(On using the courts to resolve an election). "Th'
dimmycrats ar-re right an' th' raypublicans has th'
jobs".... " 'I want a law,' he says, 'that mesilf an' all
other good citizens can rayspict,'.... Whiniver a
dimmycrat has to go to coort to win an iliction I get
suspicious...."

Philosophy, p. 121;
Boston Globe, February 18, 1900

212. On the War Expert

(More on South Africa). "A war expert," said Mr.
Dooley, "is a man ye niver heerd iv befure." ... "Th'
pa-apers says th' rapid-fire gun'll make war in th'
future impossible. I don't think that, but I know th'
expert will."

Philosophy, p. 55;
Boston Globe, February 25, 1900

213. The Archey Road Literary Club

Molly Donahue's taste in literature. Mr. Dooley says,
"A poet's a man with somethin' to say that he hasn't
thought out.... Ivery man that r-reads must r-read his
peck iv pothry."

Mr. Dooley's Chicago, p. 309;
Ladies' Home Journal, March 1900

214. On Modern Explosives in Warfare

(Mr. Dooley discounts the advances in weaponry). "I
can see in me mind th' day whin explosives'll be so
explosive, an' guns'll shoot so far, that on'y th' folks
that stays at home'll be kilt, an' life insurance agents'll
be advisin' people to go into th' ar-rmy." (The British
use of lyddite in South Africa).

Now and Forever, p. 119;

Harpers Weekly, March 31, 1900;
Hutchinson, p. 115;
Philosophy, p. 63;
Boston Globe, March 25, 1900

215. On Admiral Dewey's Candidacy

(The perils of being a candidate for President). "He'll find that a man can be r-right an' be prisidint, but he can't be both at th' same time. . . . An' he'll spind th' r-rest iv his life thryin' to live down th' time he was a candydate. . . ."

"It's no sin to be a candydate f'r prisidint."

"No," said Mr. Dooley. "Tis sometimes a misfortune an' sometimes a joke. . . ."

Hutchinson, p. 137;
Philosophy, p. 175;
Boston Globe, April 15, 1900

216. On Mr. Sheldon's Newspaper

(The pitfalls of running a Christian newspaper in Topeka). "Father Kelly was talkin' it over with me, an' says he, 'They ain't anny news in bein' good.'"

Hutchinson, p. 135;
Philosophy, p. 169 (Christian Journalism);
Boston Globe, April 22, 1900

217. On the Paris Exposition

"These here expositions is a gran' thing f'r th' progress iv th' wurruld."

"Ye r-read that in th' pa-apers," said Mr. Dooley, "an' it isn't so. Put it down fr'm me, Hinnissy, that all expositions is a blind f'r th' hootchy-kootchy dance."

Philosophy, p. 161;
Boston Globe, April 29, 1900

218. On the Methods of High Finance

(The machinations of the market). "What's th' la-ad been doin', Hinnissy? He's been lettin' his frinds in on th' groun' flure — an' dhroppin' thim into th' cellar." Mr. Dooley's definition of "hawt finance": " 'Well,' says I, 'it ain't burglary, an' it ain't obtainin' money be false pretinses, an' it ain't manslaughter,' I says. 'It's what ye might call a judicious seliction fr'm th' best features iv thim ar-rts.' "

Choice of Law, p. 95;
Philosophy, p. 155;
Boston Globe, May 6, 1900

219. On Marriage and Politics

"Th' reason th' New York jood thinks marrid men oughtn't to be in pollytics is because he thinks pollytics is spoort. An' so it is. But it ain't amachoor spoort, Hinnissy.... Ye niver see an amachoor at annything that was as good as a profissional.... Aristocracy, Hinnissy, is like rale estate, a matther iv location.... Ye talk about ye'er colleges, Hinnissy, but pollytics is th' poor man's college. A la-ad without enough book larnin' to r-read a meal ticket, if ye give him tin years iv polly-tical life has th' air iv a statesman an' th' manner iv a jook, an' cud take anny job fr'm dalin' faro bank to r-runnin' th' threasury iv th' United States. His business brings him up again' th' best men iv th' com-munity, an' their customs an' ways iv speakin' an' thinkin' an' robbin' sticks to him."

Philosophy, p. 141;
Harpers Weekly, May 26, 1900;
Boston Globe, May 20, 1900

220. On the Boer Mission

(The Boers seek support in the United States). "Th' amount iv sympathy that goes out f'r a sthrugglin' people is reg'lated, Hinnissy, be th' amount iv sthrugglin' th' people can do. . . . Th' enthusyasm iv this counthry, Hinnissy, always makes me think iv a bonfire on an ice floe. It burns bright so long as ye feed it, an' it looks good, but it don't take hold, somehow, on th' ice."

Now and Forever, p. 126;
Philosophy, p. 69;
Harpers Weekly, June 9, 1900;
Hutchinson, p. 118;
Boston Globe, June 3, 1900

221. On Platform Making

". . . whichiver won at th' iliction should commind an' congratulate an' thim that lost shud denounce an' deplore. . . . Whin he can denounce an' deplore no longer he views with alarm an' declares with indignation."

Best, p. 81;
Hutchinson, p. 128;
Philosophy, p. 97;
Harpers Weekly, July 14, 1900;
Boston Globe, July 8, 1900

222. On the Chinese Situation

(Mr. Dooley is sympathetic to the Chinese rejection of western civilization). "Annyhow, 'tis a good thing f'r us they ain't Christyans an' haven't larned properly to sight a gun."

Hutchinson, p. 120;

Now and Forever, p. 134;
Philosophy, p. 77;
Harpers Weekly, July 21, 1900;
Boston Globe, July 15, 1900

223. On a Society Scandal

William Waldorf Astor offends English proprieties by turning away a guest at his London home.

Philosophy, p. 189;
Harpers Weekly, July 28, 1900;
Boston Globe, July 22, 1900

224. Mr. Dooley's Compliments to Mr. Wu

Lying and diplomacy — east and west.

Hutchinson, p. 123;
Philosophy, p. 83;
Harpers Weekly, August 4, 1900;
Boston Globe, July 29, 1900

225. On the Doings of Anarchists

"If they was no newspapers they'd be few arnychists."

Philosophy, p. 195;
Harpers Weekly, August 11, 1900;
Boston Globe, August 5, 1900

226. On the Future in China

The German role in "civilizing" the Chinese.

Hutchinson, p. 126;
Philosophy, p. 91;
Harpers Weekly, August 18, 1900;
Boston Globe, August 12, 1900

227. On Voices from the Tomb

"Be hivins, Hinnissy, I want me advice up to date an'

whin Mack an' Willum Jennings tell me what George
Wash'nton an' Thomas Jefferson said, I says to thim,
'Gintlemen, they larned their thrade befure th' days iv
open plumbin,' I says. 'Tell us what is wanted ye'ersilf
or call in a journeyman who's wurrukin' card is dated
this cinchry,' I says."

Now and Forever, p. 141;
Philosophy, p. 209;
Harpers Weekly, August 25, 1900;
Boston Globe, August 19, 1900

228. On a Bachelor's Life

"A marrid man gets th' money, Hinnissy, but a
bachelor gets th' sleep."

Best, p. 12;
Hutchinson, p. 146;
Philosophy, p. 235;
Boston Globe, September 2, 1900

229. On the Troubles of a Candidate

(The Bryan-McKinley campaign heats up. Campaign
tricks. The role of photography): "An' did ye iver notice
how much th' candydates looks alike, an' how much
both iv thim looks like Lydia Pinkham? Thim
wondherful boardin'-house smiles that our gifted
leaders wear . . . Glory be, what a relief 'twill be fr wan
iv thim to raysume permanently th' savage or fam'ly
breakfast face th' mornin' afther iliction! What a relief
to snarl at wife an' frinds wanst more. . . 'Tis th' day
afther iliction I'd like fr to be a candydate, Hinnissy, no
matther how it wint."

Hutchinson, p. 143;

Now and Forever, p. 150;
Philosophy, p. 229;
Harpers Weekly, September 15, 1900;
Boston Globe, September 9, 1900

230. On the American Stage

"In th' plays nowadays th' hero is more iv a villain thin th' villain himsilf.... 'Tis called real life an' mebbe that's what it is, but f'r me I don't want to see real life on the stage. I can see that anny day. What I want is f'r th' spotless gintelman to saw th' la-ad with th' cigareet into two-be-fours an' marry th' lady that doesn't dhrink much while th' aujeence is puttin' on their coats."

Philosophy, p. 223;
Harpers Weekly, September 28, 1900;
Boston Globe, September 23, 1900

231. On Col. Roosevelt's Western Tour

"'Tis Tiddy alone that's runnin' an' he ain't r-runnin', he's gallopin'.... At this moment Gov'nor Rosenfelt bit his way through th' throng..."

Harpers Weekly, October 13, 1900;
Boston Globe, October 7, 1900

232. On the Education of the Young

"Nowadays they talk about th' edycation iv th' child befure they choose th' name. 'Tis: 'Th' kid talks in his sleep. 'Tis th' fine lawyer he'll make....'" Mr. Dooley disdains permissive education. "But I believe 'tis as Father Kelly says: 'Childner shudden't be sint to school to larn, but to larn how to larn. I don't care what ye larn thim, so long as 'tis onpleasant to thim.' 'Tis thrainin' they need, Hinnissy."

Best, p. 215;

Hutchinson, p. 149;
Philosophy, p. 243;
Harpers Weekly, October 20, 1900;
Boston Globe, October 14, 1900

233. On the Progress of the Campaign

(The confusion of campaign issues). "An' so it goes.
Croker an' Carl Schoortz, Altgeld an' Olney, Rosenfelt
an' Quay, Carlisle an' Stewart. What's a plain, foolish
an' thoughtless man like mesilf to do? Sure they ought
to have wan place f'r a citizen to vote f'r his principles
an' another to vote f'r his candydate."

Harpers Weekly, October 27, 1900;
Boston Globe, October 21, 1900

234. On Fame

(On the impending election): "An' what th' divvle
diff'rence does it make, me boy? Th' mornin' afther
eliction, 'tis Hinnissy to th' slag pile an' Dooley to th'
beer pump an' Jawn D. Rockefellar to th' ile can, . . .
Foolish man, th' funrals don't stop f'r ilictions, or th'
christenin's or th' weddin's. . . . Don't ye expict
Hinnissy that anny throop iv angels will dhrop fr'm
hiven to chop ye'er wood on th' mornin' iv th' siventh iv
November if Bryan is ilicted, an' don't ye lave Jawnny
McKenna think that if Mack gets in, he'll have to put
a sthrip iv oil cloth on th' dure sill to keep pluthycrats
fr'm shovin' threasury notes undher th' dure. . . .
"... I was r-readin' th' other day about a vote cast be
a lot iv distinguished gazabs through th' counthry f'r th'
occupants iv a hall iv fame. . . . I r-read th' list today,
Hinnissy, an' will ye believe me or will ye not? Much as
I know, I cudden't recall more thin half th' names. . . ."
When a new list is made out some day, "some wan may

vote f'r th' gr-reat soul that discovered how 'to make both ends meet in th' year nineteen hundhred."

Opinions, p. 109;
Harpers Weekly, November 3, 1900;
Boston Globe, October 28, 1900

235. Mr. Dooley Closes the Campaign

(Mr. Dooley on the meaning of the vote. He lists his campaign promises as opposed to those campaigning). ". . . I'll not offer to give ye th' things I'd like to see ye have, but th' things ye're sure to get."

Harpers Weekly, November 10, 1900;
Boston Globe, November 4, 1900

236. On the Romantic Novel

"Th' hero ought to be fr'm Virginia or Maryland, it makes no difference which. People will believe annything about them states."

Harpers Weekly, November 17, 1900;
Boston Globe, November 11, 1900

237. On Cross-Examinations

"They cudden't get me into coort as a witness; no, sir, not if 'twas to hang me best frind."

Opinions, p. 117;
Choice of Law, p. 7;
Harpers Weekly, November 24, 1900;
Boston Globe, November 18, 1900

238. On Thanksgiving

(Father Kelly) "says 'twas founded be th' Puritans to give thanks f'r bein' preserved fr'm th' Indyans, an' that we keep it to give thanks we are presarved from th' Puritans. . . . We're wan race, hitched together be a

gr-reat manny languages, a rellijon apiece, thraditions
that don't agree with each other, akel opporchunties f'r
th' rich an' poor, to continue bein' rich an' poor, an' a
common barnyard food. Whin iv'rybody in a nation eats
th' same things that all th' others eats, ye can't break
thim up."

Hutchinson, p. 160;
Opinions, p. 125;
Harpers Weekly, December 1, 1900;
Boston Globe, November 25, 1900

239. On the Crusade Against Vice

"Th' cit'y iv New York, Hinnissy, sets th' fashion iv
vice, an' starts th' crusade again' it. . . . As a people,
Hinnissy, we're th' greatest crusaders that iver was —
f'r a short distance. . . . A polisman goes afther vice as
an officer iv th' law, an' comes away as a
philosopher. . . . 'Ye can't make laws f'r this community
that wud suit a New England village,' he says, 'where,'
he says, 'th' people ar-re too civilized to be immoral.' "

Mr. Dooley Remembers, p. 288 (non dialect);
Best, p. 117;
Hutchinson, p. 162;
Opinions, p. 153;
Harpers Weekly, December 8, 1900;
Boston Globe, December 2, 1900

240. On High Society

New York City. The horse show, the theater and the
Palm room.

Harpers Weekly, December 15, 1900;
Boston Globe, December 9, 1900

241. Alcohol as Food

(Mr. Dooley disputes a doctor's findings). "Whiskey

wudden't be so so much iv a luxury if 'twas more iv a
necissity.... (Father Kelly says): 'It ought to be th'
reward iv action, not th' cause iv it,' he says. 'It's f'r th'
end iv th' day, not th' beginnin', he says. . . . 'Tis a bad
thing to stand on, a good thing to sleep on, a good thing
to talk on, a bad thing to think on.'" "D'ye think
ye-ersilf it sustains life?" asked Mr. Hennessy. "It has
sustained mine f'r many years," said Mr. Dooley.

Best, p. 265;
Hutchinson, p. 149;
Philosophy, p. 149

242. The Negro Problem

"I'm not so much throubled about th' naygur whin he
lives among his opprissors as I am whin he falls into th'
hands iv his liberators."

Hutchinson, p. 140;
Harpers Weekly, September 1, 1900;
Philosophy, p. 217

243. L'Aiglon

Mr. Dooley reviews a play about the son of Napoleon.

Philosophy, p. 251

244. Casual Observations

"A fanatic is a man that does what he thinks th' Lord
wud do if He knew th' facts iv th' case." "I care not who
makes th' laws iv a nation if I can get out an injunction." "Thrust ivrybody — but cut th' ca-ards." "A man
that'd expict to thrain lobsters to fly in a year is called
a loonytic; but a man that thinks men can be tur-rned
into angels be an iliction is called a rayformer an'
remains at large." "If men cud on'y enjye th' wealth an'

position th' newspapers give thim whin they're undher arrest! Don't anny but prominent clubmen iver elope or embezzle?" "A good manny people r-read th' ol' sayin' 'Larceny is th' sincerest form iv flatthry.' " "Miracles are laughed at be a nation that r-reads thirty millyon newspapers a day an' supports Wall sthreet." "I'd like to tell me frind Tiddy that they's a strenuse life an' a sthrenuseless life."

Best, 104;
Hutchinson, p. 152;
Philosophy, p. 257

245. On Recent Events in Speculative Circles

"Glory be, whin business gets above sellin' tinpinny nails in a brown paper cornacopy, 'tis hard to till it fr'm murcher." The boom and mostly bust of the stock market.

Mr. Dooley Remembers, p. 299 (non dialect);
Opinions, p. 189 (On Wall Street);
Harpers Weekly, July 1, 1901;
Boston Globe, May 26, 1901

246. On Mr. Carnegie's Gift

(Mr. Dooley marvels at millionaires giving away their money, particularly Carnegie's gift to educate the Scotch). " 'Andhrew Carnaygie's tin millyons won't make anny Robert Burnses,' he says. 'It may make more Andhrew Carnaygies,' says I. 'They'se enough to go round now,' says he. 'I don't think it makes anny difference wan way or th'other how free ye make idjacation. Men that wants it'll have it be hook an' be crook, an' thim that don't ra-aly want it niver will get it. Ye can lade a man up to th' univarsity, but ye can't make him think.' "

Best, p. 220;

Opinions, p. 145;
Harpers Weekly, June 8, 1901;
Boston Globe, June 2, 1901

247. Mr. Dooley Reviews Supreme Court Decision

"That is," said Mr. Dooley, "no matter whether th'
constitution follows th' flag or not, th' Supreme Coort
follows th' election returns."

Best, p. 72;
Hutchinson, p. 157;
Now and Forever, p. 157;
Choice of Law, p. 47;
Opinions, p. 21;
Harpers Weekly, June 15, 1901;
Boston Globe, June 9, 1901

248. On the Amateur Ambassadors

The appointment of the *nouveau riche* to cement the
ties between United States and England.

Opinions, p. 37;
Harpers Weekly, June 22, 1901;
Boston Globe, June 16, 1901

249. On the Yacht Races

". . . a yacht club which is an assocyation, Hinnissy, iv
members iv th' Bar. . . . 'Yachtin' is a gintleman's
spoort,' he says, 'an in dealin' with gintlemen,' he says,
'ye can't be too careful,' he says."

Opinions, p. 71;
Choice of Law, p. 194;
Harpers Weekly, June 29, 1901;
Boston Globe, June 23, 1901

250. On the New York Custom House

New York's custom inspectors search Hannigan upon
his return from Ireland.

Hutchinson, p. 165;
Choice of Law, p. 112;
Opinions, p. 161;
Harpers Weekly, July 6, 1901;
Boston Globe, June 30, 1901

251. On the Practice of Medicine

"I think," said Mr. Dooley, "that if th' Christyan
Scientists had some science an' th' doctors more
Christyanity, it wudden't make anny diff'rence which
ye called in — if ye had a good nurse."

Mr. Dooley Remembers, p. 279 (non dialect);
Opinions, p. 3 (Christian Science);
Harpers Weekly, July 13, 1901;
Boston Globe, July 7, 1901

252. On the City as a Summer Resort

(Mr. Dooley as an invited guest). 'I hope,' says I, 'I'm not
discommodin' th' pigeons,' I says. 'There ain't anny
pigeons here,' says he. 'What's that?' says I. 'That's a
mosquito,' says he. . . . 'Th' city,' says I, 'is th' on'y
summer resort f'r a man that has iver lived in th' city,'
I says.

Opinions, p. 45;
Harpers Weekly, July 20, 1901;
Boston Globe, July 14, 1901

253. On the Weather Bureau

Clancy's leg vs. the Weather Bureau.

Harpers Weekly, July 27, 1901;
Boston Globe, July 21, 1901

254. On an Editor's Duties

"D'ye know I'd like to be an iditor," said Mr. Dooley. . . .
"Tis a hard job," said Mr. Dooley, "but 'tis a fascinatin'
wan. They'se nawthin' so hard as mindin' ye'er own
business an' an iditor niver has to do that. . . . 'Th'
inthrests iv capital an' labor is th' same, wan thryin' to
make capital out iv labor an' th' other thryin' to make
laborin' men out iv capitalists." "I shud think th'
wurruk wud kill thim," said Mr. Hennessy sadly. "It
does," said Mr. Dooley. "Manny gr-reat iditors is dead."

Opinions, p. 55;
Harpers Weekly, August 3, 1901;
Boston Globe, July 28, 1901

255. On the Truth about Schley

Mr. Dooley reviews a revisionist history of the
Spanish-American War. He decides it's dangerous to be
a hero after a war.

Opinions, p. 101;
Harpers Weekly, August 10, 1901;
Boston Globe, August 4, 1901

256. On Life at Newport

(Eligibility for residence in the "socyal capital iv
America." The troubles of the wealthy). "Manny iv th'
cottagers ar-re talkin' iv havin' a law passed compellin'
pedesthreens to ring a bell an' blow a hor-rn on their
way to wurruk. Otherwise they won't be a whole tire
left in Newport. . . ." "Well, why do they live there if it
gives thim so much throuble?" said Mr. Hennessy. . . .
"Rich or poor, we want to be in sight an' sound iv
neighbors or they'se no fun in life."

Philosophy, p. 13;

Harpers Weekly, August 17, 1901;
Boston Globe, August 11, 1901

257. On Disqualifying the Enemy

Mr. Dooley interprets English bluster as an admission of defeat in South Africa.

Opinions, p. 29;
Harpers Weekly, August 24, 1901;
Boston Globe, August 18, 1901

258. Mr. Dooley Discusses Party Prospects

"No, sir, th' dimmycratic party ain't on speakin' terms with itsilf. Whin ye see two men with white neckties go into a sthreet car an' set in opposite corners while wan mutthers 'Thraiter,' an' th' other hisses, 'Miscreent,' ye can bet they're two dimmycratic leaders thryin' to reunite th' gran' ol' party. . . . but whin I come to silictin' a candydate f'r prisidint ivry man I think iv is ayther a thraitor or wan that th' thraitors wudden't vote f'r. If we don't get th' thraitor vote we're lost. . . . an' ivry time I mintion th' name iv wan iv ye'er fellow dimmycrats ye make a face. . . . Ye might thry advertisin' in th' pa-apers. 'Wanted: A good active, inergetic dimmycrat, sthrong iv lung an' limb; must be in favor iv sound money, but not too sound; an' anti-impeeryalist but f'r holdin' onto what we've got; an inimy iv thrusts, but a frind iv organized capital; a sympathizer with th' crushed an' downthrodden people but not be anny means hostile to vested inthrests; must advocate sthrikes, . . . an' all th' gr-reat an' gloryous principles iv our gr-reat an' gloryous party. . . . He must be akelly at home in Wall sthreet an' th' stock yards, in th' parlors iv th' rich an' th' kitchens iv th' poor. . . .' Man an' boy I've seen th' dimmycratic party hangin' to

th' ropes a score iv times. I've seen it dead an' burrid an'
th' raypublicans kindly buildin' a monymint f'r it an'
preparin' to spind their declinin' days in th' custom
house. I've gone to sleep nights wondhrin' where I'd
throw away me vote afther this, an' whin I woke up
there was that crazy-headed ol' loon iv a party with its
hair sthreamin' in its eyes, an ax in its hand, chasin' th'
raypublicans into th' tall grass. 'Tis niver so good as
when 'tis broke, whin rayspictable people speak iv it in
whispers an' whin it has no leaders an' on'y wan principle, to go in an' take it away fr'm th' other fellows."

Now and Forever, p. 164;
Opinions, p. 93 (Party Politics);
Boston Globe, September 1, 1901

259. On the Poet's Fate

He must die to become famous.

Best, p. 191;
Opinions, p. 63;
Boston Globe, September 8, 1901

260. Mr. Dooley's Dissertation on Lying

(Teaching lies at a Midway institution). "They'll be a
post gradyate coorse in perjury f'r th' more studyous an'
whin th' honorary degrees is given out we'll know what
LL.D. manes." "I lie a good manny times fr'm kindness,
more often fr'm laziness, an' most often fr'm fear. . . .
Th' most uncommon form is th' malicyous liar, an' th'
manest is th' just liar. . . . I niver deceived anny wan
half so much as I have mesilf. . . . I think a lie with a
purpose is wan iv th' worst kind an' th' mos'

profitable.... An' Father Kelly says 'tis an unsafe docthrine to thrust to anny wan but a saint."

Opinions, p. 87;
Boston Globe, September 15, 1901

261. On Athletics

"I niver knew a good card player or a great spoortsman that cud do so much iv annything else.... In me younger days 'twas not considhered rayspictable f'r to be an' athlete. An athlete was always a man that was not sthrong enough f'r wurruk. Fractions dhruv him fr'm school, an' th' vagrancy laws dhruv him to baseball.... I don't know annything that cud be more demoralizin' thin to be marrid to a woman that cud give me a sthroke a sthick at goluf. 'Tis goin' to be th' roon iv fam'ly life.... F'r, Hinnissy, I'm afraid I cud not love a woman I might lose a fight to."

Best, pp. 161, 182;
Opinions, p. 79;
Boston Globe, September 22, 1901

262. On Youth and Age

(The issue is whether President Roosevelt is too young for the office). "Well," said Mr. Dooley, "a man is old enough to vote whin he can vote, he's old to wurruk whin he can wurruk. An' he's old enough to be Prisidint whin he becomes Prisidint. If he ain't, 'twill age him."

Mr. Dooley Remembers, p. 296 (non dialect);
Hutchinson, p. 169;
Opinions, p. 181;
Boston Globe, September 29, 1901

263. On Some Political Developments

(Chicago and New York politics compared. On Croker): "He's lile to his frinds, but he has no frinds." "Rayformers, Hinnissy, is in favor iv suppressin' ivrything, but rale pollyticians believes in suppressin' nawthin' but ividince." (On reform candidates. On how Tammany gets its way). "How do they do it?" asked Mr. Hennessy. "Well," said Mr. Dooley, "nearly all th' most foolish people in th' counthry an' manny iv th' wisest goes to Noo York. Th' wise people ar-re there because th' foolish wint first. That's th' way th' wise men make a livin'. Th' easiest thing in th' wurruld is th' crather that's half-on, an' most iv th' people down there are jus' half-on. They'se no more crooked people there thin annywhere else, but they'se enough that wud be ashamed to confiss that they weren't crooked, to give a majority."

Opinions, p. 171;
Boston Globe, October 20, 1901

264. On the Law's Delays

"If I had me job to pick out," said Mr. Dooley, "I'd be a judge. I've looked over all th' others, an' that's th' on'y wan that suits. I have th' judicyal timperamint. I hate wurruk." "I don't believe in capital punishmint, Hinnissy, but 'twill niver be abolished while th' people injye it so much."

Choice of Law, p. 37;
Observation, p. 15;
Boston Globe, October 27, 1901

265. On the Celebration at Yale

(Yale's Bicentenary. Justice Brewer's speech on trusts). "D'ye think th' colledges has much to do with th' progress iv th' wurruld?" asked Mr. Hennessy. "D'ye think," said Mr. Dooley, " 'tis th' mill that makes th' wather run?"

Opinions, p. 199 (Colleges and Degrees);

207

Choice of Law, p. 52;
Boston Globe, November 3, 1901

266. On the Booker Washington Incident

(President Roosevelt invites Booker T. Washington to
the White House). "I don't suppose they have partitions
up in th' other wurruld like th' kind they have in th'
cars down south."

Opinions, p. 207;
Choice of Law, p. 59;
Boston Globe, November 10, 1901

267. Mr. Dooley as Sherlock Holmes

(Mr. Dooley compares sleuthing by the local policeman
with Holmes' deductive method). "No, sir, criminals is
th' simplest crathers in th' wide, wide wurruld, innocent, straight forward dangerous people that haven't
sinse enough to be honest or prosperous."

Hutchinson, p. 173;
Observation, p. 23;
Boston Globe, November 24, 1901

268. Mr. Dooley Again on International Amenities

(A Chamber of Commerce banquet in New York. The
Secretary of State): ". . . Diplomacy . . . has on'y to be
honest, straightforward an' manly and concede
ivrything, an' he will find his opponents will meet him
halfway an' take what he gives. . . . Di-plomacy has
become a philanthropic pursoot like shopkeepin', but
politics, me lords, is still th' same ol' spoort iv highway
robb'ry. . . . I will on'y say that hinceforth th' policy iv
this gover'mint will be as befure not to bully a sthrong
power or wrong a weak, but will remain thrue to th'
principle iv wrongin' the sthrong an' bullyin' th' weak."

(Mr. Dooley also discusses the deference our aristocracy pays to the British.)

Observation, p. 33;
Choice of Law, p. 136;
Boston Globe, December 1, 1901

269. On Art Patronage

Mr. Dooley tells American artists to paint in Europe if they want to cash in on their output.

Observations, p. 41;
Boston Globe, December 8, 1901

270. On Immigration

"Well, I see Congress has got to wurruk again," said Mr. Dooley. "The Lord save us fr'm harm," said Mr. Hennessy. "Well," said Mr. Dooley, "as a pilgrim father on me gran' nephew's side, I don't know but ye're right. An' they'se wan sure way to keep thim out." "What's that?" said Mr. Hennessy. "Teach thim all about our instichoochions befure they come," said Mr. Dooley.

Hutchinson, p. 177;
Now and Forever, p. 172;
Observations, p. 49;
Choice of Law, p. 82;
Boston Globe, December 15, 1901

271. On the Midway

". . . that f'r wan man that goes to a wurruld's fair to see how boots is made, they'se twinty goes to see th' hootchy-kootchy, . . ." (The Chicago Fair).

Opinions, p. 133

272. On Discipline from the White House

(President Roosevelt reprimands General Miles). "Ye may talk about as much as ye want, but govermint, me boy, is a case iv me makin' ye do what I want, an' if I

can't do it with a song I'll do it with a shovel. Th' ir'n
hand in th' velvet glove, th' horseshoe in th' boxin' mit,
th' quick right, an' th' heavy boot, that was th' way we
r-run polliticks whin I was captain iv me precinct."
Observations, p. 57;
Boston Globe, January 12, 1902

273. On Financial Needs in Matrimony

Mr. Dooley suggests that a salary is not one of the
sacraments of marriage.
Observations, p. 65 (Money and Matrimony);
Boston Globe, January 19, 1902

274. On Prince Henry's Visit

Mr. Dooley's suspicions as to why "th' impror iv
Germany" is sending his brother to visit this country.
Hutchinson, p. 180;
Observations, p. 73;
Boston Globe, January 26, 1902

275. On the Reception of Royalty

The stir in America over the coronation of King
Edward.
Boston Globe, Feb. 2, 1902

276. On the Condition of Cuba

"Ye can't make freedom into a stew, an' ye can't cut a
pair iv pants out iv it. It won't fry, bake or fricassee. . . .
So Cubia comes to us an' says she: '. . . if ye plaze we'd
like to thrade a little iv it back f'r a few groceries.' . . ."
(What to do about the Cuban beet).
Hutchinson, p. 184;
Now and Forever, p. 179;
Observations, p. 91 (Cuba vs. Beet Sugar);
Boston Globe, February 9, 1902

APPENDIX

277. On the Bad Man from the West

The Senate refuses to confirm the nomination of an appointee because he had been in jail. Mr. Dooley seems to suggest that the President's standards are higher than that of the Senate.

Observations, p. 97;
Boston Globe, February 16, 1902

278. On European Intervention

(Mr. Dooley discusses the question as to which of the European powers was helpful to the United States during the Spanish-American war. As to the Europeans attacking America). "I'd blockade Armour an' Comp'ny an' th' wheat ilivators iv Minnysoty. F'r Hinnissy I tell ye, th' hand that rocks th' scales in th' grocery store is th' hand that rules th' wurruld."

Observations, p. 107;
Boston Globe, March 2, 1902

279. On the Philippine Peace

Governor Taft's speech on the Philippines. Mr. Dooley reads between the lines.

Mr. Dooley Remembers, p. 292 (Non dialect);
Best, p. 62;
Now and Forever, p. 184;
Observations, p. 115;
Boston Globe, March 9, 1902

280. On the Capture of Methuen

Mr. Dooley considers the loss of a British General to the Boers a victory for the British.

Best, p. 58;

Observations, p. 191 (The End of the War);
Boston Globe, March 30, 1902

281. A Little Essay on Books and Reading

Mr. Dooley questions scholarly explanations of how the Earth began. "Most iv th' people iv this wurruld is a come-on f'r science, but I'm not." Mr. Dooley discusses the evolution of writing. ". . . an' thin th' printin'-press was invented. Gunpowdher was invinted th' same time, an' 't is a question I've often heerd discussed which has done more to ilivate th' human race. . . . Women writes all th' good romantic novels, an' reads thim all . . . th' on'y books in me libr'y is th' Bible an' Shakespere," says I. "They're gr-reat f'r ye," says she. "So bully f'r th' style. D'ye read thim all th' time?" she says. "I niver read thim," says I. "I use thim for purposes iv definse. I have niver read thim, but I'll niver read annything else till I have read thim," I says. "They shtand between me an' all modhren lithrachoor," says I. . . . Am I again' all books, says ye? . . . In modheration, mind ye. In modheration, an' afther th' chores is done." "If anny proud la-ad in th' gum business thinks he riprisints th' ideal iv his wife's soul, he ought to take a look at th' books she reads. He'll l'arn there th' reason he's where he is because he was th' on'y chanst, not because he was th' first choice."

Observations, p. 3;
Century, May 1902;
Boston Globe, May 4, 1902

282. Mr. Dooley Compares the Soldier's Life and the Policeman's

(On military justice): "Th' Supreme Coort was all right, but if ye wanted justice, hot out iv th' oven, ye shud see it administhered be three or four laughin' sub-alturns on th' stumps iv threes, jus' afther lunch."

Observations, p. 123;
Boston Globe, June 22, 1902

283. On One Advantage of Poverty

"Sickness is wan iv th' privileges iv th' poor man that he shares with no wan. . . . No, sir, if I've got to be sick, give me th' ordhn'ry decencies iv poverty. I don't want anny man to know anny more about me thin he can larn fr'm th' handiwork iv Marks, th' tailor, an' Schmitt, th' shoemaker, an' fr'm th' deceitful expression iv me face." (The rich, Mr. Dooley says, are subject to the revelations of the doctors and the speculations of the press): "He may bear himsilf with a haughty manner, but he feels that ivry man he meets knows more about him thin he knows himsilf."

Observations, p. 141;
Boston Globe, July 6, 1902

284. On the Fighting Word

(The fisticuffs between Senators Bailey and Beveridge). "Who am I to say that what wudden't be manners in a barroom is not all right in th' sinit? . . . I don't know what wud make me fight nowadays. I know lots iv things that wud make me want to fight, but I've larned to repress me desires. . . . Th' las' throuble I got into I begun to think iv th' new suit I had on, an' I knew me warryor days was over."

Observations, p. 149;
Boston Globe, July 13, 1902

285. On the Pleasures of the Rich

(A discourse on Newport society, the society column, and a monkey being invited to a society party). "Father

Kelly tells me. Says he: 'If a man is wise, he gets rich, an' if he gets rich he gets foolish, or his wife does. . . . I'm glad there is a Newport,' says he. 'It's th' exhaust pipe,' he says. . . . "Oh, well," said Mr. Hennessy. "We are as th' Lord made us." "No," said Mr. Dooley. "Lave us be fair. Lave us take some iv th' blame oursilves."

Hutchinson, p. 194;
Observations, p. 199 (Newport);
Boston Globe, July 20, 1902

286. Mr. Dooley Reviews the News of A Week

(The campanile at Venice falls, Joseph Choate, J. Pierpont Morgan, Lord Balfour, Mary MacLane, Governor Taft, stock market, etc. President Roosevelt's strenuous day, hour by hour. What is news?) "Be news ye mane misfortune. . . ." "Th' newspapers have got to print what happens," said Mr. Hennessy. "No," said Mr. Dooley, "they've got to print what's diff'rent. Whiniver they begin to put headlines on happiness, contint, varchoo an' charity, I'll know things is goin' as wrong with this counthry as I think they ar-re ivry naytional campaign."

Observations, p. 183;
Boston Globe, July 27, 1902

287. On the Home Life of Geniuses

"So it don't make much diff'rence who a man marries. If he has a job, he's safe. . . . But people, expecially women, don't want to be loved that way. They want to be loved because people can't help lovin' thim no matther how bad they are. . . . Now, what kind iv a man ought a woman to marry? She oughtn't to marry a young man because she'll grow older quicker thin he will; she oughtn't to marry an old man because he'll be much older befure he's younger; she oughtn't to marry

214

a poor man because he may become rich an' lose her; she oughtn't to marry a rich man because if he becomes poor she can't lose him; she oughtn't to marry a man that knows more thin she does because he'll niver fail to show it, an' she oughtn't to marry a man that knows less because he may niver catch up. But above all things she mustn't marry a janius. A flure walker, perhaps; a janius niver.... So ye see, Hinnissy, why a woman oughtn't to marry a janius. She can't be cross, or peevish, or angry, or jealous, or frivolyous, or annything else a woman ought to be at times, f'r fear it will get into th' ditchn'ry iv biography, an' she'll go down to histhry as a termygant."

Hutchinson, p. 187;
Observations, p. 157;
Boston Globe, August 3, 1902

288. On Reform Administration

"Why is it," asked Mr. Hennessy, "that a rayform administhration always goes to th' bad?" ... "In th' first place 'tis a gr-reat mistake to think that annywan ra-aly wants to rayform. Ye niver heerd iv a man rayformin' himsilf. He'll rayform other people gladly.... An' that's thruer in politics thin annywhere else.

"But a rayformer don't see it. A rayformer thinks he was ilicted because he was a rayformer, whin th' thruth iv th' matther is he was ilicted because no wan knew him.... So th' minyit he gets into th' job he begins a furyous attimpt to convart us into what we've been thryin' not to be iver since we come into th' wurruld. "... Laws are made to throuble people an' th' more throuble they make th' longer they stay on th' stachoo book.... Whin a rayformer is ilicted he promises ye a business administhration.... A reg'lar pollytician can't give away an alley without blushin', but a business man who is in pollytics jus' to see that th' civil sarvice law gets thurly enfoorced, will give Lincoln Park an' th' public libr'y to th' beef thrust, charge an admission price to th' lake front an' make it a felony f'r annywan to buy stove polish outside iv his store, an' have it all put down to public improvemints with a pitcher iv him in th' corner stone. . . . Ivry man ought to be honest to start with, but to give a man an office jus' because he's honest is like ilictin' him to Congress because he's a pathrite, because he don't bate his wife. . . . Another thing about rayform administhrations is they always think th' on'y man that ought to hold a job is a lawyer. Th' raison is that in th' coorse iv his thrainin' a lawyer larns enough about ivrything to make a good front on anny subject to annybody who doesn't know about it. . . . I don't like a rayformer," said Mr. Hennessy. "Or anny *other* raypublican," said Mr. Dooley.

Hutchinson, p. 190;
Choice of Law, p. 175;
Observations, p. 167;
Boston Globe, August 10, 1902

289. On the Coronation

Americans at the coronation. The sad role of a king.

Observations, p. 133 (King Edward's Coronation);
Boston Globe, August 17, 1902

290. On Work and Sport

(Mr. Dooley catalogs all the recreations that the rich endure). "A rich man at spoort is a kind iv non-union laborer. He don't get wages f'r it and he don't dhrive as well as a milkman, ride as well as a stable-boy, shoot as well as a polisman, or autymobill as well as th' man

216

that runs th' steam roller.... No, sir, what's a rich man's raycreation is a poor man's wurruk." "Why do they do it?" asked Mr. Hennessy. "I dinnaw," said Mr. Dooley, "onless it is that th' wan great object iv ivry man's life is to get tired enough to sleep. Ivrything seems to be some kind iv wurruk. Wurruk is wurruk if ye're paid to do it, an' it's pleasure if ye pay to be allowed to do it."

Observations, p. 175;
Boston Globe, August 24, 1902

291. On our Representatives Abroad

(Mr. Dooley regrets that communications has made an ambassador's job a sinecure). "To be an ambassadure all a man needs is to have his wife want to live in Europe... An ambassadure is a man that is no more use abroad thin he wud be at home."

Now and Forever, p. 199;
Dissertations, p. 87;
Boston Globe, August 31, 1902

292. On Machinery

(Mr. Dooley compares present times with the past. He notes all the mechanical wonders. A profile of Horace Greeley. But Horace Greeley's are now the tool of J.P. Morgan. Mr. Dooley notes the skyscrapers but) "I want to see sky-scrapin' men." "What d'ye think iv th' man down in Pinnsylvanya who says th' Lord an' him is partners in a coal mine?" asked Mr. Hennessy, who wanted to change the subject. "Has he divided th' profits?" asked Mr. Dooley.

Best, p. 30;
Hutchinson, p. 196;

Observations, p. 213;
Boston Globe, September 7, 1902

293. On Swearing

(Mr. Dooley comments on President Roosevelt's unkind
words to a trolleyman. T. R. doesn't always speak to
posterity). "Posterity don't begin to vote till afther th'
polls close." "I don't believe in profanity, Hinnissy —
not as a reg'lar thing. But it has its uses an' its place."
(A catalog of what trades and professions can and
cannot swear). "Th' man that swears at ivrything has
nawthin' to say when rale throubles come. . . . 'Twas
intinded as a compromise between runnin' away an'
fightin'."

Best, p. 104;
Hutchinson, p. 200;
Observations, p. 223;
Boston Globe, September 14, 1902

294. On the War Game

(Mr. Dooley chalks up the war games as a social event).
"It's a fine game. I don't know who won, but I know who
lost." "Who's that?" asked Mr. Hennessy. "Th'
threassury," said Mr. Dooley.

Observations, p. 231;
Boston Globe, September 21, 1902

295. On Arctic Exploration

(Mr. Dooley has no thought of ever going to the pole
which ironically does not exist. But a millionaire can
always get someone to go). "Fin'lly ye set off with th'
fleet, consistin' iv a ship fr ye'ersilf, three fr th'
provisions, two fr th' clothes, an' wan fr th' diaries."

Observations, p. 205;
Boston Globe, September 28, 1902

296. On Newspaper Publicity

". . . 'In th' name iv th' law I arrist ye,' says th' man seizin' ye by th' throat. 'Who ar-re ye?' ye cry. 'I'm a rayporther f'r th' Daily Sloth,' says he. 'Phottygrafter, do ye'er jooty!' Ye're hauled off in th' circlation wagon to th' newspaper office, where a con-fission is ready f'r ye to sign; ye're thried be a jury iv th' staff, sintinced be th' iditor-in-chief an' at tin o'clock Friday th' fatal thrap is sprung be the fatal thrapper iv th' family journal.

"Th' newspaper does ivrything f'r us. It runs th' polis foorce an' th' banks, commands th' milishy, conthrols th' ligislachure, baptizes th' young, marries th' foolish, comforts th' afflicted, afflicts th' comfortable, buries th' dead an' roasts thim aftherward. They ain't annything it don't turn its hand to. . . .

"They used to say a man's life was a closed book. So it is, but it's an open newspaper." Mr. Dooley then follows Malachi Hinnissy from cradle onward. "There are no such things as private citizens. . . . Ivrybody is inthrested in what ivrybody else is doin' that's wrong. That's what makes th' newspapers. An' as this is a dummycratic counthry where ivrybody is born akel to ivrybody else, aven if they soon outgrow it, an' where wan man's as good as an' as bad, all iv us has a good chanst to have his name got in at laste wanst a year. . . . A newspaper is to intertain, not to teach a moral lesson."

"D'ye think people likes th' newspapers iv th' prisint time?" asked Mr. Hennessy. "D'ye think they're printed f'r fun?" said Mr. Dooley.

Best, p. 227;
Observations, p. 239;
Boston Globe, October 5, 1902

297. On the Coal Strike

(A sardonic profile of Mr. Baer, a coal mine owner).
"But I'm with th' rights iv property, d'ye mind. Th'
sacred rights an' th' divine rights. A man is lucky to
have five dollars; if it is ten, it is his jooty to keep it if
he can; if it's a hundherd, his right to it is th' right of
silf-dayfinse; if it's a millyon, it's a sacred right; if it's
twinty millyon, it's a divine right; . . . Nobody must
intherfere with it or down comes th' constichoochion,
th' army, a letter fr'm Baer an' th' wrath iv Hivin." (An
essay worthy of Swift).

Boston Globe, October 12, 1902

298. On Education

(Mr. Dooley satirizes a speech of President Eliot of
Harvard and his despair that education has not
eradicated drunkenness, gambling, trashy novels and
common amusements. Mr. Dooley would like to gather
all educators and speak to them): "It is thrue that ye
haven't cured all th' wrongs iv th' wurruld, but nobody
ast ye to."

Boston Globe, October 26, 1902

299. On the Irish Question

(Mr. Dooley explains why the English and Irish can not
settle their problems amicably). ". . . an' it's been th'
policy iv all other gr-reat statesman. Niver start a
riv'lution without a gun. Niver ask a man f'r annything
unless ye can make him think ye're li'ble to take it
annyhow. My wrongs ar-re my wrongs, an' it's little ye
mind thim until they begin to hurt ye. . . ." "I wondher
will England iver free Ireland?" asked Mr. Hennessy.
"Niver," said Mr. Dooley. "What talk have ye? No wan

wants it that way. England will niver free Ireland, but some day, if we make it intherestin' enough f'r her, she'll have to free England iv Ireland. An' that'll be all right."

Dissertations, p. 129;
Boston Globe, November 2, 1902

300. The King in his Shirt-Sleeves

(Mr. Dooley is unhappy that the King of Belgium must share his scandals with the press). "Whin I was a boy, ... (the family) didn't say annything, but wrote it down in a note-book an' published it afther they were dead. . . . To be a king an' get away with it, a man must keep out iv sight."

Dissertations, p. 3;
Boston Globe, November 9, 1902 (On the Doings of Royalty)

301. A Dissertation on the Jews

" 'Tis ye'er idee that ivry Jew is a rich man. Maybe ye're right. Maybe all thim Jews that lives down in Canal sthreet, twinty in a room, is Rothschilds. . . . Th' raison th' Jews is all in business is because they'se nawthin' else f'r thim to do. . . . They cudden't be sojers or pollyticians or lawyers or judges. But they'se wan pursoot where prejudice has no hand. Whin a man wants to borrow money he niver inquires about th' charackter or religion iv th' fellow he touches. . . . an' not payin' back money to a Jew is a Christyan varchue. . . . In figures th' Jews is strong. Where they're weak is not carin' about money. . . . A Jew makes down town an' spinds up town. It's aisy come aisy go with a Jew. . . . Whin all th' money in th' wurruld is gathered in th' hands iv anny wan class th' Jews won't have it. Most iv it'll be in New England with a few odd dollars

221

in Scotland. . . . Why ain't th' Jew a sojer, says ye? . . .
He knows he niver cud get to be a gin'ral. . ."

Boston Globe, November 16, 1902

302. On Football

(Mr. Dooley follows Bill, who) "has a head like a walnut
on top iv a bag iv flour" (from his invitation by the
college president to profit from his amateur standing to
his fulfilling his potential to do mayhem to his fellow
man). "Why don't th' polis stop it?" asked Mr. Hennessy
testily. "They can't," said Mr. Dooley. "They can't arrist
a man f'r assault onless he commits it to get food or
money."

Boston Globe, November 23, 1902

303. Christmas Scheme

Ladies' Home Journal, Vol. 20, No. 14, December 1902

304. Adventure

(Mr. Dooley's daydreams) "The best advintures anny iv
us has is at home in a comfortable room — th' mos'
excitin' an' th' asiest."

Observations, p. 247

305. Prince Henry's Reception

(Royalty is) "like an iron lamp post, station'ry,
ornymintal, an' useful to let people know where they
are. But whin he comes to this home iv raypublican
simplicity, he's all that th' wurrud prince wud imply,
an' it implies more to us thin to annywan else." (Mr.
Dooley harshly characterizes German-Americans.)
"Whin an Irishman is four miles out at sea he is as
much an American as Presarved Fish." (A letter by the
prince to his brother, Wilhelm): "I am actually invited

222

to a dinner iv wan hundherd iv th' riprisintative business men iv New York an' a few Christyans ast in
aftherward." (Mr. Dooley contrasts his scheduled
itinerary with what he would be offered on "Ar-rchey
road.")

Observations, p. 83

306. Rights and Privileges of Women

"Woman's Rights? What does a woman want iv rights
whin she has priv'leges? . . . We have th' right to be
sued f'r debt instead iv lettin' th' bill run, which is a
priv'lege. We have th' right to thrile be a jury iv our
peers, a right to pay taxes an' a right to wurruk. None
iv these things is anny good to me. . . . I'd give all th'
rights I read about for wan priv-lege. If I cud go to sleep
th' minute I go to bed I wudden't care who done me
votin'. . . . An' so it is with women. . . . They haven't th'
right iv a fair thrile be a jury iv their peers; but they
have th' priv'lege iv an unfair thrile be a jury iv their
admirin' infeeryors."

Hutchinson, p. 204;
Choice of Law, p. 57;
Observations, p. 253

307. Avarice and Generosity

"Money won't prolong life, but a few millyons
judicyously placed in good banks an' occas'nally worn
on th' Person will rayjooce age. . . . but a millyonaire at
sixty is jus' in th' prime iv life to a frindly eye, an' there
are no others. . . . Pollytics and bankin' is th' on'y two
games where age has th' best iv it. . . . Whin a man
begins makin' money in his youth at annything but

223

games iv chance, he niver can become gin'rous late in
life. . ."

Hutchinson, p. 205;
Observations, p. 257

308. Hypocrisy

"If ye'd turn on th' gas in th' darkest heart ye'd find it
had a good raison for th' worst things it done, a good
varchous raison, like needin' th' money or punishin' th'
wicked or tachin' people a lesson to be more careful, or
protectin' th' liberties iv mankind, or needin' the
money."

Hutchinson, p. 207;
Observations, p. 267

309. The End of Things

(Mr. Dooley lists the things he would like to have said
about him when he dies). "That's what I think, but if I
judged fr'm expeeryence I'd know it'd be, 'It's a nice day
f'r a dhrive to th' cimitry. Did he lave much?' No man
is a hayro to his undertaker."

Best, p. 223;
Hutchinson, p. 207;
Observations, p. 263

310. History

"I know histhry isn't thrue, Hinnessy, because it ain't
like what I see ivry day in Halsted Sthreet. If any wan
comes along with a histhry iv Greece or Rome that'll
show me th' people fightin', gettin' dhrunk, makin'
love, gettin' married, owin' th' grocery man an' bein'
without hard-coal, I'll believe they was a Greece or
Rome, but not befure. Historyans is like doctors. They
are always lookin' f'r symptoms. Those iv them that
writes about their own times examines th' tongue an'
feels th' pulse an' makes a wrong dygnosis. Th' other
kind iv histhry is a post-mortem examination. It tells

224

ye what a counthry died iv. But I'd like to know what
it lived iv."

Best, p. 201;
Hutchinson, p. 207;
Observations, p. 271

311. Gratitude

"A man who expicts gratichood is a usurer, an' if he's
caught at it he loses th' loan an' th' intherest."

Hutchinson, p. 208;
Observations, p. 279

312. On the Carnegie Libraries

"A Carnaygie libry is a large, brown-stone
impenethrible buildin', with th' name iv th' maker
blown on th' dure." A Carnegie speech: ". . . I like hard
wurruk, an' given away me money is th' hardest
wurruk I ever did. . . . I cheer mesilf with th' thought
that no matther how much money I give, it don't do
anny particular person anny good." "Libraries niver
encouraged lithrachoor anny more thin tombstones
encourage livin'."

Hutchinson, p. 225;
Now and Forever, p. 221;
Dissertations, p. 177;
Boston Globe, January 18, 1903

313. On Royal Doings

(The romance iv th' crown princess iv Saxony). "Whin a
woman discovers she has a soul, Hinnissy, 'tis time she
was sint to a rest cure. It niver comes till late in life an'
ye can't tell what she'll do about it. . . . Whin an ol'
crazy-headed lunytic iv a woman skips out 'tis a crime,
whin an ol' crazy-headed lunytic iv a duchess does it,

it's a scandal; but whin an ol' crazy-headed lunytic iv a princess does it, it's a romance."

Dissertations, p. 11;
Boston Globe, January 25, 1903

314. Mr. Dooley Calls for an International Police Force
(Mr. Dooley doesn't think much of the international court). "A coort's all r-right enough, but no coort's anny good onless it is backed up be a continted constabulary, it's counthry's pride, as th' poet says."

Best, p. 145;
Hutchinson, p. 222;
Now and Forever, p. 214;
Dissertations, p. 161;
Choice of Law, p. 123;
Boston Globe, February 1, 1903

315. On Gambling
(The unhappiness of the professional gambler). "In ivry other business in life th' ilimint iv chance enthers in. But not in mine. Th' banker, th' dhrygoods merchant, th' lawyer, th' money lender takes risks. His days are enlivened be excitement. But there ar-re no risks in this business. It's wan dull, monotonous grind, th' same ol' percintage, th' same dhreary gatherin' in iv th' mazuma, till me heart sickens within me an' I'm almost timpted to thry some risky pursoot like pawnbrokin'."

Dissertations, p. 153;
Boston Globe, February 8, 1903

316. On the Carnegie-Homer Controversy
Dissertations, p. 145;
Boston Globe, February 15, 1903

317. On the American Family
(Dr. Eliot on the men of Harvard not producing children): "Th' av'rage fam'ly iv th' Harvard gradjate

an' th' jackass is practically th' same." (Father Kelly on the prospects of the race dying out): "Th' poor ar-re becomin' richer in childher, an' th' rich poorer," he says. " 'Tis always th' way," he says. "Th' bigger th' house th' smaller th' fam'ly. . . . A man with tin dollars a week will have tin childher, a man with wan hundherd dollars will have five, an' a man with a millyon will buy an autymobill."

Hutchinson, p. 219;
Dissertations, p. 137;
Boston Globe, February 22, 1903

318. On the Race Question

"Up here in this free North iv ours, where th' wurruds iv Windell Phillips is still soundin' in th' air, we don't see anny naygurs marryin' into our ladin' fam'lies. . . . Histhry always vindicates th' dimmycrats, but niver in their lifetime. They see th' truth first, but th' trouble is that nawthin' is iver officially thrue till a raypublican sees it." A southerner on the race question: "Th' race question, upon which I did not mean to speak, but will, can niver be settled until it is settled r-right. Th' r-right way to settle it is to lave it where it is."

Now and Forever, p. 228;
Dissertations, p. 185;
Boston Globe, March 1, 1903

319. Mr. Dooley Preaches a Lenten Sermon

"Father Kelly says 'tis good f'r th' soul, an' Dock Grogan, he says, 'tis good f'r th' body."

Dissertations, p. 123;
Boston Globe, March 8, 1903

320. On the Achievements of Congress

(Senator Aldrich on trusts, senatorial courtesy, the

filibuster). "Sinitoryal courtesy rules th' body. If ye let me talk I'll let ye sleep." Note: The Boston Globe version is much longer than the others.

Hutchinson, p. 229;
Dissertations, p. 193 (Senatorial Courtesy);
Boston Globe, March 15, 1903

321. On Diplomatic Uniforms

Diplomacy under Benjamin Franklin compared with the current crop of "waiters."

Dissertations, p. 97;
Boston Globe, April 12, 1903

322. Card Playing Among Women

Ladies' Home Journal, Vol. 20, No. 9, April 1903

323. On Mr. Carnegie's Hero Fund

"It's no use," said Mr. Dooley. "I give it up."
"What's that?" asked Mr. Hennessy.
"I can't get away from him," Mr. Dooley went on. "I can't escape me ol' frind Andhrew Carnaygie. I've avided him succissfully f'r manny years. Th' bookless libry an' th' thoughtless univarsity niver touched me.... But now he's got me at last. He's run me to earth. I throw up me hands. Come on, Andhrew, an' paint ye'er illusthrees name on me. Stencil me with that gloryous name." "... a man can on'y talk good to his infeeryors an' ye're a great stimylant to conversation." (Mr. Dooley's rationalization for saving Hennessy).... "They'se nawthin' a hayro with a medal can do f'r a livin' that ain't beneath him. Wanst a hayro, always a hayro. (Mr. Dooley talks about Clancy being saved by Mullins who becomes an albatross around Clancy's neck). "Afther awhile (Clancy) took to dhrink.

Habichool hayroes always do, an whin in dhrink he was melancholy or quarrelsome, as dhrunk hayroes sometimes ar-re. . . . Hayroes don't live long. They can't th' way they live. . . . Th' pa-apers had an account iv his fun'ral. 'Among th' mourners none was more affected thin Congressman Clancy, whose life, near forty years ago, this humble hayro had saved fr'm a wathry doom in Lake Mitchigan.' Th' rayporthers didn't observe that Clancy tamped th' grave with his foot to make sure it was solid. . . . No, sir, Hinnissy, if ye see me in disthress kindly call f'r profissyonal help. I'll be riscued be a fireman or a polisman because it's all in their day's wurruk, but amachoor hayroes is a danger whin they're riscuin' ye an' a worry iver afther. . . . There ar-re hayroes an' hayroes. We're all hayroes more or less. Ye're a hayro ye'ersilf, towin' those tired feet afther ye ivry mornin' whin th' whistle blows. An' be hivens, if ye-er wife had a medal f'r ivry act iv hayroism she's performed, she'd have so manny now as Sousa. Hayroes in th' humble walks iv life, says he? Well, there's enough iv thim to break him if he gives each wan iv thim th' on'y kind iv medals they need, th' kind th' govermint foundhry makes with an eagle on th' back."

Dissertations, p. 293;
Boston Globe, July 10, 1904

324. On the Political Situation

"Well," said Mr. Hennessy, "th' labors iv th' con-vintions ar-re at an end!" . . . "As Hogan says, th' dimmycratic convintion labored an' brought forth a muss. Th' raypublican convintion labored, too, like a cash register. . . . But, as I tol' ye, a dimmycrat has plinty iv principles that he'll fight f'r, on'y they niver get into a dimmycratic platform. A dimmycrat is a free an' indepindent citizen who thinks f'r himsilf — wrong.

229

A raypublican is a rich an' humble vassal who gets others to think f'r him — right. Ye cud hold a raypublican naytional convintion in a clothes closet, but ye cudden't r-run an orderly dimmycratic convintion in a forty-acre lot. There's a thousan' red-hot convintions inside iv ivry dimmycratic convintion. Ivry man has some principle that he'd lay down his life f'r, but wud prefer to lay down somebody else's life. . . . There isn't a platform in th' wurruld wide enough f'r two good dimmycrats to stand on without crowdin'. . . . But a man who has held office a long time is a raypublican annyhow." (Mr. Dooley discusses the sage of Princeton, Wilson, the sage of Escopus, Parker, sage Bryan, sage Hearst, "ivry sage excipt Russell Sage." Also David B. Hill).

"D'ye think th' raypublican platform is a good wan?" asked Mr. Hennessy.

"Th' raypublican platform is me frind Tiddy Rosenfelt," said Mr. Dooley. "He's standin' on himself. It's a strong platform, but he may become too heavy for it."

"Well, Parker is a safe man, annyhow," said Mr. Hennessy.

"He is," said Mr. Dooley, "but I wisht some wan else had the combination besides Hill."

Boston Globe, July 7, 1904

325. On the Duties of Vice-President

(Mr. Dooley compares V.P. candidates Davis and Fairbanks): "wan iv whom will sarve his counthry as vice-prisidint f'r th' nex' four years in Washin'ton an' th' other will sarve it jus' as much be stayin' at home. ". . . Th' prisidincy is th' highest office in th' gift iv th' people. Th' vice-prisidincy is th' nex' highest an' th' lowest. It isn't a crime exactly. Ye can't be sint to jail f'r it, but it's a kind iv a disgrace. . . . Th' way they got Sinitor Fairbanks to accipt was be showin' him a pitcher iv our gr-reat an' noble prisidint thryin' to jump a horse over a six foot fence."

"(The vice-president) has to be an all-round man. He must be a good speaker, a pleasant man with th' ladies, a fair boxer an' rassler, something iv a liar, an' if he's a raypublican campaignin' in Missouri, an active sprinter. . . . Aside fr'm th' arjoos duties iv lookin' afther th' prisidint's health . . . it is his jooty to rigorously enforce th' rules iv th' Sinit. There ar-re none. Th' Sinit is ruled be courtesy, like th' longshoremen's union."

Hutchinson, p. 216;
Now and Forever, p. 207;
Dissertations, p. 115;
Boston Globe, July 24, 1904

326. On the Comforts of Travel

(Mr. Dooley compares the travel brochures with the real thing. His trip from Chicago to St. Louis is a nightmare. For example), "in th' morning how to get into th' clothes without throwin' th' thrain off th' thrack?". . .

"I guess, Hinnissy, whin ye come to think iv it, they ain't anny such thing as luxury in thravel. . . . I can injye places betther be not goin' to thim. I think iv Italy as th' home iv th' Pope, but Hogan, who has been there, thinks iv it as th' home iv th' flee. . . . Man was meant to stay where he is or walk. If nature had intinded us to fly, she wud've fixed us with wings an' taught us to ate chicken feed."

Dissertations, p. 77;

Boston Globe, August 7, 1904

327. On the Political Prospects

"I see," said Mr. Hennessy, "that th' dimmycrats have gr-reat confidence."

"They have," said Mr. Dooley. "Th' dimmycrats have gr-reat confidence, th' raypublicans ar-re sure, th' popylists are hopeful, th' prohybitionists look f'r a landslide.... That's what makes pollytics th' gr-reat game an' th' on'y wan to dhrive dull care away. It's a game iv hope, iv jolly-ye'er neighbor, a confidence game.... Th' life iv a candydate is th' happiest there is. If I want annything pleasant said about me, I have to say it mesilf. There's a hundherd thousan' freemen ready to say it to a candydate an' say it strong. They ask nawthin' in rayturn that will require a civil service examination. He starts in with a pretty good opinyon iv himsilf based on what his mother said iv him as a baby, but be th' time he's heerd th' first speech iv congratulations, he begins to think he had a cold an' indiff'rent parent.... If he hasn't done much to speak iv, his frinds rayport his small but handsome varchues. He niver punched his wife, he sinds his boys to school, he loves his counthry, he shaves with a safety razor. A man expicts to be ilicted prisidint iv th' United States, Hinnissy, f'r th' fine qualities that th' r-rest iv us use on'y to keep out iv th' pinitinchry." (Mr. Dooley tells of the German, Smeerkase, running in an Irish ward. He was so sure he would get elected that he was breaking campaign promises. The eight votes he received were given to him. Dooley's pre-election advice to Roosevelt and Parker).

Dissertations, p. 199;
Boston Globe, August 14, 1904

328. On the Model Saloon

(Bishop Potter opens a saloon. Mr. Dooley tells the Bishop): "(The working man) goes to th' saloon an' ye go to th' club mostly f'r th' same reason. Ye don't want to go home. He don't need annywan to push him into a bar. He'll go there because that's a place where wan man's betther thin another an' nobody is ra-aly on but th' bartinder. There ought to be wan place where th' poor wurrukin' man can escape bein' patted on th' back. He ain't so bad, ye'er grace, as ye think. . . . Somehow or another, Hinnissy, it don't seem jus' right that there shud be a union iv church an' saloon. Those two gr-reat institutions ar-re best kept apart. . . ."

"Ye ra-aly do think dhrink is a nicissry evil?" said Mr. Hennessy.

"Well," said Mr. Dooley, "if it's an evil to a man, it's not nicissry, an' if it's nicissry it's not an evil."

Dissertations, p. 311 (The Bar);
Boston Globe, August 21, 1904

329. On the War

(The Russian-Japanese War. Mr. Dooley describes the progress of Japan since being opened by western civilization. He doesn't underestimate the Japanese). "Our idea iv a gr-reat man is a tall man, which lets out Napoleon Bonyparte an' Young Corbett an' lets in Fairbanks." "Ordhinar'ly a big man ought to lick a little wan. . . . In war, Hinnissy, height don't count."

Boston Globe, August 28, 1904

330. On the Automobile

(Mr. Dooley discusses the perils of the rich in their new-fangled automobiles. Algernon is hauled into court for running over some strategically placed tacks). "Now th' sign iv a haughty aristocracy is dhragged befure th' coort which proticts th' liberties iv th' people an' th' freedom iv speech iv th' magistrates. . . . 'Algernon Rex, (says the judge), this coort always timpers justice with mercy an' timpers mercy with timper. . . .' ". . . Hogan asked me to go f'r a spin as far as Brighton Park. But jus' as I was about to step into me proper place in s'ciety along with Jawn W. Gates, th' autymobill had a convulsyon. I heerd a terrific rumblin' in its inteeryer, it groaned an' coughed, an' thried to jump up in th' air. 'Something is wr-rong with ye'er ir'nhorse,' says I. 'He's et something that don't agree with him. Ye ought to take him to a vet.' . . . "I think they ought to be locked up f'r tearin' through th' sthreets," said Mr. Hennessy. "Well, maybe," said Mr. Dooley. "But don't ye think a man that owns an autymobill is punished enough?"

Dissertations, p. 67;
Boston Globe, September 4, 1904

331. On the Labor Troubles

(Mr. Dooley compares the old days of weak unions with the growth of union power).

"They ought to get together," said Mr. Hennessy.

"How cud they get anny closer together thin their prisint clinch?" asked Mr. Dooley. "They're so close together now that those that ar-re between thim ar-re crushed to death."

Hutchinson, p. 212;
Now and Forever, p. 192;
Dissertations, p. 59;
Choice of Law, p. 76;
Boston Globe, September 11, 1904

332. On the Progress of the Campaign

(Mr. Dooley puts words into the mouths of the presidential and vice-presidential candidates). "Who knows what makes a raypublican or a dimmycrat? . . . Raypublicans ar-re raypublicans because they ar-re raypublicans, an' dimmycrats ar-re dimmycrats because raypublicans ar-re what they ar-re."

Boston Globe, September 18, 1904

333. On the Bringing up of Children

(Mr. Dooley frowns on modern methods of bringing up children. Hogan won't let Dooley come near his infant). "So far as I am able to judge fr'm what he says, his is th' on'y perfect an' complete child that has been projooced this cinchry. . . . Well, ye know, Hinnissy, wan iv th' things that has made me popylar in th' ward is that I make a bluff at adorin' childher. Between you an' me I'd as lave salute a dish rag as a recent infant. . . . As f'r annybody preventin' a fond parent fr'm comin' home Saturdah night an' wallowin' in his beaucheous child, th' doctor that suggested it wud have to move. 'No, sir,' says I, 'get as much amusement as ye can out iv yer infant,' says I. 'Teach him to love ye now,' I says, 'befure he knows ye. Afther awhile he'll get onto ye an' it'll be too late.' "

"Ye know a lot about it," said Mr. Hennessy.

"I do," said Mr. Dooley. "Not bein' an' author I'm a gr-reat critic."

Dissertations, p. 51;
Boston Globe, October 9, 1904

334. On Short Marriage Contracts

(Mr. Dooley comments on George Meredith's proposal for short term marriages. Mr. Dooley characterizes marriage from the man's point of view). "We first embrace, thin pity, thin endure." (He depicts a typical marriage and then has the wife show the husband out the door as the contract is up). "In me heart I think if people marry it ought to be f'r life. Th' laws ar-re altogether too lenient with thim."

Dissertations, p. 43;
Boston Globe, October 16, 1904

335. On the War

The Russian-Japanese War. Mr. Dooley feels bad for the common soldier. He thinks "Nick Romanoff" and "Mike Adoo" should settle the matter in the ring.

Hutchinson, p. 230;
Dissertations, p. 207;
Boston Globe, October 23, 1904

336. On the Pursuit of Riches

(Mr. Dooley tells why he is not a rich man). "Life, Hinnissy, is like a Pullman dinin' car ... I've always looked on it as dishon'rable to wurruk f'r money ... Ye niver got what ye ordher, but it's pretty good if ye'er appytite ain't keen an' ye care f'r th' scenery."

Mr. Dooley Remembers, p. 282 (non dialect);
Hutchinson, p. 209;
Dissertations, p. 35;
Boston Globe, October 30, 1904

337. Mr. Dooley's Last Word to the Voters

Mr. Dooley reports on the campaign speeches of Roosevelt and Parker.

Boston Globe, November 6, 1904

338. On the Intellectual Life

"Well, sir," said Mr. Dooley, "it must be a gran' thing to be a colledge pro-fissor."

"Not much to do," said Mr. Hennessy.

"But a gr-reat deal to say," said Mr. Dooley. "Ivry day th' minyit I pick up me pa-aper afther I've read th' criminal an' other pollytical news, th' spoortin' news, the rale estate advertisements, th' invytation fr'm th' culthred foreign gent to meet an American lady iv some manes, object a matther iv more money, th' spoortin' news over again, thin th' iditoryals, I hasten to find out what th' colledge pro-fissor had to say yesterdah."

"I wisht th' iditor wud put it in th' same column iv th' pa-aper ivry day. Thin he wudden't have to collect anny other funny column ... (samples of college lectures follow): 'Speakin' iv th' Bible, it is an inthrestin' wurruk, but th' English is poor.... As f'r Shakespere, he is a dead wan.... An' he might have amounted to somethin' if he had been idjacated, but his language is base an' he had no imagination.... Me opinyon iv pollyticks, if ye shud ask me f'r it, is that we might as well give up th' experiment....' "What I like most about it is that a colledge pro-fissor niver speaks fr'm impulse.... (Professor Windhaul) didn't land on Lincoln till he was sure iv his ground. He first made inquiries an' found out that there was such a man. Thin he looked f'r his name among th' grajates iv Harvard."

"If ye had a boy, wud ye sind him to colledge?" asked Mr. Hennessy.

"Well," said Mr. Dooley, "at th' age whin a boy is fit to be in colledge I wudden't have him around th' house."

Dissertations, p. 107;
Boston Globe, November 13, 1904

339. On the Anglo-Saxon Triumph

(Roosevelt elected President). "... th' king sint f'r ambassadure Choate, who came as fast as his hands an knees wud carry him." Despite appearances, Mr. Dooley knows that it was the Hogans and Hurleys that made possible the "Anglo-Saxon Triumph."

Dissertations, p. 213;
Boston Globe, November 20, 1904

340. On Sieges

(Mr. Dooley is not upset about the siege of Port Arthur. Newspaper readers are usually more upset on reading about sieges than those being subject to them.) "Sure, Hinnissy, it's always th' same way. Wan iv th' sthrangest things about life is that it will go on in onfav'rable circumstances, an' go out whin ivrything is aisy. A man can live an' have a good time, no matther what happens to him that don't kill him.

"I lived here durin' th' cholery. I didn't like it, but they was on'y wan other thing to do, an' I didn't care f'r that. If ye're livin' in a town that's bein' bombarded, ye don't like it at first, but afther a while ye begin to accomydate ye'ersilf to it an' by an' by whin a shell dhrops near ye while ye're argin' about th' tariff, ye step aside an' if ye're still there afther th' smoke is cleared away, ye raysume th' argymint."

Dissertations, p. 285;
Boston Globe, November 27, 1904

341. On Banting

Mr. Dooley discusses the Fletcher system of dieting.

Dissertations, p. 27;
Boston Globe, December 4, 1904

342. On the Simple Life

(A review of a book by Chas. Wagner). "Th' fact iv th' matther is that th' rale thruth is niver simple. What we call thruth, an' pass around fr'm hand to hand, is on'y a kind iv a currency that we use f'r convanience. There are a good manny counterfeiters, an' a lot iv th' counterfeits mus' be in circulation. . . . Was th' wurruld iver anny more simple thin it is today? I doubt it."

Dissertations, p. 229;
Boston Globe, December 18, 1904

343. On Corporal Punishment

". . . I've come to th' con-clusion that ivry man uses vilence to his wife. He may not beat her with a table leg, but he coerces her with his mind. He can put a savage remark to th' pint iv th' jaw with more lastin' effect thin a right hook. . . As a last raycoorse he beats her be doin' things that make her pity him. . . . I look forward to th' day whin there will be a govermint whippin'-post. . . Th' govermint gives us too little amusemint nowadays. Th' favorite pastime iv civilized man is croolty to other civilized man. . . . Judges in civil coorts sometimes resign, but niver a hangin' judge in a criminal coort. . . . Th' on'y habit a man or a govermint ought to pray again' acquirin' is croolty. . . . Ye can't cure corp'ral punishmint be makin' th' govermint th' biggest kind iv corp'ral punisher."

Hutchinson, p. 233;
Choice of Law, p. 99;
Dissertations, p. 221;
Boston Globe, January 8, 1905

344. On Banks and Banking

(Mr. Dooley gives a short course on economics inspired by a Cleveland lady fleecing a bank). "Ye can be too honest to be bunkoed, but niver too smart."

"Th' wurruld is full iv crooks," said Mr. Hennessy.

"It ain't that bad," said Mr. Dooley. "An' besides lets thank God they put in part iv their time cheatin' each other."

Dissertations, p. 303;
Boston Globe, January 15, 1905

345. On Oratory

"I guess a man niver becomes an orator if he has anything to say, Hinnissy. If a lawyer thinks his client is innocint, he talks to th' jury about th' crime. But if knows where th' pris'ner hid th' lead pipe, he unfurls th' flag, throws out a few remarks about th' flowers an' th' burruds, an' asks th' twelve good men an' thrue not to break up a happy Christmas, but to sind this man home to his wife an' childher, an' Gawd will bless thim if they ar-re iver caught in th' same predicymint.... There ought to be a law against usin' th' American flag f'r such purposes... An' be hivins, I don't want anny man to tell me that I'm a mimber iv wan iv th' grandest races th' sun has iver shone on.... No, sir, whin a man has something to say an' don' know how to say it, he says it pretty well. Whin he has something to say an' knows how to say it, he makes a gr-reat speech. But whin he has nawthin' to say an' has a lot iv wurruds that come with a black coat, he's an orator."

Dissertations, p. 19;
Boston Globe, January 22, 1905

346. On the Life Insurance Investigation

Mr. Dooley analyzes the work of the New York legislative committee that exposed scandals in the insurance business. Charles Evans Hughes was counsel for the committee and this began his celebrated public career.

Collier's, Nov. 4, 18, Xmas, 1905

347. On the Power of the Press

"A few years ago," said Mr. Dooley, "I thought that if I had a son I'd make a lawyer iv him.... A law, Hinnissy, that might look like a wall to you or me wud look like a thriumphal arch to th' expeeryenced eye iv a lawyer.... Th' lawyers make th' law; th' judges make th' errors, but th' iditors make th' juries.... That's what th' Press can do f'r thim it loves. But I like it better f'r what it can hand to thim it don't love.... No, sir, as Hogan says, I care not who makes th' laws or th' money iv a counthry so long as I run th' presses. (Father Kelly) says it's against all tyrants but itsilf an' it has th' boldest iv thim crookin' th' knee to it."

Choice of Law, p. 64;
American Magazine, October 1906;
Boston Globe, November 4, 1906

348. On the Christmas Spirit

"... an' ye can't have th' Chris'mas spirit on Chris'mas onless ye've had it th' rest iv th' year. Ye must have, but ye mustn't show it."

American Magazine, December 1906;
Boston Globe, December 2, 1906

349. On Count Boney's Love Affair

On poor European royalty seeking young American heiresses, Mr. Dooley said, "The fortune took th' Count."

Boston Globe, December 9, 1906

241

350. On the President's Activities

"... th' Presidency is wan iv th' healthiest jobs in th' wurruld. No wan was iver ilicted to it that was even suspected iv a light cough." (T. R. is for spelling reform, visits Panama and Puerto Rico, keeps his cabinet on its toes, and puts Taft to work. A quiet day).

Boston Globe, December 16, 1906

351. Mr. Dooley Talks about Divorce

"Divoorce is th' on'y luxury supplied be th' law that we don't injye in Ar-rchey Road. Up here whin a marrid couple get to th' p'int where 'tis impossible f'r thim to go on livin' together they go on livin' together. . . .

" 'Ill-mated couples?' says (Father Kelly). 'Ill-mated couples? What ar-re ye talkin' about? Ar-re there anny other kinds?' " . . .

"I think," said Mr. Dooley, "if people wanted to be divoorced I'd let thim, but I'd give th' childher th' custody iv th' parents. They'd larn thim to behave."

Mr. Dooley Says p. 1;
Choice of Law, p. 87;
Boston Globe, December 23, 1906

352. Mr. Dooley Reviews the Dying Year

(Mr. Dooley is amused by reviewers of the year. Progress, disaster, Panama Canal, science, diplomacy). "I've got a kind iv an idee that I've fooled them all (the years). They think they've defaced me. . . . But d'ye know, Hinnissy, I've got a feelin' they haven't reached me. 'Fools,' says I, 'I've deceived ye. Ye've been shootin' at a decoy f'r th' best part iv a cinchry. That figure,' says I, 'was not Martin Dooley, but a scarecrow that I put up on th' breastworks to dhraw ye'er fire while I,' I says,

242

'set down here safe an' sound in th' trench an' smoke me good seegar an' laugh ivry time ye blow a limb off me riprisintative,' says I. 'Ye've niver touched me,' says I. 'I'm younger thin I iver was,' says I. 'Th' oldest I've iver been was forty years ago whin I had all th' weight iv th' wurruld on me shoulders. I've been growin' younger iver since. . . ."

Boston Globe, December 30, 1906

353. Oats as a Food

The craze for prepared breakfast foods.

Dissertations, p. 169

354. Hotels and Hotel Life

A prizefighter is turned away from a fashionable hotel. Mr. Dooley describes the scene at one of these hotels, The Waldorf. Mr. Dooley tells of his one tormented day in a hotel, and decides it is only for the rich.

"I've heerd," said Mr. Hennessy, "that this here fellow O'Brien wans threw a fight."

"I don't believe it," said Mr. Dooley; "if he had he wud've been a welcome guest."

Dissertations, p. 237

355. The Food We Eat

A Review of Sinclair's The Jungle. Mr. Dooley describes the reaction of President Roosevelt and the meat industry to this attack on food preparation. He decides that if the aristocracy wants to get him it might as well do it with the food it sells him.

Hutchinson, p. 236;
Now and Forever, p. 235;
Dissertations, p. 247;
Dissertations, p. 247

356. National Housecleaning

"It looks to me," said Mr. Hennessy, "as though this counthry was goin' to th' divvle."

"Put down that magazine," said Mr. Dooley.

(Mr. Dooley describes the effect of the muckrakers.) ". . . I've got to tell ye that this counthry, while wan iv th' worst in th' wurruld, is about as good as th' next if it ain't a shade better. But we're wan iv th' gr-reatest people in th' wurruld to clean house, an' th' way we like best to clean th' house is to burn it down. . . . (Mr. Dooley compares reformers with a compulsive house cleaner of a boarding house.) . . . "An' there ye ar-re, Hinnissy. Th' noise ye hear is not th' first gun iv a rivolution. It's on'y th' people iv th' United States batin' a carpet. . . . F'r nearly forty years I've seen this counthry goin' to th' divvle, an' I got aboord late. An' if it's been goin' that long an' at that rate, an' has got no nearer thin it is this pleasant Chris'mas, thin th' divvle is a divvle iv a ways further off thin I feared."
Best, p. 139;
Hutchinson, p. 241;
Now and Forever, p. 244;
Dissertations, p. 257

357. Socialism

(Mr. Dooley talks about the radical chic of another era: socialists selling their wares in the mansions of the wealthy). " 'What d'ye want to do?' says I. 'To make all men akel,' says he. 'Akel to who?' says I. 'If ye mane akel to me, I'm agreeable,' I says. 'I tire iv bein' supeeryor to th' rest iv th' race,' says I. . . . I'm sthrong f'r anny rivolution that ain't goin' to happen in me day. . . . I see gr-reat changes takin' place ivry day, but no change at all ivry fifty years."
Now and Forever, p. 251;
Dissertations, p. 265

358. Business and Political Honesty

". . . Ivry year, whin th' public conscience is aroused as it niver was befure, me frinds on th' palajeems (palladium) iv our liberties an' records iv our crimes calls f'r business men to swab out our govermint with business methods. . . . Whiniver I see an aldherman an' a banker walkin' down th' sthreet together I know th' Recordin' Angel will have to ordher another bottle iv ink."

Now and Forever, p. 260;
Dissertations, p. 275

359. On a Broken Friendship

An essay on the Japanese civilization and the prospects for war.

Mr. Dooley Says, p. 100;
Boston Globe, January 6, 1907

360. On the Glory of the Great

"I wanted to be famous in thim days, whin I was young an' foolish. 'Twas th' dhream iv me life to have people say as I wint by: There goes Dooley, th' gr-reatest statesman iv his age. . . An' so it goes. Whin a lad with nawthin' else to do starts out to write a bi-ography iv a gr-reat man he don't go to th' war departmint or th' public libry. No, sir, he begins to search th' bureau dhrawers, old pigeon holes, th' records iv th' polis coort an' th' recollections iv th' hired girl. . . . An' no wan will talk bad about ye afther ye ar-re dead onless ye've done something that makes people talk good iv ye.

"Which wud ye rather be, famous or rich?" asked Mr. Hennessy.

"I'd like to be famous," said Mr. Dooley, "an' have money enough to buy off all threatenin' bi-ographers."

Mr. Dooley Says, p. 14;
Boston Globe, January 13, 1907

361. On Diplomacy as a Job

Boston Globe, January 20, 1907

362. On the Army Canteen

"Th' on'y thing a Congressman isn't afraid iv is th' on'y thing I'd be afraid if, an' that is bein' a Congressman." Mr. Dooley makes fun of the effort of a women's group to abolish the army canteen. "Dhrink never made a man betther, but it has made manny a man think he was betther. A little iv it lifts ye out iv th' mud where chance has thrown ye; a little more makes ye think th' stains on ye'er coat are appylets; a little more dhrops ye back into th' mud again. It's a frind to thim that ar-re cold to it an' an inimy to those that love it most."

Mr. Dooley Says, p. 110;
Boston Globe, January 27, 1907

363. On Sir Aleck of Jamaica

An earthquake shakes up the "Anglo-Saxon Alliance."

Boston Globe, February 3, 1907

364. On Flying Machines

Mr. Dooley doesn't believe in flying machines.

Boston Globe, February 17, 1907

246

365. On Expert Testimony

"What's th' diff-rence between (expert testimony) an' perjury," asked Mr. Hennessy.

"Ye pay ye're money an' take ye're choice," said Mr. Dooley.

Mr. Dooley Says, p. 168;
Choice of Law, p. 22;
Boston Globe, February 24, 1907

366. On the Bachelor Tax

Mr. Dooley Says, p. 40;
Boston Globe, March 3, 1907

367. On Women Suffrage

" 'Ain't we intelligent enough?' says she. " 'Ye're too intelligent,' says I. 'But intelligence don't give ye a vote.' " 'What does, thin,' says she. 'Well,' says I, 'enough iv ye at wan time wantin' it enough. . . . But don't ask for rights, Take thim. An' don't ask anyone to give thim to ye. A right that is handed to ye f'r nawthin' has something th' matther with it. . . . I didn't fight f'r th' rights I'm told I enjye, though to tell th' thruth I enjye me wrongs more; but some wan did. Some time some fellow was prepared to lay down his life, or betther still, th' other fellow's, f'r th' right to vote." '

Mr. Dooley Says, p. 25;
Boston Globe, March 10, 1907

368. On Music

Boston Globe, March 24, 1907

369. On Things Spiritual

(Mr. Dooley disputes that the human soul can be weighed).

"How can I know annything, whin I haven't puzzled out what I am mesilf. I'm Dooley, ye say, but ye're only a casual obsarver. Ye don't care annything about me details. Ye look at me with a gin'ral eye. Nawthin' that happens to me really hurts ye.

"Ye say, I'll go over to see Dooley sometimes, but more often ye say, 'I'll go over to Dooley's.'

"I'm a house to ye, wan iv a thousand that look like a row iv model wurrkinmen's cottages. I'm a post to hitch ye'er silences to. I'm always about th' same to ye."

"But to me I'm a millyon Dooleys, an' all iv thim sthrangers to ME. I niver know which wan iv thim is comin' in. I'm like a hotel keeper with on'y wan bed an' a millyon guests, who come wan at a time an' tumble each other out.

"I set up late at night an' pass th' bottle with a gay an' careless Dooley that hasn't a sorrow in th' wurruld, an' suddenly I look up an' see settin' acrost fr'm me a gloomy wretch that fires th' dhrink out iv th' window an' chases me to bed.

"I'm just gettin' used to him whin another Dooley comes in, a cross, cantankerous, crazy fellow that insists on eatin' breakfast with me. An' so it goes. I know more about mesilf than annybody knows, an' I know nawthin'. Though I'd make a map fr'm mem'ry an' gossip iv anny other man, f'r mesilf I'm still uncharted.

"So what's th' use iv thryin' to know annything less important. Don't thry... Ye've got to start in believin' befure ye can find a reason f'r ye'er belief.... I'll niver get anny medal f'r makin' anny man give up his belief. If I see a fellow with a chube on his eye an' hear him hollerin' 'Hooray, I've discovered a new planet,' I'll be th' last man in th' wurruld to brush th' fly off th' end iv th' telescope."

Best, p. 1;

Mr. Dooley Says, p. 123;
Boston Globe, March 31, 1907

370. Mr. Dooley Discusses War

Mr. Dooley disparages Carnegie's peace conference. He asks where are the parades for peace.

Boston Globe, May 19, 1907

371. On the New Baby

A son is born to the Spanish throne.

Boston Globe, June 2, 1907

372. On the Call of the Wild

(Mr. Dooley on animal books that give the animals human traits). "There's th' hippypotamus. He don't look to be full iv sentiment, but ye never can tell. Manny an' achin' heart beats behind a cold an' sloppy exteeryor...."

"Well," said Mr. Hennessy. "Tiddy Rosenfelt is right. A fellow that writes books f'r childher ought to write th' truth."

"Th' little presiouses wudden't read thim," said Mr. Dooley. "Annyway, th' truth is a tough boss in lithrachoor. He don't pay even boord wages, an' if ye go to wurrk f'r him ye want to have a job on th' side."

Mr. Dooley Says, p. 180;
Boston Globe, June 9, 1907

373. On the Decay of Baseball

(A panegyric on baseball). "Baseball, like war, is for th' boys. Whin a man is twenty-five they begin to call him 'old man Kelly'; whin he's thirty th' papers advise th' aujience to be kind to him, because he has seen better days; he's not nachrally as spry as a young or

middle-aged man, but baseball must be played with th'
head as well as th' legs; an' if he lives an' holds down
a job till thirty-five, they note that his intellect is
wabbling th' same as his knees an' rayspictfully suggist
that he go off somewhere an' curl up an' die."

Boston Globe, June 16, 1907

374. On What to Do with Roosevelt

A Harvard professor doesn't think T.R. is qualified to
be President of Harvard: 'It is a very laudanum
ambition, but is he qualified f'r th' job? I think not. It
is perfectly nachral that a man who has held th'
comparatively innocint place iv prisidint iv th' United
States shud want to go higher.' ... "Yes, sir, 'tis a
gr-reat question what we'll do with our ex-prisidints.
But it ain't ra-aly much iv a question, afther all, d'ye
mind. . . But it must be a hard job to let go iv. . . . 'Tis
th' gr-reatest thing in th' histhry iv th' wurruld that a
man that's held this job shud be willin' to dhrop down
to th' sthreet level where he's li'ble to be run over be a
dhray if he isn't careful."

Boston Globe, June 23, 1907

375. On the Japanese Scare

(Mr. Dooley on American sensitivity to affronting the
Japanese). "In th' good old days we wudden't have
thought life was worth living if we cudden't insult a
foreigner. That's what they were for. When I was
sthrong, befure old age deprived me iv most iv me
pathritism an' other infantile disordhers, I niver saw a
Swede, a Hun. . . that I din't give him th' shoulder. . . .
If 'twas right to belong to wan naytionality, 'twas
wrong to belong to another. . . . There ar-re no frinds in
cards or wurruld pollyticks."

Now and Forever, p. 291;

Mr. Dooley Says, p. 193;
Boston Globe, June 30, 1907

376. On the Presidential Candidates

American Magazine, July 1907

377. On The Rising of the Subject Races

"A prophet, Hinnissy, is a man that forsees throuble. No wan wud listen a minyit to anny prophet that prophesized pleasant days. . . . We've been awfully good to (the subject races). We sint thim mission'ries to teach thim th' error iv their religyon, . . . We put up palashal goluf coorses in their cimitries. . . It's no laughin' matther, I tell ye. A subjick race is on'y funny whin it's ra-aly subjick. . . . An' nawthin' makes a man so mad an' so scared as whin something he looked down on as infeeryor tur-rns on him. . . . If th' naygurs down south iver got together an' flew at their masters ye'd hear no more coon songs f'r a while. It's our conceit makes us supeeryor. Take it out iv us an' we ar-re th' same as th' rest."

Mr. Dooley Says, p. 50;
Boston Globe, July 14, 1907

378. On the Sport of Kings

"They talk about college profissors bein' undherpaid. But how about us retail liquor dealers? A colledge profissor spills careless thoughts out iv his head to mere childher that don't dare to fight back. Ye niver heard if a misinformed gradyate returnin' afther five years to whack th' profissor in th' eye because he'd been taught that a man can make a fortune writin' pothry f'r th' pa-apers. But my classes ar-re composed iv able bodied men, manny iv thim far advanced in dhrink, an'

I've got to know what I'm talkin' about, an' that's hard,
an' I've got to know what they're talkin' about, an'
that's almost impossible. . . . I suppose ye can't stop people fr'm gambling. I don't know that I wud if I cud. It
seems to take thir minds off th' more coarse ways iv
makin' money, like wurruk an' business. . . ."

Boston Globe, July 21, 1907

379. On the Hague Conference

Best, p. 140;
Mr. Dooley Says, p. 204;
Choice of Law, p. 118;
Boston Globe, July 28, 1907

380. On Political Principles

On Fairbanks as a candidate and a lack of principles to
fight for in the coming election.

Boston Globe, August 4, 1907

381. On Drugs

"I wondher why ye can always read a doctor's bill an' ye
niver can read his purscription." (The agony of calling a
doctor when house calls were a common practice. The
use of placebos).

Best, p. 251;
Mr. Dooley Says, p. 89;
Boston Globe, August 11, 1907

382. On the Big Fine

"An appeal, Hinnissy, is where ye ask wan coort to
show its contempt f'r another coort. . . . I have great
respect f'r th' joodicyary, as fine a lot iv cross an'
indignant men as ye'll find annywhere. I have th' same
respect f'r thim that they have f'r each other. . . .
Ginrally speakin' judges are lawyers. They get to be

252

judges because they have what Hogan calls th' joodicyal timpramint, which is why annybody gets a job. Th' other kind iv people won't take a job. They'd rather take a chance."

Mr. Dooley Remembers, p. 299 (non dialect);
Best, p. 149;
Now and Forever, p. 281;
Mr. Dooley Says, p. 158;
Choice of Law, p. 41;
Boston Globe, August 18, 1907

383. On Work

"A strike is a wurr'kin' man's vacation ... I've noticed near all sthrikes occur in th' summer time. Sthrikes come in th' summer time an' lockouts in th' winter... 'Tis a sthrange thing whin we come to think iv it that th' less money a man gets fr his wurruk, th' more nicissry it is to th' wurruld that he shud go on wurrukin'. "

Mr. Dooley Says, p. 78;
Boston Globe, August 25, 1907

384. On a Prince's Visit

The Prince of Sweden visits Newport. "We cudden't injye poverty if we didn't see th' way other people injyes wealth. Ivry time I read about a socyal war at Newport I feel less disturbed about a socyal war in our back alley. . . . An' what wud be th' use iv havin' a rivolution an' desthroyin' thim. They'd on'y be more dangerous without their heads."

Boston Globe, September 1, 1907

385. On the Conduct of a Railroad

On the Illinois Central and one of their boisterous directors' meetings.

Boston Globe, September 15, 1907

386. On Ocean Travel

The myth of luxury liners.

Mr. Dooley Says, p. 67
Boston Globe, September 22, 1907

387. On Another Insult to the Japanese

An incident in Vancouver embroils Japan, U.S. and England into an international problem.

Boston Globe, September 29, 1907

388. On the Choice of a Career

(Mr. Dooley cautions adults on advising their children). "No sir, I wudden't know how to advise a young man, but I've often thought if I had me life to live over again I'd be a lawyer. 'Tis a noble profissyon. (Mr. Dooley describes the profession then and now). 'Tis a grand profissyon. An' if a man's a lawyer he can be ivrything else. Whin we want a man to do annything in this counthry fr'm conductin' a war to runnin' a polis foorce, we hire a lawyer."

Choice of Law, p. 33;
Boston Globe, October 6, 1907

389. On the President's Activities

T.R.'s tennis game; retirement speech.

Boston Globe, October 20, 1907

390. On Finances

(Mr. Dooley on a run on the banks). "Whin I see wan man with a shovel on his shouldher dodgin' eight thousand autymobills I begin to think 'tis time to put me money in me boot... Panics an' circuses, as Father

Kelly says, are f'r th' amusement iv th' poor. . . . As long
as there's a Hinnissy in th' wurruld, an' he has a shovel,
an' there's something f'r him to shovel, we'll be all
right, or pretty near all right. "Don't ye think Rosenfelt
has shaken public confidence?" asked Mr. Hennessy.
"Shaken it!" said Mr. Dooley. "I think he give it a good
kick just as it jumped off th' roof."

Best, p. 160;
Mr. Dooley Says, p. 59;
Boston Globe, November 3, 1907

391. On Corporal Punishment

(Mr. Dooley analyzes the relationship between adult
and child). "I wudden't give anny wan th' right to lick
a child that wanted to lick a child." (The issue is
whether school teachers should be able to discipline
a child).

Boston Globe, November 10, 1907

392. On the Passing Show

Mr. Dooley on the loss of anger toward the rich. Taft
takes a world tour.

Boston Globe, November 17, 1907

393. On Football

"I haven't been able to get up as much interest in
futball since I larned it wasn't played be th' murdhrous
ruffyans that I see th' pitchers iv in th' pa-aper, but be
old gintlemen who figured out varyous forms of assault
an' batthery an' deception f'r childher to practice on
each other. If I had me way I'd have all th' games
preceded be a match between th' coaches. . . . "I think
our young fellows take their game too seeryously," said
Mr. Hennessy.

255

"I don't know about that, but I know us old fellows
do," said Mr. Dooley.

Boston Globe, December 1, 1907

394. On the Spirit of Christmas

(New York is debating as to whether children should be
allowed to sing Christmas carols in school). "Th'
sufferings I endure fr'm gettin' prisints is offset be th'
pleasure I inflict in givin' them."

Boston Globe, December 15, 1907

395. On the Sailing of the Fleet

(Mr. Dooley discounts foreign criticism of our fleet
sailing in the Pacific. He appraises Japan as a world
power, and has Admiral Evans thinking) "that th' Japs
were all right gin'rally an' cud sail an' fight too, an'
they'd picked up quite a good deal about navy matthers
fr'm us, an' he wudden't be surprised if they give a good
account iv thimsilves some day." In debunking experts
on naval matters, Mr. Dooley says that "the rale naval
experts an' th' other kinds ar-re all at sea."

Boston Globe, December 22, 1907

396. On Congress

Mr. Dooley describes the creature comforts accorded
Congressmen in their new building.

American Magazine, January 1908, p. 237

397. On Hard Times

There is nothing else but hard times for the poor. "No,
sir, th' people I'm sorry f'r are th' rich. . . . To have
nawthin' an' thin to have a little less, doesn't muss ye
at all. But to have it to burn, an' think that ye got it
because ye were wiser an' smarter an' bigger thin

256

somewan else, an' thin to lose it because iv a sinseless panic, is a horrible blow to a man's pride." Mr. Dooley comments on the plight of bankers.

American Magazine, February, 1908, p. 339

398. On Philosophers

"I refer to th' Matsachoosetts not th' Missoury Jameses," said Mr. Dooley. "It's a good thing (philosophers) have an exhaust valve. If they cudden't talk they'd surely explode with gr-reat damage to surroundin' thought."

American Magazine, March 1908, p. 540

399. On the Temperance Wave

American Magazine, April 1908, p. 599

400. On the End of Life

"There's very little rale grief at a fun'ral. I've often pictured me own wind-up in me mind an' thought iv thousands iv people bein' so prostrated be me demise that they cud not attind to th' jooties iv life f'r a year.... But I know it ain't so."

American Magazine, May 1908, p. 93

401. On Diplomacy

"I'm not sure that I'd want to be an ambassadure if I iver had to come home again.... D'ye think republics are ongrateful?" asked Mr. Hennessy. "I do," said Mr. Dooley. "That's why they continue to be republics."

American Magazine, June 1908, p. 107

402. On the Democratic Party

"No wan can say what anny ten Dimmycrats will do whin they gather together f'r th' good iv th' counthry, in a hall." Mr. Dooley recites the "denounce and deplore" planks of the party out of power. Mr. Dooley discusses the candidates, Wilson included, with the usual lack of courtesy. "F'r, Hinnissy, a man is not made a Republican or a Dimmycrat be platforms or candydates. A man's a Republican or he's a Dimmycrat, an' that's all ye can say about it onless he's an indepindent, an' thin he's a Republican."

"I suppose th' counthry will be safe with ayther candydate," said Mr. Hennessy.

"It will be," said Mr. Dooley. "It will be safe with ayther candydate, or with both, or with nayther."

American Magazine, July 1908, p. 301

403. On General Grant and the Facts of History

Mr. Dooley comments on whether General Grant's drinking is a fit subject for history. The Muse of History is a "frivolous, light-headed, evil-spoken old hen that goes flyin' around fr'm house to house pickin' up all th' gossip she can hear an' writin' it down in her little note-book. An' she don't much care whether what she hears is thrue or not.... Th' splendid deeds ye have done, ye'er courage in comin' into th' wurruld at all, ye'er fortitude in stayin' in afther ye come in, ye'er almost reckless bravery in gettin' marrid, ye'er patient heroism in votin' th' Dimmycratic ticket f'r forty years, an' ye'er dauntless energy in goin' to wurruk six days in th' week an' to church on th' seventh, may be alooded to in th' inthraduction. If I had a son I'd say to him: 'Me boy, be good if ye can, but if ye can't be good don't be gr-reat, or 'twill get into histhry.' 'Tis a good thing to keep out iv what th' actors call th' spotlight, annyhow. It shows all th' spots.... D'ye suppose that if Gin'ral Grant knew what was comin' to him he wud've put in

258

four or five years chasin' haughty an' fleet rebels over bad roads, havin' himsilf shot at be people he had scarcely met, catchin' th' rhoomatism an' th' fever an' ague, bein' bitten be mosquitoes, washin' in a tin basin, talkin' to congressyonal comities an' suffrin' all th' other horrors iv war?"

American Magazine, August 1908, p. 331

404. On Big Game Hunting

"Tiddy Rosenfelt" (Theodore Roosevelt) plans a hunting trip and Mr. Dooley says some unkind things about big game hunters.

American Magazine, September 1908, p. 521

405. On the Olympic Games

(Mr. Dooley sees the Olympics as a contest between the mother country and the daughter country). "Were ye iver an athlete?" asked Mr. Hennessy. ". . . th' more me intellect an' me waist developed th' slower become me feet, an' I give it up. . . . We will niver know who's th' fastest runner iv th' wurruld ontil we have a race where ivry wan will be dhressed suitable f'r th' occasion whin he is pursooed be an insane man with a gun. . . . Rowin' is all right, but th' question ought to be . . . whether he can row a good-lookin' girl who is rockin' th' boat in Douglas Park with patent-leather shoes on his feet." "Do you think th' English are good losers?" asked Mr. Hennessy. "Good losers, says ye? Good losers? I'll back thim to lose anny time they start."

American Magazine, October 1908, p. 615

406. On Uplifting the Farmers

American Magazine, November 1908, p. 95

407. On a New Literary Light

An editor interviews "Jawn D." Rockefeller. On Jawn D.'s biography: "Jawn D. hasn't anny idee that he iver done wrong to annywan."

American Magazine, December 1908, p. 187

408. On the Retiring President

The changed attitude of a cabinet to a lame duck president. T.R., on the contrary, acts as if he might return to the White House after the inauguration of Taft.

Boston Globe, February 7, 1909

409. On Heroes and History

(The sinking of the Republic and the heroism, short lived, of the telegraph operator. Revisionists on Caesar and Nero). "Th' further ye get away fr'm anny peeryod th' betther ye can write about it. Ye are not subjict to interruptions be people that were there." (On a future historian writing about the year 1909): "Th' principal occypations iv th' people were murdher, divoorce, prize-fightin', lynching, marathon racin', abduction, burglary an' Salomying.... So intent were th' people on their barbarous pasttimes that th' name iv th' prisidint at th' time has been lost...."

Best, p. 201;
Will, p. 102;
Boston Globe, February 14, 1909

410. On the Theatre

"Well," said Mr. Dooley, "a lot iv narrow minded people who have no idee iv Art at all are makin' an attack on th' modhern stage.... Sthrange to say, both sides admit that th' theaytre is an idjacational institute. I niver thought iv it that way. I always supposed that

260

people wint to th' theaytre because they had no comfortable homes to go to or to f'rgit that th' dishes weren't washed, or to laugh or cry or have a spell iv coughing where it wud atthract attintion.... Well, annyhow, Hinnissy, Morality an' Art are clinched an 'tis always amusin' to me to see thim two great champeens fly at each other. I will say wan thing about Art. It's a great match-maker. Ye won't get Art to go on until he's counted up th' house ... Well, annyhow, it don't make much diff'rence to me. I am willin' to have th' stage made dacint or I'm willin' to have it go on as it is in th' sarvice iv art, because I niver go to th' theaytre if I can help it.... (Mr. Dooley goes to the theater) These here devotees iv th' dhrama are settin' with their coats in their laps an' their knees closely pressed agin th' seats iv th' row in front.... Th' space thus left between thim an th' backs iv th' people in front is meant f'r me thriumphal enthry."

Boston Globe, February 21, 1909

411. On the Presidency

Mr. Dooley on the electoral college.

Boston Globe, February 28, 1909

412. On the Return of the Fleet

(Court martial of an officer for drinking. The inanity of experts). "War is more a business than it used to be. Wanst it was pothry; now it's mathymatics.... Maybe 'tis a good thing, Hinnissy. Th' less war is like a picnic iv th' Longshoremen's Union, th' less wars there'll be."

Boston Globe, March 7, 1909

261

413. On Political Events

Taft appoints Democrats to his cabinet; the conspiracy against Uncle Joe Cannon.
Boston Globe, March 28, 1909

414. On the Burning Issue

(The racial implications of the Johnson-Jeffries fight). "I suppose civilization is a failure, but thin civilization always has been a failure, as far back as I can raymimber. I niver yet knew th' time whin human nature wasn't tearin' away fr'm them that wud lead it up to higher an' betther things an' runnin' into th' back yard to play in th' mud." (A portrait of "Jawn L. Sullivan). . . . Nowadays, be hivins, th' champeens are such inimies that they sildom meet. It takes as long to arrange a fight as it does to get up a European war. First there is a challenge, thin a year's engagement skippin' th' rope an' makin' faces at a lookin' glass in a variety theaytre; thin th' challenge is accipted an' th' champeens go on th' road f'r another engagement; thin a number iv our leadin' bankers are called in to fi-nance th' encounter. This takes another year. . ."
Boston Globe, April 4, 1909

415. On Women Suffrage

Mr. Dooley makes fun of women voting (polling places in department stores, etc.), but recognizes the male has no better qualification for voting. He concludes, "Annyhow it won't be a bad thing. What this country needs is voters that knows something about housekeeping."
American Magazine, June 1909, p. 198

416. On Turkish Politics

(The miserable life of royalty). "The on'y man ye need to be afraid iv is th' man that's afraid iv ye. An' that's what makes a tyrant. He's scared to death . . . I want no man to fear me. I'd hate to be more of a coward thin I am."

"What ar-re those Turkish athrocities I've been r-readin' about?" said Mr. Hennessy.

"I don't know," said Mr. Dooley. "I don't keep thim. Have a cigar."

Mr. Dooley Says, p. 214;
Boston Globe, June 13, 1909

417. On Castro's Troubles

Venezuela's troubles. The suspect role of Washington in Castro's overthrow.

Boston Globe, June 20, 1909

418. On England and Germany

(The docility of the German-American and the aggresiveness of Germany. The rumor of a German invasion of England.)

"D'ye think they'll have a war? I hope so," asked Mr. Hennessy.

"Ye can't tell," said Mr. Dooley. "They won't if they're not afraid iv each other. But ye can't tell what a proud nation will do whin it's scared to death."

Boston Globe, June 27, 1909

419. On the Tariff

(Mr. Dooley reviews the tariff bill). "Th' likes iv ye wud want to see th' tariff rejooced with a jack plane or an ice pick. But th' tariff has been a good frind to some iv thim boys an' its a frind iv frinds iv some iv th' others, an' they don't intend to be rough with it. . . . Me congressman sint me a copy iv th' tariff bill th' other day. . . 'Tis a fine piece iv summer lithrachoor. . . . I'm

in favor iv havin' it read on th' Foorth iv July instead
iv th' declaration iv independence. It gives ye some idee
iv th' kind iv gloryous govermint we're livin undher, to
see our fair Columbia puttin' her brave young arms out
an' defindin' th' products iv our soil... Practically
ivrything nicissry to existence comes in free. What, f'r
example, says ye? I'll look. Here it is. Curling
stones.... Lookin' down th' list I see that divvy-divvy
is free also. This was let in as a compliment to Sinitor
Aldhrich. It's his motto.... Well, sir, if nobody else has
read th' debates on th' tariff bill, I have.... 'I am
heartily in sympathy with th' sinitor fr'm Louisyanny,'
says th' sinitor fr'm Virginya. 'I loathe th' tariff. Fr'm
me ariliest days I was brought up to look on it with
pizenous hathred. At manny a con'vintion ye cud hear
me whoopin' again it. But if there is such a lot iv this
monsthrous iniquity passin' around, don't Virginya get
none? How about th' mother iv prisidents? Ain't she
goin' to have a grab at annything? Gintlemen, I do not
ask, I demand rights f'r me commonwealth. I will talk
here ontil July fourth, nineteen hundherd an' eighty
two again th' proposed hellish tax on feather beds
onless something is done f'r th' tamarack bark iv old
Virginya.'

"A sinitor: 'What's it used f'r?'

"Th' sinitor fr'm Virginya: 'I do not quite know....
But there's a frind iv mine, a lile Virginyan, who makes
it an' he needs th' money.'

"Th' argymints iv th' sinitor fr'm Virginya are
onanswerable,' says Sinitor Aldhrich....

"An' so it goes, Hinnissy. Niver a sordid worrud,
mind ye, but ivrything done on th' fine old principle iv
give an' take."

Best, p. 86;

264

Now and Forever, p. 268;
Mr. Dooley Says, p. 144;
Boston Globe, July 4, 1909

420. On Washington News

Mr. Dooley compares the Roosevelt and Taft methods of running the country. He suspects Senator Aldrich is in charge.

Boston Globe, August 1, 1909

421. On Books

(Mr. Dooley is not sold on Dr. Eliot's five foot shelf of books) "I don't read books. They are too stimylatin'. I can get th' same wrong idees iv life from dhrink." (But he welcomes Dr. Eliot into the) "... cillybrated univarsity iv th' Wicked Wurruld.... Th' coorse is hard. Ivry man, woman an' child is profissor an' student to ye. Th' examinations are tough. Ye niver know whin they're goin' to take place or what they'll be about. Profissor Eliot may pass ye on'y to have Profissor Hinnissy turn ye down. But there's wan sure thing — ye'll be grajated." (But Hogan prefers reading): "Ye may be right," says he. "But 'tis too late to do annything with me. An' I don't care. It may hurt me in th' eyes iv me fellow-counthrymen, but look at th' fun I get out iv it. I wudden't thrade th' injanyous, wicked people an' th' saints that I see f'r all th' poor dull half-an'-half crathers that ye find in th' wurruld," he says."

Mr. Dooley Says, p. 134;
Boston Globe, August 8, 1909

422. On Vacations

"... not long ago I made up me mind not to be th' slave iv me vacation.... I take it whiniver I feel like it....

265

While ye think ye are talkin' to me, at that very minyit I may be floatin' on me back in th' Atlantic Ocean or climbin' a mountain in Switzerland, yodellin' to mesilf.... Most iv me frinds take their vacations long afther they are overdue.... F'r a week or two they spind their avenins larnin' th' profissyon iv baggageman, atin' off thrunks be day an' sleepin' on thim be night.... Whiniver (his friend) sees her readin' advertisements iv th' summer resorts ... he takes her down to th' deepo an' shows her th' people goin' on their vacations an comin' back. Thin he gives her a boat ride in th' park, takes her to th' theaytre an' th' next mornin' she wakes up with hardly anny sign iv her indisposition.... But th' kind iv vacation I take does ye some good. It is well within me means ... I don't have to carry anny baggage. I don't pay anny railroad fares. I'm not bothered be mosquitoes or rain. In fact, it's on rainy days that I thravel most. I'm away most iv th' time.... Well, well, what places I have seen. An' I always see thim at their best. Th' on'y way to see anny place at its best is niver to go there.... An' wan iv th' great comforts iv my kind iv a vacation is that I always know what's goin' on at home.... Here's th' inside news iv a cillybrated murdher thrile blossomin' out in th' heat. Here's a cillybrated lawyer goin' to th' cillybrated murdherer an' demandin' an increase in th' honoraryum iv his cilybrated collague. Lawyers don't take money. What they get f'r their public sarvices in deludin' a jury is th' same as an offerin' in a church. Ye don't give it to thim openly. Ye sind thim a bunch iv sweet peas with th' money in it. This here larned counsel got wan honoraryum. But whin things begun to look tough f'r his protegee he suggisted another honoraryum. Honoraryum is fr'm th' latin wurruds honor an' aryum mainin', 'I need th' money.'" (Mr.

266

Dooley concludes his essay discussing President Taft's golf game.)

"What kind iv a game is goluf?" asked Mr. Hennessy. "Why do they call it rile an' ancient?"

"I don't know", said Mr. Dooley, "onless it is because th' prisidint iv th' United States has just took it up."

Mr. Dooley Says, p. 227;
Boston Globe, August 15, 1909

423. On Flying Machines

(Mr. Dooley comments on the ignominious refusal of the Wright Brothers to accept an invitation to a party while in England). " 'No wan' says this here pathrite (Hogan), 'no wan deplores more thin me th' class iv Americans wan sees so often abroad. But ye must raymimber,' says he, 'that we are not all alike.' An' it's th' same way ivrywhere in Europe. Americans, th' right kind iv Americans with loanable money, are pop'lar ivrywhere. . . ." (Mr. Dooley concludes that compared to a goose, we're poor flyers and will always be).

Boston Globe, September 5, 1909

424. On the North Pole

"Who do I think gets th' honor iv bein' there first? Faith, I'm not goin' to decide. As Doc Cook says, th' honor is great enough f'r both, an' there's little enough iv it, as it is. . . . I opened up th' pa-aper an' see that Peary had discovered th' North Pole too. Sthrange he didn't see Doctor Cook. . . . Th' most important scientific obsarvation iv ayether iv thim is that he didn't see th' other. . . . As f'r me, I believe thim both. . . . I'll take their wurrud for it. I don't ask f'r no affidavies. Th' best proof ye can have that a man done this thing is that he was crazy enough to want to do

it. . . . Th' toughest thing a man who discovers th' pole
has to face is to come home an' say he's done it. . . .
Thank th' Lord, I've niver discovered th' North Pole, an'
so me repytation f'r truth an' veracity will go on bein'
good among sthrangers. Yet I don't know that I
wudden't be aisier in me mind, knowin' ivrybody
thought I was a liar, thin if I thought ivrybody else was
a liar."

"Who will th' North Pole belong to?" asked Mr.
Hennessy. . . . "It's ondecided . . . but I think Denmark
will get it." "Why?" asked Mr. Hennessy. "It will go to
th' loser," said Mr. Dooley.

Boston Globe, September 12, 1909

425. On the Topic of the Hour

(As the Cook-Peary controversy invades Dooley's bar,
he comments): "I make out ye'er gin'ral dhrift."

"Th' other day, Hinnissy, I told ye that I thought both
iv these here inthrepid explorers had discovered th'
North Pole. . . . I'm forced to say that nayther iv thim
was at th' North Pole. . . . Annyhow if there ar-re goin'
to be medals disthributed f'r it I'm goin' to put in a
claim. No wan has suffered more in th' cause iv science
thin I have. . . . I have pushed through thousands iv
columns that separate us fr'm our pleasant readin'
in th' pa-apers."

Boston Globe, September 19, 1909

426. On the Magazines

Mr. Dooley thinks a magazine should clearly mark
what it considers to be literature. "A man don't want to
dodge around through almost impenthrable pomes an'
reform articles to find a pair iv suspinders or a shavin'
soap. . . . There ain't anny doubt iv it, whin it comes to

268

advertisin', that city iv New York is th' modhren Athens. . . ." "D'ye think lathrachoor is improved since Shakespeare's day?" said Mr. Hennessy. "It has more to eat," said Mr. Dooley.

American Magazine, October 1909, p. 539

427. On the Cost of Living

"(Idleness) saps th' moral fiber an' is th' ambition iv all." Mr. Dooley says the cost of living has "always been th' same f'r ye an' th' likes iv ye."

American Magazine, January 1910, p. 325

428. On the Political Situation

(The rise of the Democratic Party). "Gin'rally speakin' a dimmycrat was an ondesirable immygrant that had got past Ellis island. . . . Mind ye, I'm not rejoicin' over Tiddy Rosenfelt, but it's pleasant to be settin' here in me rockin' chair lookin' out th' windore an' seein' somewan besides mesilf pursooed down th' sthreet be a mob composed iv th' joodicyary, th' bar assocyation an' th' clearin' house comity. . . . Th' dimmycrat party is on'y fash'onable whin it's a kind iv a timpry shelter f'r republicans that have left home because they object to th' smell iv house clanin'."

Boston Globe, November 6, 1910

429. On Flying

(Mr. Dooley is not enthusiastic about the future of the airplane). "I'm ready to shout an' cheer over anny new invintion. . . But I ain't sure that th' man that invinted suspendhers oughtn't have a front cage in th' Hall of Fame."

Boston Globe, November 13, 1910

430. On Thanksgiving

"I don't think th' iditors pay enough attention to them. . . . Ivry year th' prisident iv th' United States, th' gov'nor, th' mayor . . . an' th' coroner goes into th' back room, locks th' dure, takes a pair iv shears in his hands an' tells us officyally, mind ye, what we've got to be thankful f'r. It's a tur-rble jooty f'r some iv these statesmen so soon afther iliction. (Mr. Dooley offers a few proclamations that executives would like to give.) . . . I'll be thankful on Thanksgivin' Day whin ivrybody is friendly accordin' to law, an' I'll be thankful th' day afther whin there's no legal raison why I shud be. . . . "Do ye think Taft and Rosenfelt are friendly?"

"They might be," said Mr. Dooley, "if they didn't have so manny friends."

Boston Globe, November 20, 1910

431. On Home Life

"Th' newspa-apers ar-re a gr-reat blessing," said Mr. Dooley. . . . If it wasn't f'r thim I'd have no society fit to assocyate with — on'y people like ye'ersilf an' Hogan. But th' pa-apers opens up life to me an' gives me a speakin' acquaintance with th' whole wurruld." (Mr. Dooley describes the peek it gives him into the homes of the aristocracy). "Th' life iv th' rich is far more home-like thin ye think." (Mr. Dooley describes the turbulent marriage of Mulligan J. Billhooley's daughter to a "Fr-rinch jook.") "Whin they set down to th' table wan night f'r supper, th' duchess happened to pass th' remark that th' jook was overthrained in th' matter iv dhrink." (Mr. Dooley also comments on the propensity of high society to marry royalty).

Will, p. 47;
Boston Globe, November 27, 1910

432. On Revolutions

"... but while they're goin' on I play thim to lose. (The Mexican Revolution analyzed. A portrait of life in Mexico and also of Diaz.) "Annyhow, whiniver I see a rivolution started th' first thing I ask is, What backin' has it got? Who is th' banker? ... A rivolution which isn't a good investment is on'y disordherly conduck. ... Ye can get anny right-minded young fellow to shed his blood in a revolution, th' same as in a fut-ball match. But till somebody will shed his money th' revolution don't ra-aly start."

Boston Globe, December 4, 1910

433. [This number reserved.]

434. On the Education of Mr. Wilson

(Mr. Dooley runs down the list of democratic candidates: Foss, Hearst, Wilson, etc.). "But somehow or other ye niver think a frind is fit to be President. ... Five months befure th' convintion meets, we've made all th' mateeryal about oursilves that th' Republicans need f'r their campaign." (A profile of Wilson and his troubles as a candidate) "Don't ye think Taft has a chance?" asked Mr. Hennessy. "I can't tell," said Mr. Dooley, "Has he iver take wan?"

Boston Globe, February 11, 1912

435. On the Orange Revolution

(Mr. Dooley on the Irish quest for home rule). " 'Tis a sthrange thing, Hinnissy, how th' Orangemen keep their prejudices an' ar-re still singin' thim foolish old songs about things that happened hundherds iv years

271

ago. . . . Relijon is a quare thing. Be itsilf it's all right.
But sprinkle a little pollyticks into it an' dinymite is
bran flour compared with it. Alone it prepares a man f'r
a bether life. Combined with pollyticks it hurries him
to it. . . . But ye'd wondher why a hero that's calkin'
seams or forgin' bolts in a Belfast shipyard wud care
who ruled Ireland. . ."

Will, p. 175;
Boston Globe, February 18, 1912

436. On Paying Homage to Royalty

"I'll say this about th' methroplis iv this counthry: It
sizes people up right. Ye can guess a man's worth
within a dollar be th' way New York rayceives him."
("th' jook iv Connaught" visits New York and gives Mr.
Dooley another opportunity to object to the American
subservience to British royalty).

Boston Globe, February 25, 1912

437. On the Friendship of Col. Roosevelt and President Taft

"But whin a man gits sintimintal over his frin'ship f'r
me I always expict ayther a touch or a punch." (Mr.
Dooley notes the cooling trend as Taft settles
comfortably into the presidency).

Boston Globe, March 3, 1912

438. On the Hundred Greatest Men

"Twas Andhrew Carnayga started it, iv coorse." (Mr.
Dooley has trouble after Shakespeare, Washington,
and Lincoln). "What makes a man gr-reat annyhow. It

isn't because he's good, though it may be because he isn't. . . It ain't because he's betther iddycated thin others . . . It ain't because he's pretty. . . . It ain't because they're brave. . . . It ain't because they're forchnit. . . . An' it ain't because they plan things in advance . . . Father Kelly says a man's great who can do th' wan thing he knows how to do betther thin most annywan else. That is, if he has th' luck to cash in. . . . I'm goin' to make out me own list . . . An' th' name I'll put down forth is th' fellow that invinted suspinders. . . . ivry time I look down at me legs an' see they're properly dhraped I think kindly iv this janius. . . . an invention that has made it possible f'r mankind to fight th' battles iv th' wurruld with both hands free." (Mr. Dooley says other countries would have different lists, and each profession would have its own preferences. Mr. Dooley suggests Mr. Hennessy): "F'r cinchries th' wurruld had been full iv talk. Now f'r th' first time there's a man who cud listen."

"But I haven't been listenin'," said Mr. Hennessy.

"Well," said Mr. Dooley, "if ye won't talk and ye won't listen ye can have ye'er trunk checked to th' Hall iv Fame tonight. Ye'er ilicted."

Will, p. 17 (Famous Men);
Boston Globe, March 10, 1912

439. On St. Patrick's Day

(St. Patrick) "niver showed his saintly character betther thin whin he fixed on th' Sivinteenth iv March f'r his birthday. . . . he named a day that was sure to fall somewhere in th' middle iv Lent. . . . But ivrybody is an Irishman on Pathrick's day . . . Annyhow, 'tis a good thing to be an Irishman, because people think that all an Irishman does is to laugh without a reason an' fight without an objeck. But ye an' I, Hinnissy, know these things ar-re on'y our diversions. It's a good thing to have people size ye up wrong. Whin they've got ye'er measure ye're in danger."

Best, p. 26;
Will, p. 186;
Boston Globe, March 17, 1912

440. On the Discovery of the South Pole

(Mr. Dooley doesn't think much of Amundsen's discovery)

"It looks to me," said Mr. Hennessy, "that there was nawthin left to explore."

"There's plenty," said Mr. Dooley. "Why, I'm explorin' all th' time. There's wan place I've sailed around a millyon times an' taken me life in me hands thryin' to map out, but all I know is what it looks like at a distance."

"An' what's that?" asked Mr. Hennessy.

"Its name," said Mr. Dooley, "is Hinnissy."

Boston Globe, March 24, 1912

441. On English Politics

(Mr. Dooley plays Hansard. He describes the workings of the British parliament). Hogan says, 'England has a constitution, but nobody iver took th' throuble to write it down, so nobody knows what is in it at anny minit, an' annything that happens is lible to change fr'm day to day. In our blessed counthry,' he says, 'we have a written constitution an' anny schoolboy can read it an' undherstand it if he has been admitted to th' bar an' follows th' decisions iv th' Supreeme coort. This here

274

vinerable docymint was wrote out be th' fathers iv th' republic whin th' republic was in its infancy, an' it's remedies ar-re good f'r teethin, rash, . . . but iv course ye can't find annything in it f'r th' gout . . . an' th' other ailments iv machured manhood, so whin th' republic has a pain in its stomach th' Supreeme coort says: At gr-reat expense we have secured a copy iv th' constitution fr'm a collector iv rare docymints an' we find castherile (castor oil) wud've been imployed by th' foundhers iv th' nation. But this wud be onsuited to th' age iv th' patient an' wud remove th' cause iv th' disease which is part iv th' nature iv r-republics. We have no doubt that if th' cold La-ads that wrote this docymint had lived to our day they wud advise a musthard plasther. Annyhow that's what we intend to slam on. Thin th' patient won't know which is hurtin' him an' will be happy, or ought to be. Holmes J., McKenna J., Hughes J., an' th' Taft judges whose names I've forgot, concurrin. But,' says Hogan, 'in England they make up th' constitution as they go along. . . . As soon as the king reads th' eliction returns an' finds out who is th' boss in th' house iv commons he says to himsilf: . . . I will make him me prime ministher. (Dooley than explains the intricate role of king and prime minister and the workings of the House of Lords).' (Mr. Dooley continues): "Th' whole idee iv a republic is that th' people should have what they think is good f'r thim. But there are more thoughtful pathrites who know that if they want it very much it can't be good f'r thim, so they stop it. Ye start a republic be ask'n' th' people what they want, but ye presarve it be not lettin' thim have it." (Mr. Dooley completes the essay by commenting on Lord Asquith's proposal as to the House of Lords).

Boston Globe, March 31, 1912

275

442. On the Recall of Judges

"Whin a man gets what Hogan calls th' judicyal timper it means he's cross all th' time.... Whin he sint a man down th' road f'r forty or fifty years he always give him such a dhressin' down that th' pris'ner was glad to get away where he'd be safe.... 'Tis funny about th' constitution. It reads plain, but no wan can undherstant it without an' interpreter.... If I iver go into coort th' polis'll have to take me in chains. I'm a gr-reat reader, an' as Hogan says, familyarity with decisions breeds contimpt iv coort.... Don't I think a poor man has a chanst in coort? Iv coorse he has. He has th' same chanst there that he has outside. He has a splendid, poor man's chanst. Annyhow, he ought to stay out iv coort, onless he's done somethin' pleasant to get himsilf there. It's no place f'r him or f'r anny man, rich or poor, to go fortune huntin'.... What is this English common law I read about?" asked Mr. Hennessy. "It's th' law I left Ireland to get away fr'm," said Mr. Dooley. "If it's pursooed me over here I'll go to Chiny."

Choice of Law, p. 168;
Boston Globe, April 14, 1912

443. On the Higher Baseball

"D'ye iver go to a baseball game?" asked Mr. Hennessy. "Not now," said Mr. Dooley. "I haven't got th' intelleck f'r it.... (Mr. Dooley has fun with the scientific explanations of baseball) "Th' two great American spoorts are a good deal alike — pollyticks an' baseball. They're both played be professyonals, th' teams ar-re r-run be fellows that cudden't throw a baseball or stuff a ballot box to save their lives, an' ar-re on'y inthrested in countin' up th' gate receipts.... They're both gr-rand games."

"Speakin' iv pollyticks," said Mr. Hennessy, "who d'ye think'll be illicted?"

"Afther lookin' th' candydates over," said Mr. Dooley, "an' studyin' their qualifications carefully, I can't thruthfully say that I see a prisidintial possibility in sight."

Best, p. 170;
Will, p. 92;
Boston Globe, May 5, 1912

444. On the Campaign

(Mr. Dooley compares compaign styles of the day and yesterdays. He has the candidates visit his bar: T. R., Hearst, Taft) "But if I was a candydate f'r prisidint ye'd niver get me into anny wrangle iv that kind. Ye cudden't see me with a tillyscope. F'r, Hinnissy, th' less ye see iv a man, good or bad, th' more ye think he's betther or worse thin th' rest iv us."

Boston Globe, May 19, 1912

445. On Roosevelt and Caesarism

Mr. Dooley discounts the college professors and editors who are predicting the fall of the American republic.

Boston Globe, June 9, 1912

446. On the Convention

"Am I goin' to th' convintion? What a question to ask a spoortin' charakter. If a fellow was to come to ye an' say: 'Here's a free ticket f'r a combynation iv th' Chicago fire, Saint Bartholomew's massacree, th' battle iv th' Boyne, th' life iv Jesse James, an' th' night iv th' big wind, an' all th' victims will be ye'er thraditional inimies,' wud ye take it or wud ye not?"

Boston Globe, June 16, 1912

447. Mr. Dooley Finds an Old Fashioned Democratic Love Feast

Copyright Chicago Tribune June 25, 1912

448. On the Fight Between Willum Jennings Bryan and Preedytory Wealth

Copyright Chicago Tribune June 27, 1912

449. On the Last Acts of Tired and Homesick Dillygates

Copyright Chicago Tribune, June 28, 1912

450. On Old Age

"Whin a man gets to be over siventy he boasts iv his age. When he passes eighty he's very lible to lie about it. An' whin he's ninety he will throw his wig in th' face iv anny man who insinyates that he ain't th' oldest man in th' wurruld . . . Manny a man that cudden't direct ye to th' drug store on th' corner whin he was thirty will get a respictful hearin' whin age has further impaired his mind. . . .

"Why," said Mr. Hennessy, "ye'd give annything to be twenty-five agin."

"I wudden't," said Mr. Dooley. "Why shud I want to grow old again?"

Best, p. 240;
Will, p. 61;
Boston Globe, July 7, 1912

451. On this Queer Campaign

Mr. Dooley on presidential electors, the intentions of our founding fathers and how they floundered, and the early heating up of the campaign.

Boston Globe, July 14, 1912

278

452. On the Hot Weather

Boston Globe, July 21, 1912

453. On the Olympic Games

(Mr. Dooley ridicules the British suggestion that our athletes are professionals). "Th' older I get th' more I've made up me mind that th' on'y reason annywan is a champeen is because enough people don't thry to take it away fr'm him. . . . Spoorts, Hinnissy, is like war. All th' excuses an' all th' complaints ye hear come fr'm th' noncombytants."

Boston Globe, July 28, 1912

454. On the Metropolis

"How wud ye like to live in New York?" asked Mr. Hennessy. "If I was younger," said Mr. Dooley, "an' more bullet-proof I'd take a chance. There's no doubt it's th' center iv American civilization . . . I'm afraid th' methropolus wud be too sthrenuse afther years iv th' relijious quiet iv Ar-rchey Road an' th' stockyards. . . . Mind ye, I don't know annything about it excipt what I r-read in th' pa-apers, . . . No church is allowed to be open within two hundred feet iv a saloon. . . . I made up me mind that about four millyon iv th' people iv New York might as well be livin' in Peewaukee f'r all they know iv th gay life iv th' capital."

Boston Globe, August 11, 1912

455. On the News of the Day

(On Standard Oil): "I've heerd that they turned out a few lijislachures an' judges fr'm time to time, as they happened to need thim, but I didn't know it was a reg'lar part iv this gr-reat industhry. But fr'm what I r-read in th' pa-apers, this is wan iv th' most extinsive plants they have." (Also on the Bull Moose, Wilson and Taft campaigning style)

Boston Globe, September 8, 1912

456. On the Origin of Man

"But nobody has iver ast me to go befure a larned society an' have me chest dhraped with medals f'r sayin' it. I cudden't fill up me time on th' program. All I cud say wud be: 'Fellow pro-fissors, th' thing that give ye an' me a shade over th' squrl an' th' grasshopper is that we have more marrow in th' bean. Thankin' ye again f'r ye-er kind attintion. I will now lave ye while ye thranslate this almost onfathomable thought into a language that on'y a dhrug clerk can understand.' . . . But afther awhile people begun to take more kindly to (Darwin's) idee an' to say: 'Well, annyhow, it's more comfortable to feel that we're a slight improvement on a monkey thin such a fallin' off fr'm th' angels.' . . . But this pro-fissor has gone further thin Darwin in pursooin' our lineage down to . . . th' jumpin' shrew . . . There's always wan encouragin' thing about th' sad scientific facts that comes out ivry week in th' pa-apers. They're usually not thrue. . . . But if he'd (the professor) f'rgit about th' origin iv th' race an' tell us not where man comes fr'm but where he's goin' to I'd take an intherpter around an' listen to him."

"These men ar-re inimies iv religion," said Mr. Hennessy.

"P'raps," said Mr. Dooley. "But they'll niver be dangerous ontil some wan comes along an' thranslates their lectures into English. An' I don't think there's a chance that cud be done."

Will, p. 82;
Boston Globe, September 29, 1912

457. On the Campaign

"... Along comes a fellow that's been a collidge profissor or a colonel iv a cowboy rigimint or a lawyer in Cincinnaty an' he says: 'Boys, I'm far an' away th' best iv all iv ye. I want ye to give me a certy-ficate acknowlidgin' me supeeryority, a hundherd thousan' dollars a year to put in me jeans, a fine three-sthory and basement house to live in, a man-iv-war f'r a private yacht, an' a guarantee to print a takin' likeniss iv mesilf f'r all time to come in th' school histhries.' ... Thank hivin, whin a man has th' owdacity to say in public without blushin' that he's qualified f'r th' best job in all th' civilized wur-ruld, to rule over a law-abidin' but haughty popylace, we'll take th' conceit out iv him befure he goes in, knowin' full well that he'll get it back th' day afther he takes hold iv th' office.... Showin' disrespict f'r th' candydates is wan way iv showin' respict f'r th' office.... There's nawthin that improves a statesman's character so much as retirement fr'm public life. (Mr. Dooley characterizes the defeated candidate and follows with an obituary by the opposition press.) ... Th' kindest things ar're always said about th' man whose votes will be counted as 'scatthrin.' ... (politics) "is a rough, able-bodied, out-iv-dures sport an' anny man that takes part in it must expict to get bumped ... We're perfectly safe so long as we go to th' polls inspired be a noble determination to vote f'r somebody, not because we think much iv him, but because he ain't as bad as somewan else. To tell ye th' truth, most iv us don't vote f'r annybody. We vote agin somebody...

"The sthraw votes seems to show—" Mr. Hennessy began.

"Ye can't take annythin' so sthrong as American pollyticks through a Sthraw vote," said Mr. Dooley.

Boston Globe, October 27, 1912

458. On Campaign Managers

"There's nawthin I'd like to be so much as a campaign manager," said Mr. Dooley. "It's th' most jovyal emplyement in th' wurruld. Nawthin' to do but laugh an' lie an' count th' money. . . . So here's a long life to th' glee-club iv campaign managers. They ought to have a good time durin' th' campaign f'r they niver have aftherward. If they don't ilict their candydate he's sure to blame thim an' if they do ilict him he wondhers how many more votes he wud-ve got if they hadn't been in his way. . . . An iliction f'r prisidint is wan iv th' great festivals iv th' poor an' it don't cost annythin.' (Mr. Dooley parodies the pre-election predictions of the presidential campaign managers).

Boston Globe, November 3, 1912

459. On Trial by Jury

"In England a man is presoomed to be innicent till he's proved guilty an' they take it f'r granted he's guilty. In this counthry a man is presoomed to be guilty ontil he's proved guilty an' afther that he's presoomed to be innicent. . . . Th' first six months iv th' thrile ar-re usually taken in gettin' a jury that will be fair to both sides, but more fair to wan side thin th' other. . . . Th' lawyer f'r th' definse on'y asks that his client shall be thried by a jury iv his peers or worse, but wud compromise if all twelve were mimbers iv th' same lodge as himsilf.

Best, p. 282;

282

Will, p. 212, (Criminal Trials);
Choice of Law, p. 1;
Boston Globe, November 10, 1912

460. On Bryan and the Administration

(Mr. Dooley has W. J. Bryan suggesting to the President that he let him run the show). "I niver agreed, Hinnissy, with thim cynics that say that ye can't believe annythin' ye see in th' pa-apers. I have always insisted that th' death notices were fairly acc'rate." (The press had been burying Bryan for sixteen years).

N.Y. Times, V 5:1, February 2, 1913;
Boston Globe, February 2, 1913

461. On Finding the Boston Chamber of Commerce

Boston Globe, May 25, 1913

462. On Drink and Statesmanship

(On the once popular role of alcohol as a political ally to Bryan's serving of non-alcoholic beverages to diplomats). (On T. R. suing an editor for suggesting he tipples): "If he'd been in pollyticks as long as I have an' was as active an' as prom'nent he wudn't have noticed th' insult. He'd know that in pollyticks th' worst men ar-re often libeled, so what can th' best expict? It's a good thing, too, fr it keeps sinsitive an' thin skinned men out iv public life an' dhrives thim into journalism."

Will, p. 43 (Drink and Politics);
Boston Globe, July 13, 1913

463. On Peace

(Mr. Bryan calls for an end to war). "It's a sthrange thing to me, Hinnissy, that with ivry wan boostin' peace there's so little iv it in th' wurruld. There've been

peace congresses an' wars goin' on side be side iver
since I can remimber . . . (Mr. Dooley feels that war is
inevitable) Besides I ain't sure that a fight ain't
sometimes betther thin a lawsuit. It laves less hard
feelin."

New York Times, V 3:1, July 20, 1913;
Choice of Law, p. 128;
Boston Globe, July 20, 1913

464. Mr. Dooley at a Summer Resort

Mr. Dooley compares the brochures on summer resorts
with actually visiting them.

Will, p. 27;
New York Times, V 9:1, July 27, 1913 (On Recuperation
at Elysium by the Lake);
Boston Globe, July 27, 1913

465. On Slang

". . . a profissor at Oxford colledge, that's about ready to
declare war on us because he says we're corruptin' th'
dilect they call th' English language in England with
our slang. . . . An' th' best way to masther th' language
iv anny furrin' counthry is to inthrajooce ye'er own.
(Mr. Dooley provides examples and suggests we pro-
duce slang in such abundance that we have enough for
export. After importation, it becomes passe in
America). Faith, whin us free born Americans get
through with th' English language we'll make it look as
though it had been run over be a musical comedy."

Boston Globe, August 3, 1913

466. On the Mexican Problem

(A political history of Mexico). "Another idee is that we
sthrike a bargain with this onaisy nation be which they
agree to finance th' disordher if we'll supply th' polis to

284

quell it. That is what is called inthervention.... We ought to lave something f'r Posterity to do besides payin' th' debts we run up f'r thim.... They have no throuble with their ex-prisidints beyond seein' that th' grass is kep cut.... We took no sides, on'y asking cash in advance f'r arms an' ammunition, an' insistin' that both parties should shoot south whin near th' Rio Grande... Madero had a sound idee iv what a republican form iv governmint shud be; it was, in a gineral way, to let on'y members iv his fam'ly know th' combynation iv th' safe."

Boston Globe, August 10, 1913

467. On Women and Politics

"... I know iv no battle in th' wurruld that's so onakel as wan between a rale lady an' a perfick gintleman.... Sure, th' bachelors will be th' boys in pollyticks if th' ladies gets th' votes. It's to us intilligent, raisonable an' handsome men that the dear things will come an' not to crusty ol' marrid men.... Th' rule iv pollyticks is, 'Do that f'r me or I'll do this to ye,' and th' prayer is not complete without both sections bein' in it. To be a succisful reformer ye've got first to be a nuisance.... An' I will say this, firmly as I believe in th' akequality iv th' sex, I dhraw th' line at puttin' thim on th' polis foorce."...

"Well," said Mr. Dooley, "I used to agree with Hogan whin he said Pollyticks was too rough f'r women. But afther readin' what they've done in England I'm afraid to give thim th' vote because they may be too rough f'r poll ticks."

Boston Globe, August 17, 1913

468. On Wills

"To be injyeable a will must be at wan an' th' same time a practical joke on th' heirs an' an advertisement iv th' ol' crust that made it."

Will, p. 3;
Best, p. 154;
Choice of Law, p. 185;
Boston Globe, August 24, 1913

469. On News from the Empire State

"I hope," said Mr. Dooley, "that Prisidint Wilson will not inthervene be foorce in New York. It may be thrue that arnychy exists there, that there is no settled govermint an' that th' lives an' property iv Americans ar-re onsafe. . . . It wud take fifty years to civilize New York up to th' level iv Arkansaw or Texas . . . It is almost th' on'y spot that has not been touched an' spiled be civilization. Th' state is large in aryea, but th' popylation is all gathered in three streets, which comprise what is known as th' city iv New York — Wall sthreet, Fifth avnoo an' Broadway . . . I niver read annything about th' rest iv th' state, so I suppose it is oninhabited. . . . A New Yorker who isn't short changed or hasn't his hat dented in at laste wanst a week be a polisman, a sthreet car conductor, a waiter, or a theaytre usher feels that he is niglictid." (Mr. Dooley also comments on the impeachment proceedings against the New York governor and the escape from an asylum of a rich, young assassin to the consternation of lawyers, alienists and other profit makers.)

New York Times, V 3:1, August 31, 1913 (On Sulzer, Thaw and the Political Situation);
Boston Globe, August 31, 1913

470. On Current Politics

Boston Globe, December 21, 1913

471. The Majesty of the Law

Not a Mr. Dooley, but one of Finley Peter Dunne's most impressive pieces. Dunne gives his impressions of a hanging that occurred when he was seventeen.

American Magazine, February 1914

472. On our Diplomacy

Mr. Dooley discusses the servilities of being an ambassador.

Boston Globe, February 8, 1914

473. On Reform Appointments

(Mr. Dooley on getting a police chief for New York City. He runs down the list that includes the man in charge of digging the Panama Canal and decides): "It takes a polisman to police a polisman."

New York Times, V 5:1, February 15, 1914 (On Col. Goethals and the N.Y. Police);
Boston Globe, February 15, 1914

474. On Dancing

New York Times, V 5:1, March 1, 1914;
Boston Globe, February 22, 1914

475. On the Pursuit of the Rich

Mr. Dooley lectures a man from Boston who deplores the attitude of the poor toward the rich.

Boston Globe, March 1, 1914

476. Mr. Dooley on the Crisis

(Mr. Dooley thinks the President should spend more time on the baseball crisis than on less significant matters such as foreign policy).

"Yes, sir. It is time f'r Dock Wilson to quit foolin' with such pollytickal croshayin' as th' rivoluchion in Mexico an' th' anti-thrust legislachion an' do somethin' that appeals to th' heart iv th' American people.

"Some people think there's too much business in base-ball . . . I don't agree with thim. Divvle a bit do I care whether a man is playin' ball f'r th' fun iv it or f'r a retainer . . . so long as he pastes thim on th' thrade-mark whin he's up an' hauls thim down with one hand whin he's in th' field. . . . I haven't a care in th' wurruld whether his constitootional rights is guaranteed, so long as he gets down to sicond ahead iv th' ball."

"I see be th' pa-aper that it's a shame that a base-ball player shud get three times as much sal'ry as a colledge pro-fissor," said Mr. Hennessy.

"He may be worth three times as much," said Mr. Dooley.

"But d'ye honestly think Tris Speaker ought to get more thin th' prisidint iv Harvard Colledge?"

"That," said Mr. Dooley, "is a matter I can't give an opinyon on. I niver see Dock Lowell play. I'd lave th' matther to a vote iv th' studints iv that great an' fash-nable resort. I'd let thim decide which athleet it gives thim more pleasure to see perform."

New York Times, V 5:1, March 8, 1914 (On the Base-ball Situation);
Boston Globe, March 8, 1914

477. On Mexico

(How to handle Pancho Villa. Wilson's and Bryan's efforts are noted. A profile of Villa.) "They (Horta and Villa) belong to diff'rent schools iv statesmanship an' di-plomacy. Horta is iv th' ol' school, fond iv pomp an' ceremony, a gr-reat stickler f'r etiket, uses bottled goods intirely, an' is particklar to have his murdherin' done be mimbers iv th' reg'lar army in uniform. Pancho Villa is more breezy an' dimmycratic, simple an' jovyal in his methods, drhrinks iv th' can, an' is not above assanaytin' his inimies or his frinds, as th' case may be, with his own hands."

"What wud ye do about Mexico, ye're so smart?" said Mr. Hennessy. . . .

"Well, sir," said Mr. Dooley, "I'd advise him to go into Mexico if I knew how he cud get out."

New York Times, V 5:1, March 15, 1914;
Boston Globe, March 15, 1914

478. On Diplomatic Indiscretions

". . . in th' old days, Hinnissy, we made a man an ambassadure to England because he'd been successful as a horse thrader. . . . But diplomacy is diff'rent, nowadays, d'ye mind. It's more like internaytional chess an' is played be cable. . . . So his name goes into th' sinit, an' th' sinitors reads his books to see that he has said nawthin that wud hurt th' feelin's iv th' south, an' he gets th' job. (Mr. Dooley discusses his uselessness.) He grajally slips down on th' program ontil th' waiters begin puttin' th' chairs on th' table whin he starts to talk."

"What is th' Monroe docthrine?" asked Mr. Hennessy.

"Large volumes has been wrote about it," said Mr. Dooley, "an' manny learned statesmen has thried to explain it. But all I can make iv it is that it manes, 'Ye keep out iv our back yard.' "

New York Times, V 5:1, March 22, 1914;
Boston Globe, March 22, 1914

479. On Ulster and the Army

"As foreigners (the Ulstermen) I despise thim; but as fellow counthrymen an' inimies I hold thim in th' highest regard ... We undherstand each other perfeckly. So we must fight. Nawthin leads to throuble so quick as a perfeck undherstandin'. Th' English don't undherstand us an' they always mess things up in Ireland. They are an onraisonable an' slow actin' people, while we're raisonable an' impetchus. (Mr. Dooley comments on a British general refusing to storm the Irish stronghold.) Lave th' makin' iv war to th' gin-rals an' we'll have peace. No gin'ral ought to go to war onless he was ready, an' no gin'ral that knows his business ought iver to be ready.... The statesmen ar-re always prepared to fly somebody else at th' throat iv th' inimy iv their counthry ... "

New York Times, VI 5:1, April 12, 1914;
Boston Globe, April 12, 1914

480. On Agitators

(Mr. Dooley discusses a riot instigated by an agitator and suspects that their value is not as intended): "But they give a good dale iv healthful out-iv-dure exercise to th' bums in th' park, they deflate, as Hogan says, th' agytators who wud bust otherwise, an' they reform th' polis departmint, turnin' thim fr'm villyans into a body iv min that wud make th' ar'my iv th' Pottymack look like a mob iv polthroons without changin' their habits."

New York Times, VI 7:1, April 19, 1914;
Boston Globe, April 19, 1914

481. On Alcohol

(Josephus Daniels, Secretary of the Navy, extends ban of alcohol to officers).

"It's hard f'r me to think iv a timprance navy.... Hogan thinks alcohol is nicissry f'r a man so that now an' thin he can have a good opinion iv himsilf ondistubed be th' facts." (Mr. Dooley argues that the world we live in will be substantially different without the availability of alcohol).

New York Times, VI 5:1, April 26, 1914;
Boston Globe, April 26, 1914

482. On Eugenics

"Look what science has done f'r horses, poulthry, an' pigs, not to speak iv cauliflower, rutybagy, turnips, an' quinces, an' think what a cinch 'twould be to superintind th' matin' iv simple, aisily managed weeds like mankind." Mr. Dooley says eugenic marriages will end courtship and lead to eugenic divorces.

Hearst's, October 1914, p. 436

483. On Dress

On Paris fashions. On the slit skirt. "I've seen thim wan year wearin' too many clothes f'r their comfort, an' another wearin' too little f'r mine.... Whin th' fashion gets as far as Wauwatosa, it disappears in New York."

Hearst's, November, 1914, p. 578

484. On the Gift of Oratory

"Ivry nation injyes some kind iv a crool spoort an' afther-dinner orathry is th' same with us as bull-fightin' is with the Spanyards...."

Hearst's, December 1914, p. 692 (see no. 490)

485. On War

"As it is, ye can tell be th' position iv anny wan in th' battle how much iv a part he had in bringin' on th' war." Mr. Dooley would like to reverse the order.

Hearst's, January 1915, p. 22

486. On Going to See the Doctor

"Annyhow most iv th' doctors has quit given' medicine an' ar-re givin' advice. It's betther too. They don't have to write it down an' it can't be used at th' inquest. . . . Ivry sick man is a heero, if not to th' wurruld or aven to th' fam'ly, at laste to himsilf. . . . If a sick man is entitled to annything it ought to be to give his own name to his own complaints" (and not to the doctor). (Mr. Dooley concludes with some nice sentiments about doctors.)

Hearst's, February 1915, p. 258

487. On Food in War

(Mr. Dooley doesn't believe you can starve a country into surrendering. He gives his version of how Lee surrendered to Grant). " 'Ye can't spile histhry be makin' it unthrue,' says Gin'ral Grant. . . . An' iver since thin th' South has been runnin' th' Governmint ayther fr'm th' inside or fr'm th' outside."

Will, p. 55

488. On the Power of Music

(Mr. Dooley bemoans Bryan as Secretary of State because it deprives the public of his oratorical skills. All a Secretary has to do is think, a task for which there are more than enough candidates. Bryan resigns. Dooley satirizes his speech on love instead of war as being given in "th' key iv G.") "I don't know whether 'twill succeed or not. I hope so. But there's wan thing I am afraid iv, Hinnissy. Ye see, me boy, th' wurruld is a pretty old hunk of mud an' wickedness, an' I've been here a long time an' I've observed this sad thruth. Ye don't have to lend a man money. Ye don't have to amuse him; ye don't have to take care iv him if he's sick; ye don't have to do annything f'r him but wan thing."

"An' what's that?" asked Mr. Hennessy.

"If he wants to fight ye, ye've got to accommodate him," said Mr. Dooley.

Will, p. 71

489. On Going to See the Doctor

(Mr. Dooley believes that most ailments are imaginary, and that a good doctor gives you a placebo only to keep you from going to an expensive quack. He describes prescription filling as practiced at the turn of the century. He finds the microbe theory excellent for the welfare of doctors). "No, sir, whin I come to think iv it, I'll not deny th' pleasure iv bein' sick. It's th' on'y way some people has iv callin' attintion to thimsilves an' bein' talked about." (Mr. Dooley concludes with some kind words about the medical profession).

Will, p. 114

490. On "The Gift of Oratory"

(Mr. Dooley frowns on an anti-oratory movement. He characterizes the master of ceremonies as an executioner and describes the nature of a banquet to Hennessy. The agony felt by after-dinner speakers. Orators seldom get the good jobs). "Orators an' iditors sildom do well in office. They have to express opinyons right off th' stove on ivry known subjick in language that ivry wan will remimber an' repeat, an' afther that they can't change without somebody diggin' up what they said." Mr. Dooley tells why he is never swayed by an orator.

Will, p. 131 (see no. 484)

491. On Golf

"Th' next pleasantest feelin' in th' wurruld to bein' perfectly happy is bein' perfectly cross. That's why it's took up be middle-aged gintlemen." (Mr. Dooley says that golf is so all consuming that it makes you forget your real troubles).

Best, p. 175;
Choice of Law, p. 198;
Will, p. 144

492. On "The Game of Cards"

(Mr. Dooley imagines a card-shark convention in Monte Carlo where they invent new games to fleece the suckers). In the old days, people played for fun "—or betther f'r indignation an' anger." He describes men and women at auction bridge. "Th' pro-fissyonal (card player) has a weary, pained look, but in th' amachoor's eyes there is a bright light iv hopeless but happy avarice." (Mr. Dooley says there is no such thing as friends at cards).

Best, p. 276;
Will, p. 159

493. On Past Glories

Mr. Dooley, who had never been to war, pictures himself as a gallant cavalry man. Dooley says the romance has now gone out of war. He concludes, "It's on'y th' prisint that ain't romantic."

Will, p. 198

494. On the Candidates

Al Smith, W.J. Bryan, and nominating a Catholic.

Boston Globe, June 1, 1924, p. 2 (edit. sec.)

495. Mr. Dooley — Prohibitionist

Boston Globe, June 8, 1924, p. 2 (edit. sec.)

496. On Women's Dress

Boston Globe, June 15, 1924, p. 5 (edit. sec.)

497. On Senatorial Courtesy

Boston Globe, May 25, 1924, p. 1 (edit. sec.)

498. On the Presidency

Boston Globe, June 22, 1924, p. 5 (edit. sec.)

499. On Vice Presidency

Boston Globe, July 6, 1924, p. 41

500. On Tennis

Boston Globe, July 13, 1924, p. 34

501. On New York

Mr. Dooley says New York is not as bad as pictured, but is well advertised.

July 20, 1924, Boston Globe, p. 7 (edit. sec.)

502. On Alienists

Boston Globe, July 27, 1924, p. 6 (edit. sec.)

503. On the Lot of the Farmer and Labor Parties

Boston Globe, August 3, 1924, p. 6 (edit. sec.)

504. On Being a World Power and Life in Russia
Boston Globe, August 10, 1924, p. 5 (edit. sec.)

505. On the Administration of Justice
Boston Globe, August 17, 1924, p. 7 (edit. sec.)

506. On Old Age
Boston Globe, August 24, 1924, p. 6 (edit. sec.)

507. On the Prince of Wales
Polo playing.
Boston Globe, August 31, 1924, p. 44

508. On the Wonders of Science
The planet Mars.
Boston Globe, September 7, 1924, p. 3 (edit. sec.)

509. On Paris Divorces
Liberty Weekly, Vol. 2, No. 40, Feb. 6, 1926, p. 7

510. On Football
"A futball star is like an ex-Prisidint — there's hardly anny way he can 'arn his livin' an' keep his dignity. . . . A man who studies th' Constitution nowadays don't bother about what Thomas Jefferson, George Wash'n'ton or Binjamin Franklin put into it. He skips all that hokum an' starts in at th' amidments . . . Manny a banker wud be made to eat th' bonds he'd sold if he hadn't disposed iv thim through an old All-American tackle weighin' two hundherd an' twinty-five pounds with a fist on him th' size iv a shovel. . . . Th' thruth is, Hinnissy, that most iv us, aven those iv us who niver went to colledge, ar-re onijacated." Mr. Dooley discusses a controversy over Red Grange, the prospects for abolishing football, and

296

asks Mr. Hennessy if he would rather be the President of Harvard or Henry Ford. "Well," said Mr. Hennessy, "if I had Foord's money, I'd rather be Eliot." "Ye cudd'nt have wan an' be th' other," said Mr. Dooley.

Liberty Weekly, Feb. 13, 1926, p. 35

511. On Youth

Liberty Weekly, Vol. 2, No. 42, Feb. 20, 1926, p. 29

512. On War Recollections

Liberty Weekly, Vol. 2, No. 43, Feb. 27, 1926, p. 45

513. On Capital and Labor

Liberty Weekly, Vol. 2, No. 44, March 6, 1926, p. 47

514. On the Income Tax

Liberty Weekly, Vol. 2, No. 45, March 13, 1926, p. 38

515. On the Pleasures of the Rich

Liberty Weekly, Vol. 2, No. 46, March 20, 1926, p. 55

516. On Mussolini

Liberty Weekly, Vol. 2, No. 47, March 27, 1926, p. 23

517. On Pride

Liberty Weekly, Vol. 2, No. 48, April 3, 1926, p. 47

518. On the Power of the Press

Liberty Weekly, Vol. 2, No. 49, April 10, 1926, p. 35

519. On a Survey of Prohibition

Liberty Weekly, Vol. 2, No. 50, April 17, 1926, p. 23

520. On the Effects of Spring

Liberty Weekly, Vol. 2, No. 51, April 24, 1926, p. 24

521. On the Descent of Man
Liberty Weekly, Vol. 2, No. 52, May 1, 1926, p. 36

522. Mr. Dooley Reviews a Book
Col. House's letters.
Liberty Weekly, Vol. 3, No. 1, May 8, 1926, p. 33

523. On Speculation
Liberty Weekly, Vol. 3, No. 2, May 15, 1926, p. 39

524. On the Women's Vote
Liberty Weekly, Vol. 3, No. 3, May 22, 1926, p. 39

525. On Conversation
Liberty Weekly, Vol. 3, No. 4, May 29, 1926, p. 19

526. On Our Moral Leaders
Liberty Weekly, Vol. 3, No. 5, June 5, 1926, p. 37

527. On Political Diseases
Liberty Weekly, Vol. 3, No. 6, June 12, 1926, p. 35

528. Mr. Dooley Talks About Gunmen
Liberty Weekly, Vol. 3, No. 7, June 19, 1926, p. 37

529. On Eugenics
Liberty Weekly, Vol. 3, No. 8, June 26, 1926, p. 39

530. On the Farmer's Woes
Liberty Weekly, Vol. 3, No. 9, July 3, 1926, p. 19

INDEX

A

Adams, Franklin P., 14, 24, 25, 54
Ade, George, 3-5
Administration of justice, 296
Adventure, 222
Advertising, magazines and, 268-269
Advocacy, art of, 98
Age, 65, 223, 249, 250
    Loneliness of old age, 178
    Old age, 44, 181, 278, 296
    Youth and age, 150, 206
Agitators, 179, 290
Alcohol, 98
    Army canteen, 246
    Currency question and, 175
    Drink and statesmanship, 283
    Drunkenness, 220
    Food, as, 198-199
    General Grant, 258-259
    Model Saloon, 233
    Navy temperance, 290-291
    Suicide, 184
    Temperance, 149
Alderman, 57
    Business and political honesty, 245
    Good man, 184
    Hanging of, 163
Aldrich, Senator, 227, 263-265
Alger, Russell A., 160
Alienists, 295
All American, 296-297
Altruists, 172
Amateur theatricals, 187
Ambassadors, 57, 169, 201, 217, 257, 287
Americans abroad, 188
    Types of, 267
American family, 226
American stage, 195
Amundsen, Roald, 274
Anarchism, 57, 146, 160, 193
Anglo-American:
    Alliance, 164
    Sports, 166
Anglophiles, 188

299

L

M

V

Vacations, 155, 265-267, 284
  (*see also* Travel)
Vaudeville, 185
Venezuela, 185
Vice, crusade against, 198
Vice President, 74, 230-231, 295
Victorian Era, 174-175
Victory, 159
Villa, Pancho, 288
Virginia, 197
Voices from the tomb, 193-194
Voting, 30, 75, 167, 187-188, 196, 223, 236, 247, 285

W

Waldorf (Hotel), 243
Wall St., 286
Wanderers, 148
War, 46, 103, 157-158, 161-168, 170, 176, 192, 238, 245, 249, 258-259,
      261-263, 279, 283-284, 290, 292-294
    Civil war, 146
    Food in, 292
    Modern explosives, 189
    Recollections, 297
    Russian-Japanese, 233, 236
    War expert, 30, 189
    War game, 218
    War maker, 167
Washington, Booker T., incident, 208
Washington News, 265
Wealth, 165
Weather:
    Bureau, 202
    Hot weather, 279
Wedding, 186
Welfare, 153, 175
Whipping post, 239
Whiskey, 175
White, E.B., 82
Whitechapel Club, 3-9
White man's burden, 164
Wife:
    Ideal, 212
    Violence to, 239